DATE DUE		
JAN. 02 1985	MAR 16 '92		
APR 11 '85	APR 15 '92		
JAN. 30 1986	MAY 15 '92		
2/11	JUL 14 '92		
SEP. 26 1986	DEC 16 1992		
FEB. 23 1987			
SEP 11 '87	MAY 16 1995		
JAN. 29 1988	AUG 01 1996		
MAR 22	AUG 05 1999		
SEP 16 '91	OCT 06 1999		
JAN 29 '92	APR 16 2001		
FEB 19			

Electric Kiln POTTERY

THE COMPLETE GUIDE

Emmanuel Cooper

B. T. Batsford London

by the same author and published by Batsford:

Glazes for the Studio Potter (with Derek Royle) (1978)
The Potter's Book of Glaze Recipes (1980)
A History of World Pottery (1981)

Acknowledgements

I would like to thank all the potters who have
talked to me about their working methods,
techniques and ideas, including potters in the
U.S.A. who have written full and copious notes.
All have given generously of their time and
expertise and without them this book could not
have been written.

In particular I am indebted to Eileen
Lewenstein, Lucie Rie, David Ketteridge and
Derek Royle (of Harrison Mayer) for reading all,
or part, of the draft manuscript and making
helpful comments and suggestions. They are in
no way responsible for any errors which have
occurred, for which I take full blame.

First published 1982
© Emmanuel Cooper 1982

ISBN 0 7134 4037 6

Printed in Great Britain by The Anchor Press Ltd,
Tiptree, Essex,
for the publishers, B. T. Batsford Ltd,
4 Fitzhardinge Street, London W1H 0AH
Photoset by Keyspools Ltd, Golborne, Lancs

Contents

List of colour photographs

Introduction

When Bernard Leach published his famous *Potter's Book* some 40 years ago, he remarked in it that small electric kilns were coming onto the market which could be fired to stoneware temperatures and, he added, by introducing thin pieces of wood into the chamber, reducing atmospheres could be induced. He also said that tests in the kiln had produced good results. This was the sum total of his references to firing in an electric kiln; it is interesting that he thought it necessary to point out how it could be converted into a reduction kiln. Many writers have since taken his lead and described the techniques, processes and firing of reduction kilns and make only passing reference to how such materials or techniques respond in oxidation.

Within the last few years serious literature on electric kilns has started to appear. Robert Fournier has written a comprehensive description of how studio potters can build their own electric kilns. Harry Fraser has produced a handbook on how to fire electric kilns in which he describes the sorts of electronic controls available to the studio potter. Both books are listed in the bibliography. Few writers have so far written in detail about the particular skills and knowledge required for producing attractive work from the electric kiln. Many potters, anxious to find out what effects can be produced in an electric firing have had limited access to information; in this book I have looked at all the processes used by the potter and written about them from the point of view of producing attractive results in an electric kiln. I have borne in mind the needs of the potter making functional pots for use in the home, as well as the needs of the potter seeking out more special or unique effects. Though there are references in this book to ware fired at earthenware temperatures, I have concentrated on the medium and high temperature wares where a greater range of colours and effects is available and where the differences between oxidation and reduction effects are at their greatest. Many of our best potters fire in an electric kiln and their work has received international recognition. It is not only the technique which leads to successful potting, it is also that the potter has to set out to understand the processes. This book is dedicated to those potters who want to find out what happens, and, armed with this knowledge, proceed to make pots which are even more beautiful than before.

1 Understanding the electric kiln

Until the development of electric kilns some 50 years ago, pots were fired in different types of flame burning kiln, using either fossil fuels like charcoal or, more recently, oil, gas or a renewable resource such as wood. The use of such fuels will create in the kiln particular sorts of atmosphere which may or may not be desirable. For instance, many potters completely enclosed their pots in clay boxes, known as saggars, to protect the pots from the effects of falling bits of grit, rough ash deposits, or to prevent the unevenness due to flame-licked pots. For some studio potters the effects associated with traditional high fired wares of the Far East are greatly admired, as are the typical glaze and body effects associated with pots fired in those kilns.

Yet for most studio potters working today, such kilns cannot be used, for a wide variety of reasons. A flame burning kiln needs space in which to build the kiln and to store the fuel. Furthermore, such kilns cannot be small; there is an important economic relationship between kiln size and the type of fuel used which tends to make the use of small flame-burning kilns impractical. The complexity of installation as well as the compliance with bye-laws and fire regulations may present problems. Instead, potters at home, in schools and in colleges have turned to kilns fired with electricity, and these present far fewer problems.

The advantages are that they can, economically, be almost any size, they are relatively easy to install (small ones will operate, in the UK, from a 13 amp domestic plug) and are not expensive to run.

Electric kilns come in a wide variety of shapes to suit many different requirements and pockets. Unfortunately, many potters have identified the electric kiln as being second best, seeing it as a workable but definitely inferior alternative to the flame burning kiln. A few potters have grasped the problems and possibilities of working with electric kilns and regard the technique as a challenge to which they respond positively. They see the electric kiln as being just as capable of producing attractive results, whether for sculptural ceramics or domestic pottery, which can be just as beautiful and exciting as that which comes out of the reduction kiln.

This book will look at the work of many different sorts of potters who fire their pots and objects in an electric kiln; it will explain their approach to their work and how good results can be obtained. No technique in itself will give beautiful objects; no method is intrinsically better or in any way inferior to any other. Nor is it

Nicholas Homoky; thrown and turned white stoneware bowls with black inlaid decoration

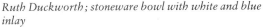
Ruth Duckworth; stoneware bowl with white and blue inlay

Ian Byers; coil pot with scratched and inlaid decoration

always possible to cling on to traditional methods; we live in a very different age. Only a few potters have the space or even the desire to use flame burning kilns and most of these potters work in the country. Potters working in cities or in workshops with no outside access often only have the choice between not having a kiln at all or only having one fired with electricity, which is also the situation in most schools, colleges and training centres, where the convenience of the electric kiln makes the firing of pottery possible.

Results from any method of making or firing vary widely. A pot which is strong in form and decoration will survive any firing process; a weak pot will still lack the necessary lively qualities, no matter what sort of firing it receives. Yet the approach to, and use of, the electric kiln affects deeply all the factors which influence the potting process, especially the composition of the clay body, the ingredients of the glazes, the decoration and, to some extent, the making techniques. There are never easy answers to successful potting, but there are many ways of firing so that the best results can be obtained. These depend upon a thorough understanding of the chemical and physical changes that are taking place, the range of materials that are available and choosing the most suitable materials for the results that are required. Despite a widely held belief to the contrary, it is

not always easy to tell whether a pot or object has been fired in an electric kiln or a flame-burning kiln. Differences in glaze quality and appearance between the one sort of firing and the other are not clearly distinguishable, though often the quality of the body, its texture and its colour can give various hints. Sometimes glazes are said to look 'oxidized', meaning they have a dry or dull surface when they have failed to fire well in a reduction kiln. To many potters this term is used in the pejorative rather than the descriptive sense. Potters who set out to make oxidised ware can produce rich and subtle results of many sorts. A 'bad' glaze from whatever sort of kiln will always be unattractive. There are also more precise differences to be identified between pots fired in different atmospheres. For instance, a glaze fired in the reduction kiln will often have tell-tale iron spots which bleed into the glaze to give the characteristic 'reduced' effects; but in an electric firing these are either absent, or may be small depending on the type and thickness of glaze, the type of clay body and the firing temperature.

Differences between electric and other sorts of firings

To change clay into pot it has to be heated until the chemical and physical structure of the clay is affected (a full explanation is given in Chapter 4). These changes start to occur at 600°C (1112°F), but only become of practical value to the studio potter at temperatures over 800°C (1472°F). When fired below this temperature most clay bodies are too soft and porous to be of much use. In fact the first firing, which is called the biscuit or bisque firing, takes the pot to the point at which the body is reasonably strong but still quite porous and easily glazed. For low temperature biscuit firing it makes little or no difference which type of kiln is used although the slowness of the firing can most easily be controlled with an electric kiln. Many potters who glaze fire with a flame burning kiln will biscuit fire their pots in an electric kiln, which can ususlly be controlled more easily. Other reduction potters build onto their kilns extra chambers so that waste heat from the glaze firing is used to biscuit the pots.

Oxidation and reduction

At temperatures above 800°C (1472°F) the differences between ware fired in the electric kiln and other kilns begin to be more distinct. Basically, an electric kiln is a completely enclosed box with special high temperature heating elements in the walls and floor. All the heat is confined within the chamber and escapes very slowly by conduction through the walls or via appertures or cracks, for example around the door. As the kiln is heated by electricity the atmosphere of the chamber is not changed, though burning organic material in the body and glazes can result in local reduction. This atmosphere is normally considered to be neutral or oxidising.

In contrast a flame burning kiln is a much more complex construction consisting of a firebox, packing chamber and chimney, all of which are designed to accommodate the sort of fuel which is to be used. Wood, for instance, needs quite a large firebox compared to a kiln fired on natural gas, which requires a comparatively small firebox. It is, however, the effect of the flame which is of greatest importance for it is this which affects the pots in the kiln. By changing the air inlets and the flue exits in the flame-burning kiln, the atmosphere in the chamber can either be oxidising, neutral or reducing. If plenty of air is present and the flues are open, the flame will burn 'clean', with all the carbon being fully burnt: this is the 'neutral' atmosphere and is close to that occuring in an electric kiln. If the air inlets and flue outlets are partially closed then the flame, deprived of sufficient oxygen for full combustion to take place,

will be 'dirty': it will become more yellow, and soot deposits (carbon) will be formed.

But the flame, hungry for oxygen to complete combustion, will try to draw it from whatever source it can – namely the clay and glazes in the chamber. Oxygen molecules in these materials will combine with the fuel and 'reduce' the amount left in the body, hence the term 'reduction atmosphere'. Typically, this affects the clay to give a darker colour often with pronounced iron spots; these also show up in the glazes as brown speckles.

Colours of typical iron glazes fired in a reduced atmosphere tend to be blue and green as opposed to the cream and yellow obtained in an electric kiln, or in an oxidising atmosphere. This is because one of the materials to be strongly affected by the flames' need for oxygen is iron, which is present in all clays and most glazes in either small or large amounts. Iron exists usually as ferric oxide; this is red in its raw state and has the formula Fe_2O_3. A typical red firing clay contains some 6–8% red iron oxide. Porcelain contains less than 0.5%. Black iron oxide, with the formula FeO, is available but at 900°C (1652°F) converts to red iron oxide in an oxidised firing. However, in a reduction firing the red iron oxide is changed into black iron oxide expressed in the following equation:

$$Fe_2O_3 + CO \longrightarrow 2FeO + CO_2\uparrow$$

red iron oxide   carbon monoxide   carbon dioxide (released as a gas)

This reaction affects the body and the glaze, and both have to be borne in mind when body and glaze formulations are being worked out.

1 The colour of the iron is changed. Typically, iron in oxidation glazes gives creams, yellows, olives, browns, blacks and reds; in reduction similar amounts give pale blues, greens, browns, blacks and reds.
2 In the Fe_2O_3 (ferric) form iron does not readily act as a flux, but in the FeO (ferrous) form it becomes an active flux, causing bodies to vitrify more readily and glazes to be more fusible and to flow.

Earthenware and stoneware

The kiln atmosphere can be effective at both earthenware and stoneware (including porcelain) temperatures, that is from around 1000°C (1832°F). Earthenware, usually fired to around 1050–1150°C (1922–2102°F), shows little difference at these temperatures whether fired in

electric or in a reducing kiln. The major exception is in special sorts of lustre glazes or lustre decoration which will only yield their colour when fired in a heavy reducing atmosphere at about 750°C (1382°F). Recently a few potters have started to fire earthenware in reduction kilns, often using wood as a fuel, but they aim for temperatures in the region of 1150–1200°C (2102–2192°F) rather than the lower range.

For most pots fired in earthenware temperatures there is little advantage to be gained with the reduction kiln. By careful blending of various clays to make special bodies and the sensitive use of colouring oxides in the glaze, rich and subtle effects can be obtained. One of the major differences between earthenware and stoneware is the extent of the vitrification of the body. By and large the earthenware body remains softer and less vitrified; in contrast the stoneware is harder and more vitrified. There are other important distinctions which include the reaction between the body and glaze and the creation of an 'intermediate' glaze/body layer. At earthenware temperatures this layer is thin and hardly noticeable; at stoneware temperatures this layer is much more pronounced and, in the case of some thinner, more reactive glazes (such as ash glazes), there is hardly any glassy layer formed. (This is the case whether the firing has been oxidised or reduced.) The effect is more significant at higher temperatures, when the body is much more affected by the kiln atmosphere.

Paul Philp; agate ware teapots press moulded from stained white clay, covered with clear glaze, 1180°C (2156°F)

This body/glaze interaction becomes more apparent as the body softens, which depends as much on the body mixture as the temperature; it can take place with some earthenwares as well as at the higher stoneware temperatures. It is possible, for instance, by the addition of suitable fluxes to the clay body, to produce vitrified earthenware which, for all intents and purposes, has most of the qualities of stoneware, but is achieved at a much lower temperature. With the ever increasing cost of fuel such bodies are being used more and more by the ceramic industry, but they are not sufficiently plastic or workable to be suitable for the processes used by the studio potter, though this is an area well worth investigating.

The separation therefore, of wares into 'earthenware' and 'stoneware' is very much a convention based on temperature limitations and the type of clay used, as well as on the qualities such as the hardness and softness of the fired body. Some clays such as red terra cottas, which contain quite large amounts of red iron, are often known as earthenware clays. They will rarely withstand a temperature much above 1150°C (2102°F), at which point they become hard, vitrified and a dark purple red colour; pots made from these clays and fired to such temperatures, when tapped, give a pleasant, clear ringing note. These clays, which occur in great abundance, may become quite vitreous at 1050°C (1922°F). If taken above their vitrification point the colour darkens even further and the body begins to bloat, sag and deform.

Stoneware clays have a much higher and usually wider vitrification point; some are sufficiently vitrified at 1200°C (2192°F) but can withstand a further 60°C (140°F) before they will start to bloat, soften, distort and eventually collapse. Clays of this type fired to the lower earthenware temperatures, will give a porous, physically weak, nonfunctional body on which most glazes will in time craze. When tapped the bodies will give a dull, unattractive thud. There is, however, huge scope for intermediate stoneware fired to around 1200°C (2192°F) (described in Chapter 11).

Neither studio earthenware nor stoneware should be confused with the terms used to describe the types of ware and the processes used in industrial ceramics. These are very different to those of the studio potter. It is, perhaps, ironic that the majority of pots produced by the ceramics industry are fired in electric kilns, albeit of a continuous as opposed to the intermittent type used by the studio potter. Production and firing techniques used by industry have the aim of producing large amounts of work as efficiently, cheaply and reliably as possible, and much of the individual skills used are rarely apparent in the finished item. The ceramic industry's main product is industrial earthenware made from a specially (and often secret) formulated white body which, depending on the making technique used, will usually have a low level of plasticity. This body is formed out of carefully selected and cleansed materials so that it will vitrify sufficiently at 1140–1160°C (2084–2120°F) to become hard with a low level of porosity; it is to this temperature that the first, or biscuit (bisque) firing is taken. This is partly for economic reasons. (More pots can be packed into the biscuit chamber than in a similar sized glaze chamber.) The hard fired bisque enables the ceramic industry to employ methods of glost placing which allow the use of low temperature glazes for the subsequent glaze firing. Lead and alkaline based glazes which give smooth practical surfaces are applied to the vitrified biscuitware fired to a temperature around 1060°C (1940°F).

Industry, in fact, reverses many of the traditional procedures of studio potters who, if they have two firings (as opposed to a single 'raw' firing which is explained in detail in Chapter 12) take the first to a temperature of around 1000°C (1832°F), which renders the clay sufficiently firm to handle

James Richardson; thrown and carved stoneware bottle with tenmoku glaze

easily but porous enough to absorb glaze. At this stage the clay has the qualities of traditional flower pots. The second (glaze) firing takes the glazed wares to a higher temperature; the body continues to mature and, depending on the temperature, reaches a practical level of vitrification.

Porcelain, like 'earthenware' or 'stoneware', is an equally vague term. Traditionally it refers only to those objects or wares made from a special mixed porcelain clay which becomes hard, vitrified and translucent when fired. This is taken to a high temperature, often above that of stoneware, at which point the body becomes translucent. With the introduction of lower firing porcelain bodies the term has broadened to include so called semi-porcellaneous wares, some of which are fired to temperatures as low as 1240°C (2264°F). With many traditional bodies such qualities are not achieved below temperatures of around 1300°C (2372°F). Porcelain clay is made up from a mixture of three main ingredients: feldspar, quartz and china clay. In addition, depending upon the plasticity of the china clay, small amounts of ball clay may be added. At the top temperature sufficient glassy material is formed in the body to give it its main characteristics. However, at temperatures below this point, because of the fluxing action of the porcelain, the reaction between glaze and body is very different to that occurring between stoneware and glaze. On porcelain some glazes will be runny and over fluxed; others will be richly coloured. On stoneware some porcelain glazes will be dry and matt; others will be dull and lifeless.

For the electric kiln potter, porcelain clays offer opportunities for either rich or subtle colour effects on delicately made forms which can only be achieved in the clean and controllable conditions of this type of kiln.

There are various approaches to potting which potters working with electric kilns can take. They can set out to imitate the effects that are produced in a reduction atmosphere; this is done by the careful blend of clays with suitable additions to give a 'toasted' appearance, and of glazes and slips which aim at typical 'reduced' effects. Secondly, they can turn the electric kiln into a reduction kiln by creating a reducing atmosphere in the kiln chamber; this is done either by introducing combustible materials such as wood chips into the kiln or by the introduction of a suitable gas into the chamber. Thirdly, potters can set out to discover effects, such as various colours, that are unique to the oxidised atmosphere of the electric kiln and make full use of them. They can exploit the whole range of oxidised glazes, seeing them for what they are rather than for what they are not. In the various chapters of this book I will detail all these different approaches; it is up to individual potters as to which they choose.

2 The electric kiln

In contrast to most flame burning kilns in regular use in pottery workshops, those fired by electricity are relatively simple in construction. What is very different is that with a kiln being heated with wood, coal, coke or oil, however complex the structure of the kiln, the flame can usually be seen, which gives a physical involvement in the firing process. This is not possible with the electric kiln. The way in which electricity produces heat or energy is complex, and we can see the effects of the heat at work and control it by various means. At around 600°C (1112°F) it is first possible to see colour develop in the kiln; this appears as a deep dark velvet red which moves to a dull red at around 730°C (1346°F) and gets brighter and more intense as the temperature rises. With the use of a pyrometer system, which indicates the temperature inside the kiln, it is possible to observe the increases as they occur and relate them to the visible colour. The input of electrical power into the kiln can be observed, either by keeping a track of the units as they register on the electricity meter or by counting the revolutions of the meter wheel, which turns at various speeds depending upon the amount of electricity being used; both give guidance as to what is happening inside the kiln.

When firing the electric kiln there is little to do for most of the time except to check regularly that the temperature is rising, to see that a fuse or a kiln element has not burnt out and to adjust the controls as and when necessary. Only towards the end of the firing, when most careful temperature checks and 'soaking periods' (long periods at a pre-arranged temperature) are required, is skilled assessment needed. Despite many sophisticated switch-off systems, many potters still prefer to attend to this process manually. It is at this time that an accurate and carefully kept log of previous firings can be a useful guide to what is happening.

How different this is to the drama and heat of the flame kilns when the firing process can make or literally break the ware packed within it. Weather, chance, the careful regulation of temperature rise as well as the intricacies of controlling kiln atmosphere all involve great skill and often hard work. Electric kilns require a very different sort of skill, for the kiln will only provide the amount of heat necessary by radiation; there are no surges of scorching flames or suchlike to affect the pots. The kiln will only produce the work that goes in to it; body, glaze, decoration, as well as kiln packing, have to be decided before the door of the kiln is closed. Nothing will be given by the actual heat of the kiln except to work the physical changes in the materials. No amount of nursing the electric kiln, carefully peering into the glowing spyholes or nervous tapping of the pyrometer indicator will have much effect upon the results of the firing, nor is it possible to throw on more wood, adjust the dampers or open the gas taps.

Basically, the electric kiln consists of a box made from refractory material which is heated by some sort of electric elements secured to the inside of the walls. The box can be almost any size, ranging from 0.01 cu m ($\frac{1}{2}$ cu ft) to 2.3 or 2.8 cu m (80 or 100 cu ft). Electric kilns used by most potters range from about 0.11 cu m (4 cu ft) to 0.34 cu m (12 cu ft), but this depends on the type and quantity of pots being produced. Studio potters making repetition domestic ware and working with one assistant may find a kiln 0.34–0.4 cu m (12–14 cu ft) a manageable and useful size. To keep production moving, a potter concentrating more on individual pieces may prefer a kiln of half this size or even smaller, whilst an artist modelling large sculptures must choose a kiln of suitable dimensions.

Unlike most electric kilns used in the ceramic industry, potters fire their kilns intermittently; that is, they pack them when cold, or cool, fire them to the required temperature and let them cool down before unpacking them. The ceramic industry fire the majority of their wares in intermittent kilns loaded with trucks. Some, however, fire their kilns continuously. These are constructed like huge tunnels through which slowly pass trolley-loads of pots; these move from low, to medium, to top temperatures in the kiln and then to cooler again before emerging at the other end. The firing method affects the design of the kiln. Studio potters' kilns, for instance, are more heavily worn by the cooling and heating process, which puts a much greater strain on the fabric of the kiln. For instance, unless the wire elements are firmly held in supporting grooves they fall out of their supports; brickwork, which is continually expanding and contracting, develops splits and cracks in roofs and walls, particularly around the door. Equally, studio potters' kilns have to be well sealed; the door has to be well fitting and constructed so that it can be easily swung into position. This is made more difficult if the door is fitted with heating elements, which will make it heavier, and this can demand some fairly exacting engineering work.

Yet not all electric kilns need be so complex; depending on the size of the kiln required and the temperature to which it is fired, it can be relatively simple to construct out of lightweight refractory materials. Recently materials have been developed which are considerably lighter in weight and have far less bulk.

For the inside of the kiln, 'hot-face' materials still tend to be the traditional lightweight bricks. These range in constitution and density according to the temperature at which the kilns into which they are fitted are intended to be fired. The higher temperature bricks have a greater alumina content. An advantage of these bricks is that, while they cannot carry heavy loads, they will support themselves, and as such can be built into a metal frame to hold them together. The bricks are fairly soft and can be cut with a hacksaw blade. Such bricks are used for the inside surface only and are backed up with more cheaply produced bricks and/or the recently introduced ceramic fibre materials which have excellent insulating qualities.

Ceramic fibre is produced by blowing a high velocity gas jet onto a molten stream of high-purity aluminium silicate. Fluffy, white, cotton-like fibres are produced which can then be made up into various forms such as blankets, felt, brick modules, board, wool and so on. Depending on the precise alumina-silica ratio, the ceramic fibre will withstand very high temperatures. As the fibre does not readily absorb or retain heat, it is not always possible to use it as a hot face material in electric kilns as its excellent properties can cause the elements to overheat. However, as a back up material or on inside surfaces which do not carry

elements (such as the roof) ceramic fibre is excellent.

Kiln elements

There are two main types of electric heating elements, both of which resist the flow of electric current and, in so doing, generate heat. The most common and the one with which many people are familiar is the metal spiral wire of the type used in electric fires. The other type is in the form of a silicon carbide rod, and these are discussed in the next section. Wire elements used in kilns are made out of a special mixture of metals which can withstand the high temperatures of stoneware firings; unlike the elements in an electric fire which loses heat through radiation and convection quickly, the chamber of the kiln traps in the heat and the elements get very much hotter. No one metal alone can normally withstand high temperatures without burning out or collapsing and so kiln elements are made from alloys of such metals as nickel, chrome, cobalt and iron. Depending upon the metals used and in what proportion and thickness (gauge), element wire can be designed to fire to different temperatures. Nichrome elements, made from nickel and chrome, will only withstand a kiln temperature of about $1050°C$ ($1922°F$) though the elements themselves go to a much higher point. In kilns fired to higher temperatures the wire will quickly burn away. The largest manufacturer of wires for kiln elements are Kanthal of Sweden and the wire is sold under license in various part of the world. Kanthal 'A' wire has an operating limit of $1250°C$ ($2282°F$) while Kanthal 'A1' has an effective maximum of $1300°C$ ($2372°F$).

Commercially built kilns are carefully designed to be as economical and efficient as possible. The size of the kiln chamber and the maximum firing temperature will determine the requisite number, length and type of elements. The element will be of a specific metal mixture, will be of a specific thickness gauge, and will be of a particular length wound into a spiral with 'tails' protruding at each end. The elements required by a kiln must be replaced with identical elements if evenness of temperature is to be maintained.

Metal elements need to be firmly supported inside retaining grooves in the kiln because they soften at high temperatures and would collapse if not held in position. They will also become brittle and fragile after several firings.

Silicon carbide rods

So far I have been discussing the exposed wire elements with which most electrical kilns are fitted. These can clearly be seen in the kiln and are held in position by grooves, though some may be supported by porcelain tubes which run down the middle. Elements can be concealed inside tubes, or behind muffles, and this has the advantages of protecting them from the effect of the atmospheres in the kiln and helping to prevent accidental damage.

An alternative to the wire element are silicon carbide (SiC) rods. These have certain advantages: they can operate at much higher temperatures, up to 1600°C (2912°F), and are not affected by reducing atmosphere in the kilns. The disadvantages of silicon carbide rods lie in that they are very much more expensive to buy (up to ten times, or more, the cost of wire) and need quite complicated arrangements within the kiln as they are not so flexible in use. Most are made in the form of hollow rods (those for lower temperatures are solid) and are self-supporting in the kiln. Each rod is usually housed in a protective brickwork enclosure to prevent it getting knocked and broken as it becomes very brittle in use. Rods can be mounted either vertically or horizontally.

Over a period of time the rods start to fail, that is, they become less resistant and their heating ability decreases. When this happens they need to be replaced. If a rod accidentally gets broken, it must be replaced with one of a similar age as a new rod will upset the balance of the kiln element. If no suitable replacement is available all the rods should be changed, and the good ones stored for possible future use. Rods are connected by means of a looped wire and, as with all elements, all screw joints have to be tight.

Types of electric kiln

While the actual box construction of a kiln built within a frame is a relatively simple procedure, there is not the space in this book to describe in detail how this is best done and how the kiln can be fitted with electric elements in order to fire evenly and, very importantly, safely, to the required temperature. Robert Fournier's book, *Electric Kiln Construction*, is a clear and accurate account of how to build electric kilns. Potters wishing to do so would be advised to follow Robert Fournier's instructions, which are based on many years of experience. There is, as Robert Fournier points out, a marked saving in costs,

often of up to 50%, to be achieved by building your own kiln.

Manufacturers produce a wide range of kilns, many of which are illustrated in their catalogues. It is surprising to note how little variation there is between examples of the same type, though in terms of construction and performance levels there are differences, which are worth investigating. Apart from the different type of elements used, there are two basic types of kiln on the market: top loading with a hinged or removable lid, or side loading fitted with a door.

Top loading kilns

Kilns which are packed from the top have many advantages: they are usually simpler to construct, can be made more airtight because there is no side door and can be fitted with continuous elements which go round the walls to help achieve even, allover temperatures. The lower cost of such kilns reflect these production benefits. There are disadvantages with such kilns: some potters find

Lucie Rie's top loading kiln fitted with a lid which has a counter-balance arrangement to enable it to be lowered into position

that leaning over and reaching down into the kiln makes them difficult to pack, though others say this becomes much easier with experience. There is a physical limit imposed on the size of this type of kiln determined by how far it is possible to lean down into the chamber. Some potters find a depth of 90 cm (3 ft) quite sufficient, especially when bulky kiln shelves have to be manoeuvred gently into position so that no damage is done to pots already in position. Elements are rarely included in the roof of the kiln and this may make high temperatures difficult to obtain.

Some lids on top loading kilns are arranged to lift upwards, where they are held in position by a hinged bracket. However, because of the compact weight of the lid this is often a precarious arrangement, particularly after the kiln has been in use for some time. During the firings steam, fumes and, to some extent, heat escapes through the join between the lid and the chamber; this affects the metal hinges, which can be considerably weakened by rust. Hinged lids are fitted onto many of the quick-fire electric kilns recently introduced onto the market. Regular servicing of the kiln is necessary to prevent deterioration. Alternatives to the hinged lid involve solid slabs of refractory material (which can be bulky and heavy to move around) or layers of different material which are lifted manually into position. Cantilever devices which enable the lid to be lifted mechanically can be constructed so that the heavier weight lids can be used.

The size of top loading kilns is also determined by the span of the kiln, for there is a limit to the strain that a flat roof will withstand.

Manufacturers make two main types of top loading kilns. One is the square box type which is set into a solid metal frame and may be finished with a thin metal cladding. Hard asbestos board or a similar material now on the market may be used as cladding instead of more expensive, and cosmetic, metal; recent worries about the dangers of some types of asbestos have tended to discourage its use. The introduction of ceramic fibre insulating material has enabled kiln walls to be reduced in thickness though such materials, because of their low mechanical strength and their ability to retain heat, cannot house the elements. Such kilns are therefore lined with a thinnish layer of white firebrick (about 5 cm, 2 in) backed up with ceramic fibre either in the form of blocks or blanket.

Ceramic fibres have particularly influenced the design of the second type, thin walled, hexagonal shaped or round 'dustbin' top loading kilns. These

Top loading kiln

are simply constructed: the metal shell supports the layers of insulating material which are literally wedged into place. Costly and complex brickwork is eliminated, making the price of such kilns economical. Equally important is the rapid firing (and cooling) cycles achieved by the use of such efficient insulation, which can represent substantial saving in firing costs. Faster (or slower) firings affect the maturing of the body and glaze and this has to be taken into account. Such kilns are also much lighter in weight and therefore more portable than the heavier, more traditional structures.

A particular feature of one series of top loading kilns is the facility to add or remove sections. This enables kilns to be enlarged to house more work or taller pieces, or to be reduced in size according to requirements. Each section sits on the one below and is separately wired, so no complicated procedure is needed in order to change the size of the kiln.

Many of the smaller sized top loading kilns with the thinner walls are produced at low prices and are fitted with only the necessary minimum of electrical control equipment. Some have a kiln control which can be preset to operate the cut-off switch. These work by means of a bar made from ceramic material; these bars, like pyrometric

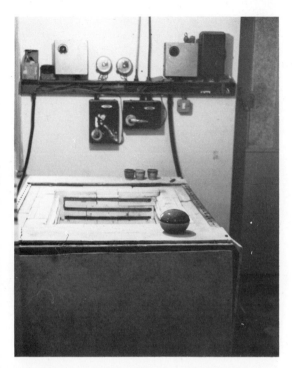

Sally Dawson's top loading kiln which she built herself; the controls can be seen in the background

Small earthenware kiln; absence of elements in door indicates this is for earthenware temperatures

cones, are available in different grades, all designed to soften at specific temperatures. The selected bar is placed inside the kiln so that it supports a trip switch. When the softening temperature of the bar is reached, the bar, or 'setter', softens and bends; this automatically operates the switch and turns off the kiln. Economical and fast to fire, these kilns often need a setter of 20–30°C (75°F) above the required temperature to allow time for a soak period so that the glazes are able to mature. Underfired glazes look dry and dusty but can usually be refired if necessary.

Side loading kilns

One of the advantages of side loading kilns is that they can be located at waist level and for most people this makes for easier packing. There is no need to lean over in order to peer into the kiln, though again there is the depth – front to back – limit. The placing of heavy kiln shelves at the back of a deep kiln can be tricky and be a strain on back muscles. Some deep kilns are fitted with a trolley on rails. This can be loaded outside the kiln chamber and then gently pushed into the kiln.

Most commercially manufactured kilns are fitted with a single side door, though on larger kilns, depending upon the space available, double

'French' doors are fitted. Because of the sheer weight of firebrick built into the door they are quite heavy and put a large strain on the kiln framework. This strain can, in time, result in a badly fitting door, which in turn creates 'cold spots'. It would seem that little can be done about this but as a precaution it is advisable to keep the door closed and securely fastened whilst the kiln is not in use. This lessens stress on the frame as well as protecting elements from workshop dust.

Some kilns are fitted with a cumbersome drop door which can be operated by means of a counterweight system. These doors are useful in cramped conditions or where kilns are placed close to each other. With the introduction of ceramic fibres, door weights will be reduced and better, and a more lasting door fit will be possible.

Depending on the firing temperature for which the kiln has been designed, elements may be fitted into the floor, side walls, back wall and door of the kiln. This will ensure all round heat and the possibility of even firings. Kilns intended for a maximum temperature of 1100°C (2012°F) may only have elements in the side walls and floor. As mentioned, elements are rarely fitted in the roof, though some manufacturers do fit them on their heavy duty kilns. The problem with this is that at top temperature the element wire gets very soft

Stoneware kiln, 0.34 cu m (12 cu ft)

and, when worn, often falls out of its support.

When elements are fitted into the door of the kiln, for the sake of safety, the connecting cable should be carried within a flexible conduit tube to protect it from damage. Equally, the catch which locks the kiln door in position should be of the type which can be tightened to ensure as snug a fit as possible. The edges of the doors are usually tapered to provide close joins; as the brickwork heats up it expands and, in theory, an airtight fit is achieved. In practice this rarely happens and inevitable cold spots will occur on the bottom front shelf where air is drawn into the kiln. This is one disadvantage of side loading kilns.

Depending on the size of the kiln, the roof will either be flat (on the smaller kilns) or arched (on larger kilns) to achieve a wider span. Because of the lack of movement of air in the kiln, the arch can be quite a cold spot and this has to be taken into account when packing the kiln.

All side loading kilns are fitted with some sort of vent or damper. These are either at the top back of the arch, the centre of the roof or in the back wall of the kiln. On smaller kilns this is simply a firebrick which is placed into position; on larger kilns a more complex arrangement, with an opening flap which can be adjusted, is fitted. The

purpose of this vent is to allow fumes and vapour to escape in the early stages of the firing and, after switching off, to speed up the cooling cycle. A well fitting flap or brick is essential if cool spots are to be avoided. Through currents of air in an electric kiln should be avoided; cold air entering at the door, and leaving via the vent will not only waste heat and cause uneven temperatures, but it may also prevent the top temperature being reached.

A spy hole, or holes, some 5 cm (2 in) across in the door enables the inside of the chamber to be observed during the firing. These holes are fitted with either a ceramic or brick bung, or a metal flap, which can be removed when necessary to look into the kiln or aid ventilation.

Some potters seal or clamp their kilns round the door jamb and vent outlet with a mixture of sand, clay and water, but on a well made and maintained kiln this should not be necessary.

Trolley kilns
It is just not possible to load such objects as heavy sculptures into a front loading kiln; they can only be fired in a trolley kiln. This consists of a bogey or trolley which forms the base of the kiln, set on rails which run into the firing chamber. Such kilns are usually built on site, are expensive to construct and are usually large in size. They are beyond the means of most small workshops. However, such kilns can be useful in colleges and schools, or for larger production workshops, since they enable quantities of small pieces to be packed more quickly and, with the all round access, more efficiently. The firing or operating of such kilns is exactly the same as the other front loaders.

Top hat kilns
Top hat kilns are fitted onto a winching device and are literally lifted off or placed over the ware. The kiln will serve several bases, each one fixed. When the base is loaded the chamber of the kiln is lowered onto it. The system has several advantages: the chamber can be removed while still warm and taken from one kiln base and placed over another base waiting to be fired. The arrangement is geared to large output, is mechanically complicated and is of limited use for the studio potter.

Tunnel kilns
Equally complex in structure are the tunnel or continuous kilns which are used widely in the heavy clay and domestic pottery industries. The truck or trolley loaded with ware is moved slowly on rails through the kiln. The elements are

arranged so that the temperature increases until the firing cone is reached. Heat from the hot part of the tunnel is transferred towards the cooler parts, the kiln structure is not subjected to the stresses of cooling and heating and evenness of firing can be obtained.

Kiln controls

The temperature inside the kiln has to be controlled so that it will rise at the required speed, and this speed will depend on many factors. These factors include the type of firing (for example, whether it is a biscuit, glaze or on-glaze firing), the type of clay that is being fired, the density of packing in the kiln and the types of pots in the kiln (for example, whether they are small or large, or thick or thin walled). Equally the rate of temperature rise may need to be altered as the firing progresses; it may need to be speeded up, slowed down or maintained at a constant level (soaked). Control of temperature in the kiln is achieved mainly by controlling the input of electricity and this can be done in several ways.

1 The simplest and most direct method is by means of an on-off switch which is manually operated. As a general practice it is best to ensure that ware is as dry as possible before firing, but even bone dry pieces still contain some moisture which needs to be driven off slowly. By the simple expedient of switching the kiln on for a few minutes at a time and then off, the temperature can slowly be increased. This is effective in small kilns. It is not advisable to use this method on large kilns where the electrical input is considerably greater. For automatic control, or for larger kilns, more sophisticated equipment is required.

2 The supply of electricity can be interrupted on a regulated basis by the use of an intermittent switch system. A typical example in widespread use is the Sunvic control, which is operated by a dial knob marked with a scale of 1–100, spread over 1 minute; when the dial is set at 50 the kiln is on for 30 seconds. It is on for 50% of the time and could be said to be at a medium setting. Set at 75 the kiln would be on for 45 seconds, off for 15 seconds. On 100 the kiln would be on continuously. A low setting would be 10 (on 6 seconds, off 54 seconds).

This system involves the use of quite complex time/heat switches which, although noisy in operation and costly to install, are a very effective means of control; they allow for a slow build-up of heat and, with experience, excellent firing programmes can be worked out.

3 Separate switches for each element (or banks of elements) can be installed so that they can be switched on one at a time. This is a relatively inexpensive method but has the disadvantage of heating up the kiln unevenly. With improved electronic engineering and, more recently, with the introduction of the silicon chip, quite complex methods of controlling the temperature rise in the kiln have been developed. The three methods described above, for instance, are all manual in that the kiln has to be switched on and off, the controls adjusted by hand. Such a system means that potters are tied to their firings. This may be a big disadvantage if, for example, a cheap rate of electricity is available overnight and special visits to the workshop have to be made. Automatic switch-on or even switch-off devices can make firing kilns much easier and convenient.

The time clock

This relatively inexpensive device widely used on central heating systems. It will not control the input of electricity but will switch the kiln on, or off, at a desired time; for example, the clock can be set to switch the kiln on in your absence. It can also act as a safety device. With experience it is possible to estimate how long it will take to fire a particular kiln and this will depend on such factors as the amount of ware, the density of packing and the number of kiln shelves. If a firing takes, say, 12 hours, the clock can be set to switch off automatically shortly afterwards; if for any reason the kiln is not attended, the automatic clock will end the firing. Not a method of firing a kiln, but a useful safety check.

Heat fuse

Safety devices which avoid waste and prevent damage are often incorporated into kilns. The heat fuse comes into operation if the kiln overfires. They can be set for any temperature; mine is fixed at 1300°C (2372°F) – some 40°C (104°F) above my usual firing temperature. They are similar to a thermo-couple in that they consist of a ceramic sheath which projects into the firing chamber of the kiln, and this is wired into the kiln circuit; a fuse burns out if the maximum safe temperature is reached. This cuts off the electrical supply to the kiln, protecting pots, shelves and kiln from excessive damage.

Safety devices

Potters working by themselves should fit devices to their kilns to prevent accidents from heat or electric shock, but if people are employed then full legal precautions have to be taken. The most useful safety device is a door switch which, when the door is open, automatically cuts off the electric supply to the elements. There are more sophisticated variations which are fitted with a key which operates a lock on the door; this can only be removed when the door is locked shut and used to switch on the electric supply. Safety precautions for kilns in schools and educational establishments are detailed in the Appendix.

Outlined here are only the kiln controls which, though quite complex in themselves, are controlled by the person firing the kiln. There are electronic firing systems which are much more complicated and allow more sophisticated firing patterns. For instance, a 'soak' control will maintain any pre-set temperature for a specific length of time, which can vary from 15 minutes to 8 hours. A programme controller can determine the whole firing cycle from start to finish. It can control temperature rise according to any determined cycle, maintaining, speeding up or slowing down the rise in temperature, and when final temperature is reached the controller will switch the kiln off.

Other devices will switch the kiln off at pre-set temperatures but will not automatically control the temperature rise. Many potters find such controls very useful.

Choosing your kiln

The decision facing most potters, once they have decided to purchase an electric kiln, is which kiln to choose. Decisions about size, firing temperature, electrical loading, wire element or silicon carbide rod, top or side loader, cost and so on, will all have to be made. Many questions will resolve themselves but there will still be many variables. The first thing to take into consideration is the fact that the kiln is a major and necessary investment. The kiln which you choose should be as perfect as it can be, since it has to last many years. Kilns are not cheap and so all factors have to be taken into consideration. First, study the catalogue. Manufacturer's catalogues may look and sound very impressive and give masses of information, some of which is not always exactly relevant to what you require to know. Always check on the type of control equipment that is fitted to the kiln. There is a sequence of questions which are worth asking which may make the decision easier.

Size
This will depend partly on your requirements, partly on your electric supply and partly on cost. If you want to work by yourself producing one-off pieces and yet have enough space in your kiln to pack in quite a few pots, then a kiln with a firing chamber measuring some $30 \times 30 \times 30$ cm ($12 \times 12 \times 12$ in) will give you a small kiln which can be fired frequently. For most potters a kiln of this size is too limiting; the next practical size is $45 \times 45 \times 45$ cm ($18 \times 18 \times 18$ in) which will, if well packed, hold quite a lot of pots. This is a useful average-size kiln.

For potters planning larger scale production of pottery a larger kiln will be required. Depending upon output, some potters prefer a kiln with say, a large firing chamber of 0.37 cu m (13 cu ft), whilst others will choose a smaller kiln which will then be fired more frequently. Such choices are not easily made, but it is worth bearing in mind that a large kiln may take a potter working alone a long time to fill, and will on the whole discourage experimental work. Smaller kilns fired more often will give shorter periods between firing and quicker feed-back information from finished work.

Electricity supply
Size will also depend on the electric supply available. Most houses in the U.K. are equipped with a single phase electric supply of 240v which will accept up to 30 amps on the electric cooker and water immersion heater circuit. These will, without difficulty, carry a kiln with a rating of less that 6.75 kilowatts, which, on a full load will consume about 28 amps on a 240 volt supply. This will accommodate a kiln capacity of around 0.08 cu m (3 cu ft).

Most houses in the U.K., however, have the possibility of providing a much larger supply such as a 60 amp or even a 100 amp supply, and this can be tapped without incurring great expense. Contact with your local electricity board is essential in order to establish what is readily available. In towns and cities for example, heavier supplies may be cheaply installed. For the rural potter it may be very expensive if new cable has to be laid. A 15 kilowatt supply will limit the size of the firing chamber to about 0.2 cu m (7 cu ft) for stoneware firing and 0.25 cu m (9 cu ft) for a lower temperature earthenware-firing.

Some properties are fitted with a three-phase supply and this will usually allow for a much greater possible consumption. When ordering a kiln, the manufacturer will require information as to what sort of electric supply is available and you will need to check carefully to ensure that you are making the most economic use of fuel. For instance, the larger kilns tend to be more economical and so the cost of firing will be proportionately less, an important factor when doing long term planning. Thin-walled kilns which incorporate highly efficient insulation will fire much more quickly than the heavier walled kilns constructed from more traditional firebricks. On kilns up to 0.28 cu m (10 cu ft) this can give a saving of up to 25%, though it has to be remembered that the speed of firing will affect the melting and maturing of the glaze.

Cost of kilns
The price of a kiln depends on various factors such as the size of the kiln, whether it is standard or custom built, the maximum temperature at which it is intended to operate and whether the kiln is to be installed by you or by the kiln manufacturers. Kilns built on-site are by far the most expensive, being approximately double the price of a similar kiln built at the manufacturers. Check, therefore, as to whether factory-built kilns can be taken into your workshop, and choose accordingly.

Kilns, whether built with the newer ceramic fibres or with traditional materials, will still be quite heavy when installed. Whilst some of the smaller lightweight kilns are advertised as being portable, most workshop kilns are permanent fixtures and need to be placed on a firm, load-bearing floor. Ideally they should be on a ground floor made out of concrete. On wooden floors the kiln may need to be placed in a corner so that its weight is distributed around two walls; the least safe place would be in the centre of the room. If in doubt check with a structural engineer or architect.

The catalogue
Before making your final choice study carefully the manufacturers' specification, attempting to compare like with like. One method is to draw up a table listing size (bear in mind the outside dimensions of the kiln as well as the firing chamber size), the kilowatt loading, firing times (these are not always given) and maximum firing temperature. Check that the control equipment and delivery charges are included in the price. Note also any mention of guarantee and the availability of service for new elements or repairs.

Finally, ask around. Potters in your area may have such kilns and be able to advise on their performance, a factor which is both personal and difficult to measure. Some manufacturers will give the names and addresses of potters in your area who have already installed the kiln in which you are interested.

Kiln installation

Once you have decided on which kiln to buy you have to choose where in the workshop is the best place to put it. Potters with production workshops should divide the space into distinct working areas, such as clay storage and preparation, making, glazing and firing. With flame burning kilns the siting of the kiln is crucial; there has to be sufficient room for fuel storage, a clear access, good fire safety and access to a suitable flue outlet. With electric kilns the considerations are different. The cable supply can be taken to almost any position and the heat from the kiln can be used to warm the workshop as well as for drying pots or clay.

But fumes, and steam, given off during firing, can be quite strong and the kiln room must be well ventilated to allow for these to escape. In no circumstances is it wise to install the kiln in a tiny room with poor ventilation. A 25 cm (10 in) extractor fan fitted in a window or wall will move a considerable volume of air, and even open windows will give through draughts. Over large kilns a metal hood with a flue outlet fitted with an extractor fan is advised, but for most kilns this is not necessary.

Space is the final consideration. Kilns should have sufficient room around them so that they can be easily inspected; 76–91 cm (30–36 in) from the wall is a workable minimum. This will also give sufficient space between the kiln and the wall to allow air to circulate. On cooling, kilns give off considerable amounts of heat over long periods of time. The kiln controls, which are often located behind the kiln, must have plenty of space so that regular check-ups can easily be made. A tight squeeze will discourage this and make the replacement of elements more difficult; 91 cm (36 in) would be the minimum distance.

With a properly maintained kiln there is little fire risk. Naked flames are not involved and heat is given off slowly over a period of time. However, this heat can have a considerable drying effect on the walls and ceilings and this has to be borne in mind. The more space there is between kiln and ceiling, the safer the installation; again a minimum of 91 cm (36 in) is suggested. One safety precaution is to install a baffle made out of fireproof material above the kiln on the ceiling. A gap of about 15 cm (6 in) between ceiling and baffle will provide an air space to protect the ceiling from direct heat rising from the kiln.

Wherever possible, the space under, around and above the kiln should be kept neat and tidy, with

racks provided for kiln shelves and props.

Kilns which require more than a 13 amp supply should be installed by a qualified electrician and all installations should be professionally checked. Ensure that the electric cable is properly laid and that it is fitted with its own fuses and mains switch, so that the kiln and its controls can be isolated. A qualified fitter will also be required to connect the kiln to the electricity supply. With heavy electrical loads it is essential that this is done correctly.

Firing costs

The cost of firing kilns by electricity can be as competitive as those fired by any other sort of bought fuel, particularly when the advantages of automatic firings are taken into account. The cost of electricity is charged according to the amount consumed and is measured in units of kilowatt hours, that is, one kilowatt used for one hour. An electric fire rated at 2 kilowatts, if switched on full for 1 hour, will consume 2 units of electricity. If a unit costs 5p then the cost of this would be $2 \times 5p = 10p$. The cost of electricity consumed by kilns is slightly more complicated to work out, a 15 kilowatt kiln will cost, on full power, $15 \times 5p = 75p$ per hour to run. Over a period of 10 hours this will amount to £7.50. The periods when

Corrosion on the metal framework of a kiln

the kiln will be on half power can be recalculated accordingly.

Electricity, however, is charged for at different rates at different times of the day and night and commercial or home consumers will pay at various rates; it is always worth checking with your local electricity board as to what rates are available. There may, for instance, be a private and an industrial tariff, or a rate which will decrease dramatically after a certain number of units have been consumed. For most potters the off-peak night-rate, sometimes called the white meter rate, are usually applicable between the hours of 11 pm and 7 am, and will be most economic.

Systems on the night rate are operated by a time clock, which comes on and goes off automatically, and the units used in this period are charged accordingly; any units used outside these set times are calculated at the higher rate. To use these periods economically your kiln needs to be switched on at, say 11 pm and for the firing to be over by 7 am. This is where automatic time switches are useful. Rates and times do vary considerably and only your area Electricity Board can advise.

Electricity will also bear some sort of 'standing-charge' in addition to the cost of units actually consumed. This may be calculated in various ways, but it is a charge that has to be taken into account when reckoning costs. Ideally it is best to have a separate electricity meter for your kiln. The turning wheel enables you to check, by its speed, that sufficient electricity is being consumed and that none of the elements has burnt out. Also, by recording the number of units of electricity consumed over a number of firings, you can calculate the number of units consumed in one firing. This is not only a correct indication of the cost of the firing, essential information when you are working out prices and the costs of production, but is also an excellent guide to the progress of the firing and a good indication of when the desired temperature has been reached. This will be discussed at greater length in the next chapter.

Kiln care

For most potters a kiln represents a major capital investment and should be looked after and maintained accordingly. Not only should the fabric of the kiln be kept clean and, as far as possible, free of dust and grit, but the electrical wiring and connections need to be checked regularly to ensure that no rusting or arcing has taken place. *Whenever work is being done on the kiln the mains supply should be switched off.* When major maintenance is carried out remove the fuses. This is a basic and essential safety procedure. A household vacuum cleaner nozzle is ideal for removing dust and small pieces of grit which accumulate in corners or grooves; do not disturb the elements any more than is necessary as they become brittle after a few firings and break very easily. Check they are all in good condition and note any burnt spots which could indicate that they are wearing out.

To check the electrical wiring the safety covers have to be removed. Follow each circuit as far as possible making sure all joins and connections are clean and tight. The steam and gases liberated during firings will, over a period of time, eat into both the brick and metal fabric of the kiln, corroding the metal and causing edges of bricks to discolour and crumble. While there is unfortunately little that can be done to prevent this, it is essential that the effects of the corrosion should be regularly monitored and the kiln kept as clean and safe as possible.

Brickwork is also affected by the heating and

Cracks and wear on the brickwork of the kiln

cooling processes and will develop alarming-looking cracks and splits. In my experience there is not much that can be done about this. During the firing the brickwork expands and the cracks close up, and they indicate the amount of movement that takes place. Small bits and pieces do fall off the edges of these cracks and this is where a stiff brush is useful to remove loose edges. Filling the cracks in the brickwork or between the roof and walls with high temperature refractory cement is not recommended as it will quickly fall out and may ruin a special pot. Bricks on the edges of doors or walls often get broken; they tend to get weakened by steam and fumes as well as being knocked when kiln shelves are being placed into position. Sometimes these bricks can be replaced successfully but, again, this is not always possible.

Wire elements
Some kiln suppliers will guarantee the fabric of the kiln, but very few will say how long the elements should last. Principally, this is because the life of the element will depend on the number of firings (the working life), the maximum temperature to which the wire is taken, and the contents of the kiln, all of which are highly individual and variable conditions.

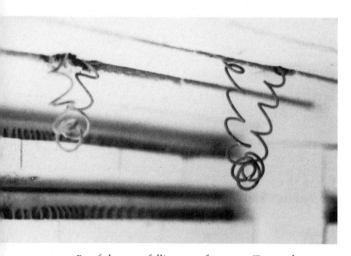

Roof elements falling out of grooves. To put the element back in position, first turn the kiln on for a few minutes, as the element is brittle when cold. Turn the kiln off and squeeze the coils together using pliers

Elements do have an average working life and most potters will establish a knowledge of this based on their own experience. In my kiln the average life is 9–12 months. By firing to a slightly lower temperature the working life of the elements will be extended. Elements which are fired regularly to their recommended maximum temperature will have a much shorter life. Newly installed elements are at their most efficient and give out maximum heat for electrical input. Such a situation will last for only some half-dozen firings before there is a dramatic fall off in performance, after which they settle down to give a steadier temperature rise. Rapid firings affect the result, particularly when glazes are being fired, and most potters prefer a slower firing to give the glaze and body time to mature, factors which are worth bearing in mind when the kiln is new or elements have been replaced.

All potters do not agree on the benefits, or otherwise, of complete element replacement. During the life of the kiln the elements gradually get thinner; eventually they will start to flatten and become relatively inefficient. Some may fall out of their supporting grooves; as the elements get hot they soften and unless firmly supported and held in place they very easily lean out and stretch, hanging down the wall of the kiln. Once an element has fallen from its groove it is very difficult to put back into place, as the wire is brittle when it is cold, and any attempt to bend or move it will cause it to break. Some potters have found that after softening the wire by heating with a blow torch it can be pushed back into place with a pair of pliers,

but I have never been able to do this successfully. Gradually with each firing any loops of wire which have fallen from their groove will stretch more and more and can hang down the wall at a distance of some 20–25 cm (8–10 in). Provided that the kiln shelves can still be placed into position and the element continues to function it does not have to be replaced. The danger is that this element will eventually touch another element and make a short circuit which may, at its worst, burn out both of the elements, or fuse the kiln. In practice the element can be left as long as there is little likelihood of it touching another.

As the elements become thinner and less efficient it will be worthwhile considering the benefits of fitting a complete set of new elements. The advantages are that there will be an increase in the speed of the firing, but this can be slowed down if desired. A complete new set will ensure that evenness of firing throughout the kiln will be maintained, and there will be less risk of wasted firings as the result of a burnt-out element. It takes quite a lot of courage to take out perfecty good, but old, elements and replace them with new ones, particularly as the cost of wire increases, but I am convinced that for a production pottery overall savings are made.

The alternative procedure is to replace individual elements as they burn out or become too flattened to work efficiently. A burn out, which occurs usually in the middle of the firing, will effectively break the circuit of that series of elements. Some kilns are fitted with an indicator light which stays on as long as all circuits are working correctly. When an element fails the circuit is broken and there is little that can be done. The kiln will usually not reach temperature (i.e. the required working temperature) and it is best to switch off and accept that the firing is wasted. If the exact element which has failed is known connections can be made in the wiring section of the kiln with jump wires which will by-pass this element and complete the circuit. This, in emergencies, will work, but is not recommended as it imposes a much heavier load on the other elements and may cause other burn outs. A further disadvantage of this procedure is that during the time that the kiln is switched off in order to find the faulty element a drop in temperature will occur.

Removing elements, like all inspections of the kiln, is done only when the main electrical supply is switched off. Different kilns have various systems but all have a method of connecting the element wire to the circuit. This is done by means of a screw or nut and bolt arrangement which holds the wire firmly; connections must not be loose or arcing will occur. Once the connections are loosened the old element can be lifted out and every trace of the melted metal in the brickwork must be removed, using old chisels, screwdrivers and so on, as makeshift tools. Sometimes the burnout is quite dramatic with globules of metal and slag some 2.5–5 cm (1–2 in) across may be formed. All must be carefully dug out from the brickwork and any iron metal deposits scraped off. Large holes can be filled in with pieces of soft firebrick carefully cut to size, although they often fall out during the firing. Some manufacturers recommend filling holes with refractory cement, but this can shrink considerably during the firing to form a dense material which forms a hot spot in the groove. Porcelain support tubes which can be wedged in position to support the element are also available. All of these measures, of course, are a further argument for changing elements before they become liable to burn out.

simple burnout

ends interlocked

One method of joining together a burnt-out element. Stretch the wire and interlock; dab the join with water. Turn on the electricity supply, which will cause the wire to arc at the joins and to fuse together

New elements need to be of the exact type specified by the makers. Different elements in the kiln will be made from different lengths of wire and it is essential that the correct one be fitted. In other words, unless specified, elements are not interchangeable, even in the same kiln. Make sure that the screws holding the element tails in the connection are as tight as possible and that surfaces of the metal are clean and free from deposits. A rub with a wire brush or piece of emery cloth will serve as an effective cleaner. When placed in position, new elements need to be under slight tension. This will ensure that as they soften in the firing they will settle into the groove. If the element is slightly too long for the groove it will tend to buckle outwards and may fall down the kiln wall; the coils of the element need to be pushed firmly together.

If you have an accident and break an old element in the kiln, a temporary repair can be made by linking in together the broken ends of the two halves. This will be effective with new wire but less so with old wire, which builds up on the surface an oxidised layer which does not conduct electricity. When this happens the two elements have to be forced together to form a proper connection. This can be done by means of electric welding, involving the use of an oxy-acetylene flame and a flux such as borax. A cheaper, and less professional method, is to put a wad of wet clay on the join, which will hold the two ends together for a short period. Another method is to turn the kiln on for a few minutes to heat up the elements. Then turn the kiln off and, with pliers, squeeze the two ends of the elements together and interlock them. Dab the join with water and turn the kiln back on. The water will cause the wire to arc and fuse together, thus completing the circuit.

Regular cleaning of the kiln will prevent dust and bits of grit falling onto pots and ruining work. When elements have been replaced, of whatever type, the kiln should be checked to ensure it is working correctly. The current should be switched on and any indication lights checked. (Beware of a failed bulb; always make sure by replacing an unlit bulb with a working bulb.) Listen for any arcing or spitting noise. All Kanthal wire elements will omit a humming noise when first switched on; this will decrease and finally stop as the temperature increases. Listen for any arcing noises; these are produced when electricity jumps across a narrow gap, for instance in a loose connection. Sparks are formed and a sharp cracking or spitting noise can be heard. Heat is generated, and if the gaps are left they will either weld together or burn apart. A bright spot of light is also emitted as a result of the heat formed. If this happens, isolate the kiln at the mains, disconnect and clean the joins before tightening them up.

Finally, if no indicating lights are fitted, a simple check to ensure all the elements are working is to switch the kiln on for 3 or 4 minutes, then *switch off at the mains* and dab each element with clean water. A sizzling sound will issue from those which are working.

3 Packing, firing and controlling the kiln

Unlike kilns fired by flame-burning fuels, there is comparatively little movement of air inside the electric kiln. As mentioned already, during the firing fumes, steam and gases are given off and these need to be allowed to leave the kiln, either through the ventilation hole or by seeping through brickwork. Unfortunately, such spaces will also allow heat to pass through them and so they need to be carefully controlled for two reasons. The first reason is that they represent heat lost, when the aim of an electric kiln is to retain as much heat as possible. The second reason is that this escape of kiln atmosphere indicates movement of air upwards, and this will inevitably draw in cold air at the bottom of the kiln. This is a particular feature of many front loaders. So, packing and firing an electric kiln does require certain skill and an understanding of how the heat is distributed in the kiln.

Electrical elements give off heat which is dispersed by conduction, convection and radiation. Conduction is the passage of heat through solid materials both inside the kiln and, to some extent, through the kiln walls. Convection is heat transferred by the movement of air currents; hot air rises and cooler air moves in at the bottom to replace it. (A typical example is an electric convection heater which warms the room by air movement.) Because, for most of the firing, the electric kiln is sealed, little convection takes place, but in the early stages of firing, when the damper at the top of the kiln is open, convection can keep the bottom of the kiln much cooler than the top. Radiant heat is given off in straight lines and is the main method by which heat is passed into an electric kiln. After 800°C (1472°F) convection and conduction cease and the bulk of the heat given off from the elements is radiant. (The exposed bars of an electric fire, for instance, give off radiant heat which we can feel on our skins.) Inside the kiln this radiant heat has to be passed as evenly around the kiln as possible. Interior walls heat up and irradiate the kiln shelves and the pots, which in turn pass on some of their heat. For this reason it is essential to have elements in as many walls as possible so that the heat can be evenly distributed. Kilns which are badly designed or are too large for the number of elements present may scorch the pots which are adjacent to the elements because the heat is not sufficiently evenly distributed.

In kilns designed to fire to low temperatures (usually with a maximum of 1110°C, 2012°F) elements will be fitted in the side walls only; for higher temperatures, elements will need to be fitted into as many walls as possible, and in front loaders usually in the door and the floor. Whether elements are fitted in the floor or not, there should always be a gap of 13 mm–2.5 cm ($\frac{1}{2}$–1 in) between the floor of the kiln and the bottom shelf. This makes possible the movement of air, and the direct conduction of heat through the floor shelves. Some manufacturers fit elements in the roof to help eliminate the cold spot in the arch at the top of the kiln but, in time, these have a tendency to fall out during the firings. This cool spot in the top of the kiln is also a good illustration of the lack of convection that exists in the closed conditions of the firing chamber, and very careful packing is needed to ensure it does not occur. In top-loading kilns which have elements round all four walls as well as the floor, more even firings are possible, although cool spots may exist in bottom corners.

Silicon carbide rod kilns usually have fewer elements because each rod gives off a proportionally greater amount of heat, up to six times as much as an equivalent wire element. The correct packing of these kilns is even more essential if an even temperature throughout the chamber is to be achieved.

Kiln furniture

Electric kilns are open packed, that is, the pots are placed on batts or shelves supported by various sorts of props. Normally, saggars (closed containers) are not used. Batts, props, pot supports, tile or plate cranks are defined as kiln furniture.

Manufacturers will recommend suitable furniture for use in the particular kiln they supply and this will depend upon the maximum firing temperature and the size of the chamber. There are, basically, two sorts of kiln shelves, those made from ceramic material and the others from silicon carbide. The latter can be recommended for use in electric kilns because, though silicon carbide will conduct electricity, the batts are bonded together by clay and this makes them safe. Unfortunately the cost of these shelves is considerably greater than ceramic shelves, and although they withstand the effects of the heat without warping they become very brittle and can easily be damaged during kiln packing. They are excellent for use on the floor of the kiln as in this position they need to be removed only occasionally for cleaning. Unfortunately, all kiln shelves get the odd glaze drip on them and silicon carbide shelves are no exception. This problem will be dealt with later in the chapter.

Ceramic shelves, usually called batts, are made in two grades – high temperature and low temperature – both of which are available in many sizes and thicknesses. Most potter choose the high temperature batts because, although they are slightly more expensive, they tend to warp less in use. Most high temperature kiln furniture is made from high grade alumina refractories and will withstand working temperatures of up to 1300°C (2372°F). It is generally accepted that the total weight of the kiln furniture is likely to be greater than the combined weights of the ware, which means that over half of the heat of the firing is taken up by the kiln furniture. The moral, therefore, is to keep the amount of furniture to a minimum. Industry tends to use highly specialised kiln furniture, such as tile cranks which support the tiles at each corner, or plate cranks, the use of which can give important weight and space savings. Such equipment is worth considering but is often not used at temperatures much above 1200°C (2192°F). At this temperature most clay bodies used by the studio potter start to soften and need firm, even support to prevent warping.

Thicker kiln shelves will warp less and therefore give a longer working life than thinner ones, but against this must be set the fact that they are heavier and more bulky. From a handling point of view, thinner shelves present fewer problems and can be lifted in and out of the kiln with far less difficulty. Any savings in fuel consumed may be more than offset by the cost of more frequent replacement. In my kiln, which has a placing chamber 61 cm (24 in) high, and usually holds six shelf levels, each one made up of four batts, a total of 24 batts are used. With shelves of 13 mm ($\frac{1}{2}$ in) thickness, this gives a total solid mass 30 cm (12 in) tall. With shelves of 19 mm ($\frac{3}{4}$ in) (which is the thickness I use) the total height of the kiln shelves themselves is 46 cm (18 in). These shelves have a useful working life of about 18 months, during which time they will be fired some 150 times to temperatures of 1260°C (2300°F), not including biscuit firings.

Thickness is not the only consideration; the span of the shelf is also important. Some batt manufacturers suggest for stoneware temperatures a maximum span of 25–30 cm (10–12 in) between supports. Larger kiln shelves may not be the answer to prevent bending, as the greater the span the heavier the load the shelf has to bear. To reduce costs some kiln shelves are pierced, which reduces bulk and firing cost, but unless ware is designed specially to fit over the holes the shelves are not satisfactory.

Manufacturers will recommend batt sizes suitable for the kilns they supply, but generally speaking there should be a minimum of 13 mm ($\frac{1}{2}$ in) gap between the shelf and the kiln wall.

Batt supports are made in a variety of styles, the most common of which are the tubular props, castellated props and castles. Some manufacturers recommend the use of flat discs, sometimes called collars, which help spread the load on the batt and so prevent warping.

Special kiln furniture is worth considering for production firings. Flatware cranks for instance, consist of flat round batts supported by three legs which slot into the batt. Each batt has a central hole to ensure good heat spread, a feature which manufacturers claim assists in overcoming dunting (splitting) when firing large pieces. It is a system which is economical on space but may give too dense a packing for high-temperature firings.

Some pots need to be glazed all over and so must be supported above the kiln shelf. This is particularly important in the case of some earthenware pots where the body is not vitrified. Various sorts of stilts are available, the most popular of which are refractory spurs. These are three-armed supports which end in fine points. Stilts which are tipped with high temperature wire giving sharper points are available in the U.S.A. Stilts cannot be used to support pots at stoneware temperatures as the body of the pot becomes pyroplastic and needs support round the entire footrim or base otherwise distortion will take place.

To avoid pots sticking to the kiln shelf and to allow them to contract over the surface of the batt (which, having already been fired, will not contract further) it is necessary to coat or dust the batt with some sort of wash or sand. Most manufacturers supply a ready prepared batt wash which is prepared by mixing with water and applied by painting, spraying and rolling onto the kiln shelf. Usually such mixtures are 50% china clay and 50% alumina, though some recipes include zirconium silicate sand. After each glaze firing, kiln shelves should be brushed top and bottom with a wire brush and any drops of glaze should either be rubbed off with a carborundum stone or carefully chipped off with a hammer and chisel. Further coats of batt wash will be required but, as a build-up occurs over a period of time, the wash bonds itself to the shelf and the surface may crack and flake, leaving it rough and uneven. This is a disadvantage and is caused by the difference in contraction rates between the wash and the batt.

An alternative to batt wash is the use of a fine dusting of calcined alumina, a fine white sand which can be lightly sprinkled onto the shelf before it is placed in position. This material is sometimes sold under the name of 'placing sand', and works extremely well. It does not cause a layer to be built up, and can be brushed off (or left on) at the end of the firing. It also has the advantage of enabling pots to 'roll' over the surface of the batt during firing. Shelves which have bent slightly can be brushed off and fired upside down next time to correct this. The big disadvantage of alumina is the need to handle the dusted shelves with care, otherwise the dust will get tipped onto pots already in position. Rapid closing of the kiln door can also disturb the powder and cause it to fly about; with reasonable care, however, such disasters can be avoided.

Packing

Kilns are packed so that the most economical use is made of the available space, and packing is done differently for biscuit or first firings than for glaze or gloss firings. If you bear in mind the positions of hot and cool spots in your kiln, then knowledge will come with experience. Props are kept to a minimum, with each batt supported by only three props; this not only reduces the amount of kiln furniture required, and therefore gives more packing space, but will also prevent wobbling or rocking of the shelves. Various arrangements of props are illustrated and it is essential that props

are placed directly above each other so the batt does not have to bear heavy, unevenly distributed loads.

For stoneware firings the greater the support given to the kiln shelf, the less likely is the shelf to split or warp. One prop can for instance, support the four corners of the shelves, and here a disc (or collar) is required on both the top and bottom of the shelves to spread the load evenly.

The biscuit packing

The terms biscuit and bisque are used to describe the first firing of the ware before the glaze firing. In practice the two terms are freely interchanged, but while both refer to the first firing, they do describe different temperatures. Bisque (sometimes written bisc) describes the industrial process whereby the ware is taken to the point of vitrification which, depending on the clay body used, is around 1150–1180°C (2102–2156°F). This represents certain savings in that the bisque can be packed tightly with ware inside each other or stacked in piles. The later glaze firings are usually taken to a lower temperature.

From the studio potter's point of view this method has many disadvantages. The vitrified ware, being non-absorbent, is difficult to glaze and is only useful for low temperature, earthenware firings. Instead, the lower temperature or soft biscuit firing of around 950–1000°C (1742–1832°F) is preferred. At this temperature most bodies are porous and lacking in strength but can be glazed easily.

Biscuit kilns are packed using the minimum amount of kiln shelves. By carefully packing pots rim to rim or foot-ring above foot-ring so that weight is carefully and evenly distributed, considerable heights can be built up, resulting in savings in firing costs. Illustrated are various methods of stacking bowls, mugs and so on. Because the pots are not glazed they can be stacked like this, but bear in mind that during the first 200°C (392°F) the ware does expand before it begins to contract. For this reason small gaps should be left between the stacks and space left between the stack and roof of the kiln to allow for expansion upwards.

Ideally all pots should be bone dry before biscuit firing, but depending on the size and thickness of the ware this is often difficult to achieve, and even bone dry pots will still retain some water. For these reasons the initial firing period should consist of a very slow rise in temperature. Firing schedules are discussed later in this chapter.

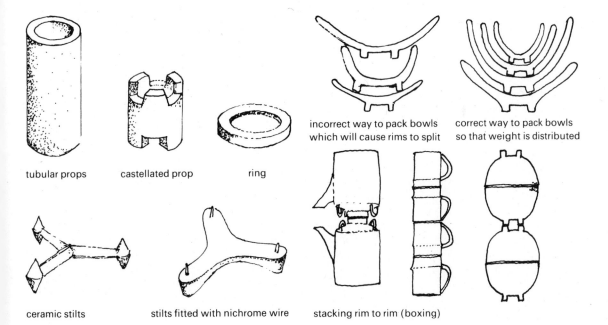

tubular props   castellated prop   ring

ceramic stilts   stilts fitted with nichrome wire

incorrect way to pack bowls which will cause rims to split

correct way to pack bowls so that weight is distributed

stacking rim to rim (boxing)

Kiln furniture   *Packing pots in a biscuit firing*

The glaze packing

Once the pots have been glazed, fettled (had streaks and unwanted glaze removed) and dried, they are put back into the kiln for the second firing, which is the glaze or gloss firing. In contrast to the biscuit packing, where pots can be stacked, glazed pots must not be allowed to touch each other, and the skill lies in utilising the space as economically as possible. For example, ware of the same height should be carefully selected and the spacing of shelves planned before packing starts. The aim when packing the chamber will be to achieve evenness of heating throughout, and this is obtained by balancing dense areas with more open areas. The positioning of kiln shelves, more than the ware, enables this to be done evenly, so it is important to work out their distribution through-out the kiln before hand. For example, if you have to fire a large quantity of flat ware such as plates or tiles, it is unlikely that the kiln could be filled from top to bottom with shelves some 2.5 cm (1 in) apart. In theory this system would make the fullest use of space; in practice the density of the load may prevent temperature being reached. The best solution here would be to spread the flatware over several firings, balancing the closed and open spaces.

Most potters find that the kiln has hot spots and cooler areas and any pack has to take this into account. A common feature of some kilns is that the bottom tends to be cooler than the top and this can be balanced by leaving a space of say 8–10 cm (3–4 in) at the bottom of the kiln, with narrower spaces of 2.5–5 cm (1–2 in) above it. To avoid a cool spot at the top a gap of at least 8 cm (3 in) needs to be kept at the top wall of the kiln to enable temperature to be achieved. This is particularly important in front loading kilns fitted with an arch. The closer the shelves, the longer they will take to reach temperature. The more open the gaps are, the quicker will be the firing.

If your kiln consistently gives a cool area on the bottom shelf, then the gap has to be bigger between the batts. The number of pots you put in will also have some effect upon the way the heat is distributed; since they are hollow and fairly lightweight they quickly take up the heat and help distribute it through the kiln. As a general rule, the denser the packing of the pots, the more evenly they will be fired. It is very noticeable that the glaze on a pot fired alone in a kiln will respond in a different way to a similar pot fired in a dense pack. Often the glaze looks drier, which may be partly due to lack of a slow maturing period; this can be avoided by soaking the kiln. The dryness may also be due to some volatilisation of the glaze at high temperature. Without other glazed pots around it this takes place to a greater extent. Glaze flashing is often noticeable on unglazed surface areas which pick up orange flashes.

Once the best shelf arrangement to fit pots that have to be fired has been worked out then packing can start. First, check that all circuits in the kiln are working and that no elements have been broken or burnt out. Sometimes this happens right at the end of the previous firing and may not have been noticed. There is nothing so annoying after having carefully packed a kiln, as to find that you have to unpack it again due to the discovery of a faulty element.

Place the props in position and then put pots round them; leave a gap of about 2.5 cm (1 in) between the wall of the kiln and pot; this is to prevent scorching of the glaze by the element, though the pots can be placed very much closer together. Pots which have been glaze fired once and are for some reason being refired should be at least 13 mm ($\frac{1}{2}$ in) clear of any other pot as they expand in the kiln and can touch adjacent ware. Pots which touch during the kiln firing and stick are described as having 'kissed'.

Build up each shelf making the fullest use of the space available.

Firing the kiln: temperature checks

Temperature rise in the kiln can be controlled by the wide variety of electrical equipment, either manually operated or automatic as described in Chapter 2. There are two main types of heat indicator: one is the pyroscope, which measures heat-work achieved, and the other is the pyrometer, which indicates temperature. Before the development of such pieces of equipment, potters relied on a variety of methods to assess temperatures in order to indicate whether or not the desired one had been achieved. They are all worth listing as they can still be useful to us today.

Colour
At around 600°C (1112°F) a dark red colour will develop in the kiln. As the temperature rises this will get brighter, moving through a dull to a bright cherry orange to a dark yellow, to a light yellow, and to a very bright white at around 1260°C (2300°F). At higher temperatures the colour becomes very incandescent and takes on a bluish tinge. With practice temperature can be read from the colour in the kiln. *Never* look in the kiln without using a dark glass at temperatures over 1150°C (2102°F); the light is very intense and can damage your eyes. A pair of suitable spectacles should be worn or a light shield used. This is an excellent tool for the purpose, and is easily made from a round bat, rather like one used for table

tennis, with a 5 cm (2 in) hole in the centre over which is fixed a dark blue piece of welder's glass. Such a tool has the advantage of also protecting your face from the heat of the kiln. Sunglasses should not be used to look into the kiln as they only eliminate the blue, violet and red light, which makes the expanded iris more vulnerable to the ultra violet light, which can seriously damage the eye. Again, never approach an open spyhole from above, always from below, and never have two spyholes open at once.

Time
For the same kiln pack and the same amount of fuel used, the time taken to fire the kiln will be fairly constant. Slight variations will occur according to density of pack (always count and record the number of kiln shelves in a kiln) and the weather. A kiln will take longer to fire on a cold day than on a hot day.

Draw rings
Special glazed rings some 2.5 cm (1 in) in diameter placed inside the kiln near the spyhole can be 'drawn' (removed on a rod) from the kiln when it is thought the glaze has matured. They will cool rapidly and indicate whether or not the firing is complete. This procedure can only take place in an electric kiln if the spyhole is clear of the electric elements. Equally, it is important that the kiln is switched off while the rings are removed so that the danger in a metal rod touching an element is eliminated.

Firing log
Finally, a method which is not old, and is fairly simple, is to record the number of units of electricity used. A record must be kept of the meter reading before the firing starts and again when the firing is finished. One reading subtracted from the other reading will give the number of units consumed. This amount will vary according to the age of the elements (though after the first six firings they will give fairly constant results) and the number of kiln shelves present, but it is still a reliable guide.

Pyrometric indicators
Most potters require a more sophisticated guide, and the most common devices used are pyroscopes. These are made from ceramic materials, and are similar in composition to glazes. They are compounded so as to soften and bend over when a certain amount of heat work has been achieved. They are coded under a sequence of letters and

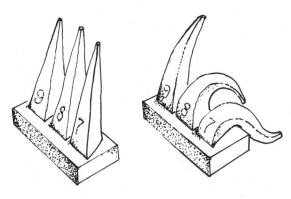

Cones set for a stoneware firing (left), *and after firing* (right)

Cones indicating temperature has been reached

numbers which relate to specific bending temperatures, provided that they are used according to the manufacturer's instructions.

Cones are the most popular and most widely used type of pyroscope used by studio potters. They are in the shape of a tall, tapering triangular form about 5–8 cm (2–3 in) high, and have a code number imprinted on the widest side. When they have reached their appropriate temperature they soften and bend over. They are usually placed in front of the spy hole which is in the door of the kiln, and they need to be regularly observed towards the end of the firing. Because cones are made from ceramic materials they behave in the kiln very much as pots do; that is, they respond to the heat work absorbed and, to give reproducible results, need a constant firing sequence. For instance, in a very slow firing the cones will bend over at temperatures 5–10°C (41–50°F) below their stated temperatures; if the cones are fired very rapidly they may need an extra 10°C (50°F) to bend over.

For this reason many potters find them a much more relevant indicator of heat temperature in the kiln than instruments, and list their glazes under cone numbers rather than temperatures. The disadvantages of this system are that not all potters use cones, and cone numbers will differ according to manufacturer.

A common practice, when firing by visible cones, is to use a sequence of three cones, each maturing at a consecutively higher temperature; one as a warning, one for the required temperature and one to indicate any overfiring. This system is particularly useful in large kilns fitted with two spyholes (top and bottom) where one set can be compared with the other. For example, to fire to 1260°C (2300°F) using Staffordshire cones you would use cones 8 (1250°C/2282°F), 8A (1260°C/3200°F) and 9 (1280°C/2336°F). These are set in sequence either in special stands or in soft clay, and are carefully placed in front of the spyhole so that when they bend over the numbers are clearly visible and a check can be made if necessary. Most manufacturers suggest that the cones should be tilted slightly so that they bend over to reveal their numbers. They must be firmly supported and the clay supporting them allowed to dry or it may explode during the early part of the firing. Cones are said to have fully matured when they have 'touched their toes'. Once you have established a regular firing schedule you can usually manage quite well with only one cone, which may take 15–30 minutes to bend over, or squat.

Give the cones sufficient space inside the kiln; do not sacrifice cone space to pot space. Always place the cones the same distance inside the kiln and check their position using a lighted candle inside the kiln or from outside with an electric hand torch once the kiln is complete. Different manufacturers have different recommended firing sequences for their cones; however, by keeping your firing schedules the same they should give reliable results and it is these which are important. Peering into a hot kiln, as I have mentioned before, should only be done with care; if the cones are difficult to see a gentle blowing of cool air into the kiln will cool and 'freeze' them for a better view.

Cones are made in two sizes, standard 6 cm (2.5 in) high and miniature, or junior, about 2.5 cm (1 in) high for use in limited spaces. The two sizes of cone, though given the same number, will not necessarily bend at the same heat temperature point, and it is best to stick to those you know work. All cones should be kept dry as any dampness can affect their performance. Cones, having been fired once, cannot be reliably used again even if they did not reach their bending temperature. Orton cones are made in the U.S.A., Seger cones in West Berlin and Harrison cones (sometimes known as Staffordshire, or British Standard cones) are produced in the U.K. Cones from different manufacturers are not automatically interchangeable; reference numbers should be checked and the cones tested in a firing before changing from one brand to the other.

Another sort of pyroscope are Holdcroft's bars. These, like cones, are made so as to soften and sag at specific temperatures, but are fired supported horizontally at each end in a refractory stand. Like cones they give a visible indication of heat temperature reached.

A recent introduction is the use of kiln sitters. These are made, like bars and cones, out of ceramic materials; they will soften and sag at the specified temperature. They are positioned in a kiln so as to prop up (open) a switch so that when they soften and sag they will switch off the kiln automatically.

Other types of pyroscope that are useful are Bullers rings, and these are also made out of ceramic materials. They consist of a flat ring about 8 cm (3 in) in diameter about 6 mm ($\frac{1}{4}$ in) thick, with a hole in the centre. Unlike cones and bars they do not give a visual indication; during the firing they contract and, after removal from the kiln, this contraction is measured on a special gauge which give a Bullers ring number. From this a temperature can be deduced. Temperature °C (approx) $= (960 \times BR\ No. \times 7)$. Rings can either be lifted out of the hot kiln (difficult to do in an electric kiln) or checked when the kiln has cooled. If rings are placed in different parts of the kiln, they can be used to record temperatures achieved in these positions.

Pyrometers

These are instruments which indicate temperature, consisting of a thermocouple and an indicator, sometimes called a galvanometer. They have many benefits for the studio potter. To start with they show clearly the temperature in the kiln at any time and indicate whether the temperature is rising. A graph of pyrometer temperature readings against time can be made up from several firings and used as a control against which subsequent firings can be checked. Pyrometers also serve as a clear warning to indicate when the firing is nearing its end; finally, they can form part of an automatic switch-off system which will ensure

regular and reliable firings. Many potters fire their kilns using both pyrometers and cones, though for production pottery many potters find the use of a pyrometer to be a simpler method of determining temperature.

Pyrometers, though relatively simple to use, are finely and sensitively made. The thermocouple, which protrudes into the kiln, consists of two lengths of wire made of dissimilar metals or alloys. At one end the wires are joined by welding and the other ends are connected to the galvanometer. On heating the thermocouple generates a small voltage dependent upon the temperature. This is indicated on the galvanometer (i.e. millivolt meter) which is calibrated with a temperature scale. As the temperature in the kiln rises the voltage generated by the thermocouple increases and this causes the needle on the indicator to move. In the kiln the thermocouple wires are protected by a porcelain sheath and are connected to the millivolt meter by a length of compensating cable which is of a measured length (and therefore electrical resistance) to ensure correct readings. Pyrometers measure the temperature in the kiln, or at least that part where the tip of the thermocouple is, and can be linked to the kiln control in order to switch off, soak or control the firing cycle.

Thermocouple readings will not precisely indicate the state of glaze maturation, but with experience you will find that with your kiln a specific pyrometer reading will be required to achieve the effects you want. This will also depend on the speed of the final hour or so of firing.

The types of metals used in the thermocouple will depend on the temperature at which you wish to fire and may be alloys of chromium, nickel, aluminium or platinum. Make sure you have a thermocouple which will go to the highest temperature that you are likely to use. Installation is through a hole in the wall of the kiln, in the back or the roof, and the porcelain sheath protects the wire against physical damage. On the outside the thermocouple terminals are connected by the cable to the indicator, which should be placed as far away from the kiln as possible. Do not change the length of this cable and do not run it parallel to any other electric cable, as this may induce an additional current and falsify the readings. Handle the instruments with care and they will last many years. Ensure that the thermocouple is positioned correctly; some are meant to go only in side walls, some can be inserted in the roof of the kiln.

Check your instruments regularly and in the case of a new kiln use cones as well as a pyrometer for the first few firings. For instance, at room temperature the indicator should read 20°C (68°F); check any discrepancies, make sure all connections are secure and tight and, if in doubt, consult the manufacturer. Any calibration should be done by them or their representative.

Firing schedules

Once packed, the kiln is ready to fire. It is always safe to assume that some of the pots are slightly damp; it is rarely safe to assume they are not. Therefore, begin by firing slowly. Lock the door, check that the cones can be seen and open the top vent.

Firing the biscuit

The initial temperature rise for the biscuit is probably the most crucial stage, for it is this period that water in the clay is converted into steam, and if this is done too rapidly the pot will explode. In a kiln up to 0.34 cu m (12 cu ft) in size, packed with normal ware, this rise should be about 40°C (102°F) per hour, i.e. less than 1°C (34°F) per minute up to 200°C (392°F). This will enable the heat to spread through the kiln and for proper drying to take place. Larger kilns may take longer.

When 200°C (392°F) is reached in about 4 hours, the rise in temperature can be increased slightly to 60°C (140°F) per hour until 600°C (1112°F) is reached. At this point the ventilation hole can be closed and the rate of temperature increase speeded up to around 100°C (212°F) per hour until 850–900°C (1562–1652°F), when the rate should be slowed down until top temperature is reached. This soaking period at the end of the firing enables any carbonaceous matter in the clay to burn away before the particles of clay start to sinter and trap in the carbon. At this point some potters open the air vent to let out any fumes in the kiln. Depending on the clay used, considerable amounts of fumes can be liberated.

When temperature is reached and the kiln switched off, all vents should be firmly closed until the kiln has cooled down to 400°C (752°F), when the top vent can be opened if faster cooling is required. The door should not be opened until 150°C (302°F).

A biscuit firing can take from 6–8 hours to reach top temperature and 24 hours to cool – for domestic pots. Sculptural or heavy pieces may need a longer firing. With practice you may find the faster and more economic schedules adequate.

The glaze firing

Once the pots have been biscuit fired, the initial

Sophisticated electronic controls for firing a kiln

rate of heating can be speeded up providing that the pots are not still damp from the glazing process. Rapid firing of glazed pots which are still damp can cause the glaze to crack and either fall off, or crawl on, the surface of the pot. With biscuit pots there is little further change below 900°C (1652°F), and so the kiln controller can be turned on to the maximum setting after 1–2 hours on a medium warming-up setting. All vents should be firmly closed at this stage.

As the temperature rises the rate of temperature rise slows down considerably. For example, on maximum the kiln may rise at 150°C (302°F) per hour in the early stages, but this rate will not continue much above 1000–1100°C (1832–2012°F). Towards the end of a stoneware firing the rise in temperature may be less than 60°C (140°F) per hour, a rate which allows the body and glaze to mature. Some potters decrease this rate even more, down to 30°C (86°F) per hour, or introduce a soak period of 30–40 minutes at the end of the firing, with the aim of maintaining but not increasing temperature. This is done by turning down the electricity input to 80% or less. Again, kilns vary and the need to soak will depend on the temperature rise you achieve.

Probably the most difficult decision for the potter to make is when to switch off the kiln. The obvious answer is to switch off when the correct temperature is reached, but this is not always easy to decide. The pyrometer may give one indication whilst the cones may give another. Provided that the cones were placed in a reliable position, that is, not too near the spyhole, I would place more trust in the cones as the indication they give has more to

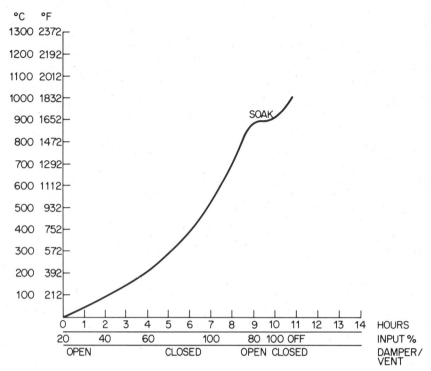

Typical biscuit firing with carbon soak. (The
measurements in this and the three following graphs
are for a 0.34 cu m (12 cu ft), electric kiln.)

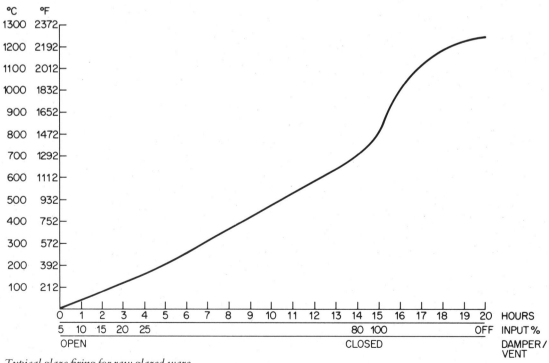

Typical glaze firing for raw glazed ware

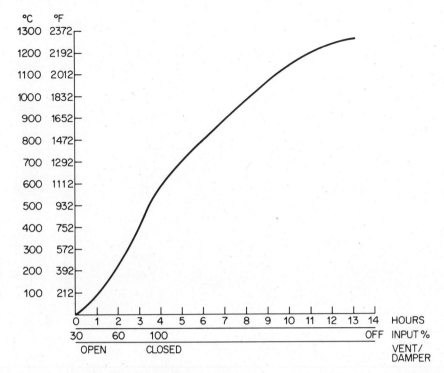

Typical stoneware glaze firing of biscuited pots

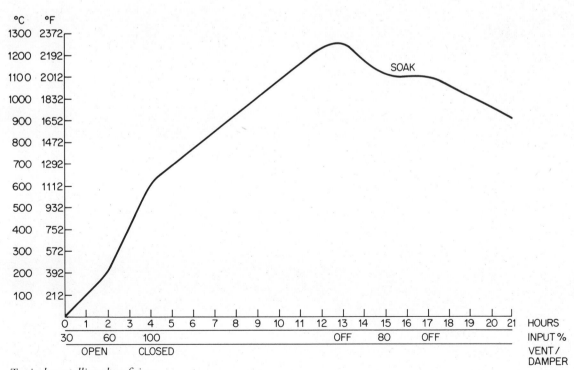

Typical crystalline glaze firing

do with the effect of heat work, which is what is required. With experience the relationship between the number of kiln shelves used, the way they are packed in the kiln, the length of the firing and the cone and pyrometer readings will be clearer and the final decision easier to make. In my 0.34 cu m (12 cu ft) kiln, following a well established kiln pack and with a constant number of kiln shelves, I can set the automatic switch off which is linked to the pyrometer and get reliable results.

Once switched off, leave the kiln to cool slowly. Continue to ventilate the kiln room for 2–3 hours as more fumes are discharged. Once this stage has passed the heat can be useful in the workshop and will be fume-free. Rapid cooling, by opening the top vent, will help to ensure clear glazes, but these are rarely of interest to studio potters. I keep the vent closed until the temperature has dropped to at least 400°C (752°F) and do not open the door a crack until 200°C (392°F). Despite impatience to find out what has happened in the firing, it is worth waiting in order to save the wear and tear of rapid cooling on your kiln as well as avoid the possiblity of pots cracking or dunting (splitting caused by silica inversion).

David Morris's kiln cooling after being fired

4 The clay body

Clay is a naturally occurring earth which is found, in various forms over most of the surface of the world. When soft or 'muddy' it has the ability to be moulded into a wide varitey of shapes by the use of many different techniques without crumbling or falling apart and, after drying, to 'set' to retain that shape. This moulding ability is known as plasticity. The other significant quality that clay has is that, when it is heated in a fire or a kiln to a temperature above red heat, i.e. about 600°C (1112°F), it changes physically and chemically to become pot. The higher the temperature, the harder and more vitrified the clay will become. Fired clay can no longer be softened in or be affected by water – the change is irreversible.

Clay, which is formed from the decomposition of an igneous rock, such as granite, is defined chemically as hydrated silicate of alumina. It is made up of very small plate-like hexagonal particles which, when mixed with water, slide over each other to give clay its plastic quality. Clay may be divided or classified into many types: according to colour, working qualities or firing temperature, and all these factors have to be taken into account. A most important distinction to be made is that between primary and secondary clay.

Primary clays are deposited where they were formed from the parent rock. Such clays are relatively pure in composition and their large particle size makes them less plastic than secondary clays. The most important primary clay is china clay, which is formed in nature from the decomposition of igneous rocks, and is valued chiefly for its purity and whiteness. It is the clay whose composition comes nearest to the theoretically pure clay formula $(Al_2O_3.2SiO_2.2H_2O.)$.

Secondary clays are clays which have been moved by ice or water from the site on which they were formed, and deposited over long periods of time. Most clays fall into this category and they are particularly useful to the studio potter because of their fine particle size, which give a high level of plasticity, and for the various 'impurities' picked up as the clay was moved. Such clays will contain some iron (a red earthenware as much as 8%) as well as organic matter. Their unfired colour may range from cream to grey/brown, red, yellow or black.

Fireclays are another broad range of clays and are so called because they will withstand high temperatures without distortion or bloating. They are usually low in fluxes and high in alumina and

Lucie Rie; thrown stoneware bottle, beaten into a square, with thickly applied textured glaze

silica. Most are found under coal seams and were the underclays for coal forest vegetation. Some fireclays are reasonably plastic but most have a low level of plasticity. They are useful to the stoneware potter for blending with plastic ball clays to give workable high temperature plastic clays. Many prepared stoneware clays offered by suppliers are based on fireclays and are not as plastic as ball clay based bodies.

Earthenware clays are usually red clays, sometimes called terracotta, which fire to 1000–1100°C (1832–2012°F); they contain some 8% iron (Fe_2O_3) and, depending on the firing temperature, give a typical orange brown colour. Darker shades develop at higher temperatures. Most earthenware clays remain relatively porous (from about 5–15%) and for this reason need to be glazed over as much of the surface as possible if they are to be in regular use. Because of the relatively porous nature of the body consistent with its low level of vitrification, earthenware is mechanically weaker than stoneware and is consequently usually made thicker than stoneware in order to compensate. Some red earthenware clays, particularly those to which flint has been added, will withstand higher temperatures and become vitrified without collapsing or bloating. Their colour is very much darker, and to all intents and purposes they are classified as stonewares.

Clays prepared specifically for use at stoneware temperatures can be fired to 1200°C (2192°F) and above, when they become hard and vitrified, with a low level of porosity. Their colour may vary from cream white to grey/brown, buff or dark red. Some stoneware clays occur naturally but most are prepared by blending together several clays. This clay should not be confused with porcelain; as mentioned before, this fires white, vitrified and, when potted thinly, is translucent. (This clay will be discussed in more detail later.)

All potters, no matter what method of firing they employ, use similar materials, but the firing method used will help them to decide which materials will work best. Although all clays go through the same physical processes in the early stages of firing when an oxidation atmosphere is essential for all the changes to occur, the clay is affected in the later stages by the method of firing.

Though it is more convenient to list separately the changes that occur in the clay during firing, they are all dependent on each other and occur over a wide range of temperatures. These changes depend for example on the speed of the firing, the density of the kiln pack and the type of clay being fired.

The firing changes

1 Though the clay body may feel bone dry when it is put into the kiln (it is advisable to let the pots dry naturally before being packed), they will still contain the moisture they absorb from the atmosphere (usually about 5%). In the first stage this physically combined water must evaporate and be given off as steam. This should be carried out slowly. Some potters estimate a rise as low as 1°C (34°F) every two minutes – about 30°C (86°F) per hour. This rate depends very much on the size of the kiln (the larger the slower), the thickness of the walls of the pot (the thinner they are the faster they can give up the water) and the density of the pack.

Vents on the top of the kiln should be open to allow the steam to escape. It is during this phase that any explosions of the clay will occur when the change from water to steam, with a corresponding increase in volume, is too rapid. For this reason it is far better to err on the side of caution. This stage, known as the water smoking period, is estimated to last up to 150°C (302°F). During this period any vegetable additives to the clay, such as dye, will also start to burn away, as will gums present in the glaze, and wax or water emulsions used as resists.

2 Changes occur in the structure of the clay, particularly to the cristobalite, which is a form of silica, between 200°C and 300°C (392°F and 572°F). At around 573°C (1063°F) any quartz present alters its form and this change is accompanied by an increase in volume of up to 3%. This change is reversed when the clay is cooling. Although these changes in size are relatively small, they need to be taken into account when the kiln is being fired. On large pots, or thick-walled pieces, for example, the firing should not be too rapid.

3 Starting at around 200°C (392°F) changes begin to occur to the structure of the clay crystals, although these are usually still reversible until around 500–600°C (932–1112°F). After this the clay crystals begin to decompose and the water which is chemically combined in the structure of the clay molecule is given off as steam, thus irreversibly changing the molecular structure of the clay. A cubic foot (0.0283 cu m) of pots can give off as much as 570 cc (1 pt) of water. It is necessary, therefore, for the kiln to be adequately ventilated to allow this steam to escape rapidly rather than forcing its way around door jambs and between bricks. By 600°C (1112°F) this reaction slows down and by 700°C (1292°F) it has virtually been completed. At this point though the clay has

been turned to pot, and it is at its weakest physically. The particles are only just held together and if the firing was stopped the resultant clay fabric could be easily crumbled and broken. A normal biscuit firing, to 900–1000°C (1652–1832°F) ensures that the sintering continues beyond this point, at which the pot starts to vitrify (around 800°C, 1472°F).

4 Most clays contain vegetable matter in various stages of decay and this begins to decompose at around 200°C (392°F). Carbon and sulphur present in the clay start to burn out at around 400°C (752°F), a process which lasts until 800–1200°C (1472–2192°F). For this to occur fully, the atmosphere must be thoroughly oxidising, and for this purpose electric kilns are excellent. Both the carbon and the sulphur combines with oxygen to form monoxide, dioxide and trioxide gases and these should not be allowed to concentrate in the kiln room. Any pale blue smoke that hangs in the air usually has a strong acrid and pungent smell which catches the back of the throat. In theory all the carbon can burn out by 900°C (1652°F) but this rarely happens in practice; the sulphur is much slower to burn away and can still be given off at 1200–1250°C (2192–2282°F).

Some potters recommend that the firing be held at 900°C (1652°F) for an hour or two to ensure that all the carbon has been oxidised. Carbon trapped inside the body by vitrification will still attempt to turn to gas; when the body becomes glassy and softened by further increases in temperature (pyro-plasticity) the gas will form and bubble in the body and bloating will occur. When this happens it is particularly noticeable on stoneware bodies covered with a shiny glaze. If the glaze starts to mature and melt at around 1200°C (2192°F), or lower, it traps in the carbon, which tries to escape when the body softens. On matt glazes which do not seal the surface until a very much higher temperature this fault is more rare.

All the gases liberated during the firing are harmful to health and should be extracted from the kiln room. Whilst they are unlikely to collect in large concentrations (unless the kiln room is very small), they can be particularly irritating to people who have sensitive chests or suffer from asthma. Fluorine gas tends to attack the surface of window glass giving it a slightly blue, etched surface which cannot be removed. A wipe over with a light oil will serve as an effective glaze to protect the window.

5 Vitrification of the body starts at 800°C (1472°F). The fluxes start to weld together the free silica in the clay; glass is formed, and the body

David Morris; thrown stoneware pots with fly-away handles

starts to contract. During the production of vitrified material the chemical changes cause simultaneous physical changes. As well as the decrease in total volume, the pores are filled with molten liquid, which also reduces porosity. According to the amount of liquid formed, there will be an increase in hardness and strength. Clays used by studio potters tend to vitrify between 1100–1150°C (2012–2102°F) for red earthenware clays, and 1250–1300°C (2282–2372°F) for stonewares and porcelains.

The colour of the clay is also affected by vitrification; most clays darken with harder firing, particularly red earthenware, which can change at over 60°C (140°F) from a bright terra cotta to a dark purple brown. Iron is the material which most affects the colour and this is present in all clays (porcelain is the exception) in amounts which vary from 8% for red earthenware, to 2–3% for stoneware. The usual form of iron oxide is red iron oxide with the formula Fe_2O_3 which, in theory, acts as a refractory material in the clay (and the body) in oxidation. In a reducing atmosphere the iron, deprived of oxygen, converts FeO, which acts as a flux. For this reason a clay which is to be fired in a reduction atmosphere can accommodate a lesser amount of iron. However, even in oxidation iron does act as a flux, though less powerfully than in reduction. It is the way in which the iron behaves which is one of the major differences between the different firing atmospheres.

The rate of temperature increase in most kilns

Caroline Whyman; thrown porcelain pots with slip trailed dots and carved decoration, under a dolomite glaze with a small amount of copper carbonate

of clear glazes, whilst slow cooling promotes crystal formations, resulting in opaque or matt effects. Decorative crystalline glazes can be produced by making use of this phenomena by holding the temperature of the glaze at around 1100°C (2012°F) to encourage the growth of crystals. By 1000°C (1832°F) stoneware bodies behave as a solid. At 573°C (1063°F) and between 300°C (572°F) and 200°C (392°F) the free silica undergoes further physical change. Both temperatures need to be passed slowly. At both points the silica changes from one crystalline form to another, accompanied by a reduction in size. Too rapid cooling at these temperatures can cause pots to crack or dent. At around 500°C (932°F) the glaze ceases to be molten.

Clays which are less refractory, such as red earthenwares, develop a liquid phase much earlier and the crucial vitrification range may be much narrower. This is in contrast to refractory clays, which are low in fluxes and only vitrify slowly at very high temperatures.

Preparing clay bodies

Bodies are prepared from blends of the different sorts of available materials, and these include china clay, ball clays (red and white) and refractory fireclays, with additions of fillers or fluxes which improve working, handling and drying properties as well as raising or lowering firing temperatures.

Potters who use electric kilns tend to work in small potteries tucked away in the basements of houses, or into small commercial units or shops. This usually means that space is at a premium and this presents clay mixing problems. Ideally, clay bodies need to be mixed and then stored for as long as possible (at least several months) before use, though this is not always practical. The addition of such organic substances as yoghurt or vinegar (to cause the development of acid bacteria) are said to help the formation of bacteria in the clay and increase its plasticity. Time, however, is the prime requirement. Raw materials are cheapest if ordered in bulk, and this demands dry storage facilities. Finally, the actual mixing of the body does require a considerable amount of space, especially if amounts of any appreciable size are to be made.

Bodies can be mixed in two ways: either by adding them to sufficient water to make them plastic (and this is often easiest to do with a machine such as a dough-mixer) or by reducing the mixture to a liquid slip by hand, in a ball mill or

slow down towards the end of the firing, particularly at high temperatures, though some potters soak for up to an hour at top temperatures. There is often great benefit in this. This soaking period allows the heat to penetrate completely to increase the amount of fused matter; it also reduces the number of pores in between the particles and renders the material more impermeable. Reactions between body and glaze are also increased. Too long a soak, or too high a temperature, may result in the formation of too great an amount of liquid, which in turn may give rise to bloating or boiling of the clay, often with a resulting loss of shape and finally sagging or squatting of the pot.

6 Cooling is part of the firing cycle and the rate at which it occurs can affect the shine of the glaze, its colour and matt by promoting or preventing the formation of crystals. Too rapid cooling can cause pots to crack, or dunt, while too slow a cooling period can cause materials in solution to crystallize out. At top temperature stonewares and porcelains are slightly soft and the glaze is liquid; at this point reactions between the body and glaze occur which form an integral part of the strength of the finished piece. Cooling from a top temperature of around 1260°C (2300°F) down to 1100°C (2012°F) can be rapid. This will prevent crystallization of cristobalite, and lessen the tendency of the glaze to come off the edges of the pot (known as shelling).

Rapid cooling also encourages the development

in a blunger. The more liquid the clay, the more plastic will be the body. The slip is then either de-watered to a plastic consistency in a filter-press or poured into absorbent plaster troughs and allowed to stiffen slowly. The slip process is the best as it ensures that the mixture is homogenous and that all the particles are thoroughly wetted. Clay bodies are mixtures of clay, free silica and fluxes, but ideally one would find a natural clay which vitrifies at the required temperature and use this, rather than make up a composite body. Few natural clays, however, will satisfy the requirements of studio potters. They may be too plastic, which will make them slow to dry and tend to warp. After firing, their texture may be too dense, and their overall shrinkage from plastic to high-fired state too high, resulting in cracking and warping in the kiln.

The remedy for all these problems is to either add clays which have the opposite sorts of qualities (i.e. are less plastic) or to add an opener such as a grog or sand. China clay, if mixed with a little water to a slip, can then be added in amounts of up to 15% without noticeable loss of plasticity, with great benefit to properties such as shrinkage, fired strength and colour. Clays are said to be 'short' if they have a low level of plasticity.

When no specific suitable clay is available a blend of one or more ball clays with other materials will provide a suitable body. In the U.K. the two large clay suppliers are English China Clays Ltd and Watts, Blake Bearne & Co., who offer a wide range of clays and will provide chemical and physical data on request. 'Hyplas 71', English China Clay (E.C.C.) is one ball clay which will give a good strong pale firing body at 1280°C (2336°F) when combined with 25% china clay and 1% Cornish stone (to serve as a flux). To lower the vitrification temperature an increase in the amount of Cornish stone would be necessary. Other pale firing ball clays which have proved to be an excellent base are Hymod SMD (E.C.C.) which is good when mixed with 10% china clay and 10% grog, TWVD and HVAR (Watts, Blake, Bearne & Co.).

In the U.S.A. the Tennessee and Kentucky ball clays have proved to be excellent bases for stoneware bodies with additions of a flux and with sand or grog. For coloured bodies and for red earthenware Jordan and Redart clay are in widespread use.

There is not the space here to go in detail into the chemistry of bodies nor to give precise recipes for such mixtures; generally speaking, many ball clay based mixtures will be as workable, easier to handle and more successful to fire, if not better, than most of the commercial bodies on the market.

Ready-mixed bodies

Despite the great numbers of plastic clay bodies available from potters' suppliers, there is not a great deal of difference between many of them. Most are based on fireclay bodies which are cheaper to buy and easier to prepare; ball clays have a much finer particle size and this makes them more difficult to mix thoroughly and more expensive to buy. Potters who purchase bodies in the plastic state are not only buying the clay but also the water (about 25%) it contains and the cost of the labour used in the production of the body. It is not unreasonable, therefore, to expect that such a body will be immediately ready for use without any further addition. Yet in practice this is rarely the case. Most potters make additions to these bodies to give them their own 'unique' quality and also to improve their handling and working qualities.

With such a wide range of different bodies on the market it is not possible to describe them in detail but some general recommendations are necessary. A distinction must always be drawn between red terracotta clays and white earthenware bodies. Terracotta clay is intended for, and usually will only withstand, earthenware temperatures without bloating, distortion and collapse. Most will fire to 1100°C (2012°F); some will go higher, up to 1200°C (2192°F)

Earthenware bodies

Most red clays, unless stated, are likely to be blends of various red marls and some have an addition of 10% flint, which increases the firing temperature. They usually have a high level of plasticity and are suitable for all pottery making processes. Many local clays are suitable for use at these temperatures. Most red earthenware clays will remain quite porous unless taken to higher temperatures, at which point they lose their attractive bright red colour.

White earthenware bodies rarely occur as a single clay but are blends of various sorts, and are intended to vitrify at around 1150–1180°C (2102–2156°F). Some of the very white bodies are specially blended for industrial working methods and often have a relatively low level of plasticity; they are difficult to throw on the wheel or to use for hand building techniques. Such bodies are intended for slip-casting in plaster of Paris moulds or for jiggering and jolleying production methods. These white earthenwares contain only very small quantities of iron and will fire to a bright cream white. In the ceramics industry they are taken to a high temperature (to achieve vitrification) in the first firing and are then glaze fired at a lower temperature. These bodies become very hard. In the U.K. they are sometimes called hotel-ware bodies and are usually potted with fairly thick walls.

Industrial earthenware bodies should not be confused with ivory or cream coloured mixtures which are more plastic and are intended for use at earthenware or medium temperatures. These bodies usually vitrify at around $1150–1180°C$ ($2102–2156°F$). When fired at lower temperatures they will be porous and may cause glazes to craze. They will often withstand slightly higher temperatures and can give interesting results at around $1200°C$ ($2192°F$) or even higher.

Stoneware bodies

It is convenient to divide the higher temperature clay bodies into the smooth, buff grey or cream coloured mixtures intended for use as throwing bodies, from the rougher more textured clays sometimes known as crank mixtures or sculpting marl, designed for handbuilding or raku work. Most prepared stoneware bodies are blends of at least two or three clays plus sand or fine grog. Few suppliers will give detailed descriptions though many do supply details of chemical formulae. Generally the information is limited to vague descriptions of working qualities, fired colour and maximum and minimum firing temperatures. Some suppliers will provide an analysis of the body on request. Two typical ones, both of which work well in oxidation, are:

Emmanuel Cooper; thrown porcelain bowl with dolomite glaze and matt pigments on rim

instance the high level of iron in the Albany slip would indicate a low temperature clay. What the analysis does not tell us however, is that Albany clay contains very fine particles which will enter into fusion and produce reactions much more readily than bodies prepared from whiter ball clays. Neither does it describe the handling qualities of these clays, how they are affected by moderate changes in temperature, and so on. Equally, the relevance of much of this information depends not only on the temperature, but also the speed of firing, the length of soak (if any) as well as the glaze fit. Some glazes, particularly matt glazes, weaken the body; most are slightly crazed and have little physical or mechanical strength. A tap on the side of a bowl glazed with such a glaze will give a dull thud. In contrast, shiny glazes which are under slight compression (not all shiny glazes do

	SiO_2	Al_2O_3	TiO_2	Fe_2O_3	MgO	CaO	Na_2O	K_2O	Loss
Moira stoneware clay (U.K.) (Moira Pottery)	59.7	25.55	1.6	1.44					9.46
Special stoneware (U.K.) (Potclays Ltd)	61.3	26.3	0.65	1.02	0.31	0.65	0.44	1.31	7.62
These compare with Hymod SMD Ball clay:	65.0	23.0	1.4	1.0	0.4	0.2	0.4	2.4	6.8
Grolleg China clay (E.C.C)	47.7	37.2	0.03	0.7	0.25	0.1	0.1	1.95	12.06
Jordan Stoneware (U.S.A.) (Minnesota clay)	67.2	20.2	1.18	1.73	0.52	0.16	0.23	2.0	6.7
Albany clay (U.S.A.)	57.64	14.66	0.4	5.2	2.68	5.78	0.8	3.25	9.46
Fremington clay (U.K.)	52.66	18.17	1.02	6.22	3.42	4.69	3.68		

The analysis of the clay is only a starting point for determining working and firing qualities; for

this, some craze badly) will strengthen the body. A tap on the side of a bowl glazed with these glazes

Alix Leff; thrown porcelain bowl with faceted side and oil spot glaze, 12.7 cm (5 in) wide

will give a pleasant sharp note if the glaze and body fit well together.

There is really only one way to find out what a body is like and that is to test it out thoroughly in your own workshop, and under your usual firing conditions. Adequate tests cannot be carried out on samples of less than 5 kg (10 lb) of clay. Not only does the body have to be tested for larger pieces of ware, but also on different shapes with various glazes and in all the parts of the kiln. Finding the right body is often a slow process but one which it is essential to get right. Glazes and slips can be varied easily; it is much more difficult with clay bodies. Results can only be assessed over a long period of time. Often for regular production it is better to go for a bland, but reliable body; more exciting experiments can be reserved for individual pieces.

Many suppliers offer a range of dark coloured, smooth bodies which need precise firing temperatures. Above these temperatures the bodies are likely to bloat and deform.

Textured, crank and sculpting mixtures are usually made up of refractory clays which have been opened up by the addition of coarse grogs. They usually remain slightly porous at stoneware temperatures but are excellent for hand building and so on. They can also be usefully added to throwing bodies when larger pots are to be thrown, as they give 'tooth' or 'grip' to the clay to enable it to be pulled up more firmly.

All clays can be altered, doctored or adapted, and few potters find that they can use a plastic clay body without having to make an addition of some sort.

Fillers

Materials such as grog and sand are sometimes called fillers. These materials, which are non-plastic, reduce the plasticity of the body and decrease the shrinkage (as they do not absorb water and may have already been fired). Excess contraction causes warping and cracking of pots and this can best be remedied by the addition of an inert material or filler to the body. Grog and sand are ideal for this purpose. In comparison to the particle size of clay, grog and sand are coarse, which can make the body easier to work as well as having an effect on the density. Grog is ground up clay which has been fired to vitrification point and is available in many different sorts. Molochite is ground china clay which has been fired to 1400°C (2552°F); it has a high fired strength and a low thermal expansion. It is sold in various sorts, carefully graded, from dust to 1.6 mm ($\frac{1}{16}$ in) and coarser. White or cream, it lightens body colour and can be added to a plastic ball clay to give a strong body. It can also usefully be added to porcelain as well as to stoneware body to raise the firing temperature. One U.K. firm, Watts, Blake, Bearne & Co., supply a calcined finely ground high-alumina ball clay, 'Kalbrite 2K', which can usefully be added to clay bodies (or even glazes).

Most grogs however, are made from a wide variety of fired ceramics including ground up pots and fired crushed fireclays, so they are usually marketed as high temperature grog and graded for size. For a body to be used for throwing, a fine grog, dust – 60's mesh – is used. Coarser grogs are suitable for use in bodies intended for hand working methods and raku bodies but they do make clay hard to throw. Red earthenware grog can be added for a speckled effect in stoneware clays. Coloured grogs can best be made in the workshop. A high manganese slip, for example, can be made and allowed to dry. This is then crushed and fired to biscuit temperature. A small quantity of this added to the body will bleed into the glaze to give attractive results.

Calcined alumina, which is used as a shelf dust to prevent pots sticking to shelves, or as packing for bone china, can also be added to clay bodies. As a high alumina sand it serves to open up the body and raise the firing temperature. All grogs are best moistened before being added to the clay body.

Sand is a natural quartz and varies in composition from almost pure silica (such as silver sand) to mixtures of silica, clay, calcium and various soluble salts, as well as iron and manganese. Builders' sand is usually too coarse for use in a body, though it may be suitable after sieving and washing. Beach sand, too, is rarely suitable. Outcrops of sand inland, however, can offer interesting and cheap sources. As well as the

Ewen Henderson; handbuilt stoneware beaker with runny glaze, 11 cm ($4\frac{1}{4}$ in) high

purity of the sand, its grain size must also be considered. If it is too fine the silica enters into solution and acts as a flux in the body; if the particles are too sharp it can make handling painful. Coarse sand can be classified as a grog in that it will not go into solution in the body. Sand is often added to bodies intended for reduction firing, but for oxidation firings the sand has to be fine and clean. If the sand is coarse it will make a very workable body but when fired can result in a brittle body which chips easily.

Coarse zirconium silicate makes an adequate substitute for quartz sand; it is a highly refractory material and, unlike silica, has a smooth rate of thermal expansion without sudden transition points.

Adding various clays

Different clays can be used to affect the body in various ways. Some, like earthenware clay, lower the vitrifying point of the body; some, like china clay, will increase it. Others will colour the body either by darkening or lightening it. The clay, being plastic, will usually increase the plasticity of the body, though not necessarily its strength.

China clay

Added in amounts of 10–20%, this will lighten the body without decreasing its plasticity. Lucie Rie blends 10% china clay into the prepared plastic body she uses. Most ball clays will increase plasticity. All clays should be prepared in the form of a slurry and wedged into the clay; if mixed in dry a lowering of the plasticity will result.

Bentonite

Bentonite is an unusual sort of clay in that it has a very high level of plasticity – a superplastic clay. It has extremely fine particle size and can be added to bodies to increase plasticity, and it can absorb large amounts of water, almost twice as much as ball clay. In the process of absorbing water the bentonite swells and gives a greasy slurry. For this reason it is best mixed separately and then added to the body, either at the blunging (mechanical mixing) state (if appropriate) or wedged into the plastic clay.

Fluxes

To become hard and vitrified clay bodies need to contain a fluxing material. Some mixtures, especially if the particle size of the clays is small, will flux on their own and no special addition is required. Others need a flux addition. Generally feldspar, nepheline syenite or cornish stone will fulfil this function at low cost and be operative over a relatively wide firing range. Amounts required vary according to temperature and on the make-up of the body, but 5–10% would be considered to be an average addition. A body recipe composed of 70% ball clay calls for the inclusion of 1% cornish stone, which should be sufficient to flux the body. More dramatic fluxes are frits, which start to fuse at relatively low temperatures and encourage the vitrification of the body. The addition of 5% frit would be a suitable starting point.

Other body additions

Some materials, such as the lithium bearing feldspars, petalite and spodumene, can be added to clay bodies to serve as a flux, in that they cause vitrification at a lower temperature. Because lithium has a very low thermal expansion it will enable the body to withstand changes of temper-ature without cracking. A suitable fitting glaze must be used. Such a body is useful for ovenware. The addition of spodumene will also colour the body, giving it an attractive rust colour similar to the toasted effect of reduced stoneware. (Amounts of 10–20% will give this effect.) Quantities in excess of this will considerably lower the vit-rification point of the body.

Talc works in much the same way as spodumene in reducing the thermal expansion of the body. Some outcrops of clay in Turkey occur as mixtures of clay and mica; they feel soapy to the touch and are not easy to work, but when fired will withstand, without cracking, the direct heat of a flame. Talc bodies present similar problems to the potter but are worth experimenting with. Coarse mica waste, if available, is probably much easier to work with and just as effective as talc. This also has the advantage of improving the resistance of the body to chipping. Muscovite mica, after firing to stoneware temperatures, will develop needle-shaped mullite crystals whilst retaining its lamel-lar (plate-like) structure.

Some materials, such as spodumene, colour the body. Various metal oxides can also be added to darken or tint the body. Most clay bodies contain iron which, when fired, will produce shades of cream, tan, grey and brown; additional iron can be added either as red iron oxide, yellow ochre or crocus martis. However, these amounts must usually be kept below 5% as they do act as fluxes in the body, even in oxidation conditions. The chief danger is that they can cause the body to bloat. Yellow ochre, a soft variety of iron ore which may contain up to 5% clay as well as iron and other impurities, can be added to white firing bodies (such as semi-porcelain) to give attractive pale colours. Additions of other body stains and oxides to produce coloured bodies are dealt with in Chapter 9.

Body blends

As I noted earlier, very few potters will use one of the prepared clay bodies by itself; most modify it in some way. The most popular method of doing this is to blend different bodies together whilst they are plastic. This can easily be done by wedging the weighed clays together, or by putting them through a pug mill if one is available. At Briglin Pottery newly delivered clay is pugged together with a mixture of reclaimed clay as this gives it more tooth for throwing.

Many potters find commercial stoneware bodies are too pale in colour and try various ways

of overcoming this. Many add 10–15% red earthenware clay to counteract the colour and give variety. Robert and Sheila Fournier, at Lacock Pottery, use a mixture of five parts buff firing stoneware with one part red earthenware, and find that this gives them a tough, stone-like body which only bloats if overfired. Sarah Bodine, a potter in New York, describes most prepared bodies as having a dull, smooth monotony, and she adds extra fine grog for tooth. Some potters mix a smooth stoneware with a small quantity (about 10%) of coarse body, such as crank or raku body, to achieve much the same effect.

In the U.K. there are special 'speckle' bodies available which contain small grains of a material which fuses during the firing to form 'iron spots' in the glaze, giving a similar appearance to reduction effects. Most of these clays contain too much 'specking' material and the resulting effect in the glaze is that the spots are too evenly distributed. A blend of 40% of this body with a plain body gives more interesting results.

Porcelain

So far this chapter has dealt with stoneware and earthenware clay bodies which are prepared from

Peter Lane; thrown and turned porcelain bowl with pinched and indented rim. Manganese dioxide painted on the biscuit before spraying a white dolomite glaze (feldspar 50, china clay 25, dolomite 20, whiting 5), 1280°C (2336°F). 15.2 cm (6 in) diameter

mixtures of ball clays, grogs and so on; when fired they are strong, opaque and dark coloured. In contrast, porcelain is white and, although translucent, is still strong. It is made from iron-free materials which include china clay and quartz and is fluxed by feldspar. Porcelain has normally been fired to high stoneware temperatures, but additions of larger amounts of flux can lower the firing temperature. The distinction is often made between hard paste or 'true' porcelain, which is fired to high temperatures usually in excess of 1260°C (2300°F), and soft paste or low temperature porcelain, which matures at around 100°C (212°F) below this temperature. A further difference is that hard paste porcelain has a low biscuit firing and a hard gloss, while soft paste has a relatively hard biscuit with a lower glaze firing.

Most potters who fire in an electric kiln do not concern themselves with the translucency of porcelain, and tend to use it more as a white, high-fired body. The particular interest of porcelain lies

1 Above *Emmanuel Cooper; porcelain bowl with dolomite matt glaze with copper carbonate pigment under the glaze. Rim painted in black and pink pigment*

2 Right *Emmanuel Cooper; thrown porcelain lidded pot with matt nepheline syenite glaze containing 1.5% copper carbonate*

3 *Eileen Lewenstein; thrown porclain plate with matt feldspathic glaze coloured with cobalt oxide and iron oxide*

4 Above *Lucie Rie; thrown porcelain bowl with transparent glaze containing uranium. The rim is painted in gold bronze pigment*

5 Above right *Phyllis Ihrman; thrown porclain bottle with crystal formation. The glaze has a higher feldspar content with zinc oxide, 17% bentonite B (Millwhite Company, Texas) and 3% titanium dioxide; the bottle is glazed raw fired to Orton cone 10. Then the temperature is dropped to 1149°C (2100°F) and held for three hours. The white clay body is made from Kamic Kaolin 3, Ball clay (OM 4) 4, Potash feldspar 2, Flint 1*

6 Below *Alison Britton; slab built jug with inlaid colour and painted decoration under the semi-matt clear glaze*

7 Right *Christine Anne Richards; thrown porcelain bottle with copper glaze containing silicon carbide and colemanite*

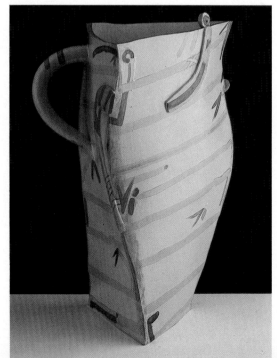

in its ability to be worked finely without loss of strength, and its whiteness, which enables a range of colours to be obtained from soft, subtle whites and creams to rich tenmokus. Porcelain fired in an electric kiln will take on a creamy white, sometimes an ivory colour, while the same body fired in reduction will give a blue, grey white shade; both effects are caused by the presence of minute quantities of iron in the body.

Traditionally the high temperature porcelains made in China were formed from a blend of 50 china clay, 25 quartz and 25 feldspar and fired to temperatures of 1300°C (2372°F) and above. But such temperatures are hard to obtain in most electric kilns and have a very wearing effect on the wire elements and fabric of the kiln. Additions of a white firing bentonite to the body not only helps to lower the firing temperature but also makes the body more plastic and very much easier to work. Some potters add small quantities of white firing ball clay to make the body more workable; however, both bentonite and ball clay contain small amounts of iron and this will tend to colour the body.

Bernard Leach used a body composed of china clay 45, feldspar 25, siliceous ball clay 16.66 and water ground quartz 13.33, which after storing, becomes sufficiently plastic to work with. David Leach, son of Bernard, using bentonite, has devised a highly plastic body which matures at 1260–1280°C (2300–2336°F); it has the following recipe: china clay 55, potash feldspar 25, quartz 15, white bentonite 5 and in the U.K., is available commercially. Other potters have worked out variations of this mixture. The plasticity of all porcelain bodies improves with age and they are best stored in a cool, damp cellar, well wrapped in sheets of polythene for as long as possible before use.

Porcelain, like any other clay body, is reclaimed in the usual manner, but care needs to be taken to keep it clean and free from contamination. However, depsite the most careful efforts, contamination of the body often occurs. A pleasant grogged porcelain can be made by the addition of white molochite or, for a more textured body, an ordinary high firing grog.

Some potters find the density of porcelain bodies too difficult for easy throwing, particularly if the object to be made is large. Here the addition of grog made from the porcelain body will give it strength without changing its fired qualities. This grog can be made by crumbling the dried clay and passing it through a fine sieve (60–80 mesh). The powder is then fired in a biscuit bowl to a temperature slightly below the temperature at which the body matures. The resulting grog can be added to the plastic clay in amounts up to 15%.

Commercially available porcelain bodies range from the expensive fine, pure, high temperature mixtures to semi-porcelain and white stoneware. They represent great savings with regard to the time taken in mixing and storing and, as porcelain is rarely used in great quantities, are well worth investigating. Formulation of these bodies varies from one manufacturer to another, and consequently not all glazes will fit them. The most difficult problem is that of the crazing of clear glazes. If the body is acceptable, then to prevent crazing it is better to adjust the glaze slightly according to the advice given in Chapter 8.

Body faults

Finding a clay body which has the right colour and quality, handles well and gives consistently reliable fired results can take a long time. Tests cannot be done quickly and have to be carried out over a wide range of shapes. Once found, few potters are willing to change their clay body formulation, but sometimes faults arise which cannot be ignored. These can result from slight changes in the clays used in the body and may require adjustments in the proportions of the other ingredients. There is not the space here to discuss these in detail but only to outline the main faults and changes.

Spiral or ring crackings
The condition where the body cracks and splits in a spiral formation as though bursting apart is due

Ian Godfrey; handbuilt stoneware object with dry glaze

to either the glaze having too low a thermal expansion which is putting the body under too great a tensile stress (see Chapter 8) or conversely, because the body has too high a thermal expansion because it contains too large a quantity of silica. Reduce the silica in the body by adding more china clay or by replacing some of the ball clay with one which is lower in silica. The addition of molochite to the body may help.

Chipping of the edges
A body which is too brittle is liable to chip in use. This can be caused by sand in the body which does not go into a sufficiently intimate mix in firing. Replace the sand with a grog.

Spit out
Clay bodies which are contaminated with small pieces of plaster of Paris can suffer from spitting as a result of small areas of clay being lifted off. This fault can occur either at the green stage or after being biscuit fired. The clay in this case, unfortunately, has to be discarded or reduced to a slip and sieved. Small particles of calcite (calcium carbonate) in the body can cause similar problems.

Porosity
To be hygienic and strong a fired stoneware body should have a porosity of less than 3%; bodies which are too porous either require firing to a higher temperature or require the addition of a body flux such as feldspar. Bodies, however, which are slightly porous, if covered with a well fitting craze-free glaze, often make good ovenware bodies. Porosity rarely presents a problem at stoneware temperatures, and in the case of red earthenware can be an acceptable quality.

Vitrification
The opposite of porosity. Ideally a matured body should be well vitrified and this process should occur slowly over a wide range of temperature. Vitrification is the furthest point to which a clay body can be taken without deformation. A body taken to its maximum state of vitrification can be brittle in use and needs either a lower temperature firing or an addition of alumina. This can be added in the form of china clay or as alumina hydrate.

Deformation
When clays reach their maturing temperature they become slightly soft, or pyroplastic, and, depending on the shape of the pot, sagging and deformation can occur. This can only be avoided by firing the body to a lower temperature, increasing the alumina in the body, or by improved making. Flat lids, for instance, should be made with a slight arching to prevent sagging and the walls of pots need to be made with an even thickness.

Bloating
This is a bubbling and swelling of the body at high temperatures and is caused by the presence of bubbles of trapped gases. During the firing the body gives off carbon monoxide, sulphurous gases and fluorine, and this continues through the duration of the firing. Any gases trapped by the vitrified body will be released at top temperature, when the body becomes pyroplastic, and a bloat is then formed. The solution lies in either slowing down the rate of firing, particularly at around 900°C (1652°F), so that the gases formed can escape without problem, or firing to a slightly lower top temperature.

Splitting and cracking
Large pots which split or crack on the base may have been fired too quickly or biscuit fired while still slightly damp. Always ensure that large pots are bone dry before firing. (This can take much longer than you think.) During the glaze firing place them on a layer of alumina sand to enable them to move and contract.

5 Pottery production

Some potters choose to work with electric kilns and some potters, by force of circumstances, do not have a choice. Living in a block of flats, or in a crowded city will almost certainly rule out the use of any other sort of kiln. Yet among all the potters I have spoken to, none has expressed regret at not being able to use reduction kilns, and most of them like the challenge of obtaining good results with electricity. The development of suitable working methods, the selection of materials and the acceptance of size limits can all play an important part in the creative process. In this chapter I will discuss how potters have resolved many of these production problems, for, whilst the basic making processes are the same irrespective of how the work is to be fired, there are some important differences between making work for different firing processes, as well as a different emphasis which can suggest alternative solutions.

Lack of space, for most potters, is a major problem and few are lucky enough to have too much. Choosing to work in a tight and compact urban environment where every square foot of space has to be paid for either in high rents or in local taxes often forces a close examination of working methods and workshop layout. The luxury of large, sprawling workshops are to be found in the country rather than the town. City potters almost seem to be a race apart. Their desire to live in an urban setting yet continue with an occupation which has traditionally been rurally based means working in small rooms and using electric kilns. It is unlikely that production will be huge or the workshop team large; most city potters work by themselves or with only one or two assistants.

Yet there are advantages to such a geographical position. Cities and large towns provide a market for their goods as well as a ready access to shops and galleries. Deliveries of work can be made relatively easily and visitors can be welcomed, though this may often need some control. Far from being isolated, many urban potters have to fight to ensure that their work programme is not lost in a social, if pleasant, round of exhibition openings, visits and visitors. Potters working on a small scale of production will make important decisions very early on about the sort of ware they want to produce. There is, for instance, no use in planning a huge production schedule of a wide range of domestic wares if there is just not sufficient workshop space to store the pots or kiln space to fire them.

Lucie Rie; a set of stoneware cups with a white tin glaze unpacked from the kiln

This is in strong contrast to country potters with large workshops who can plan such a production and who may for example design a wide range of quickly made domestic wares which are thrown but not turned. Glazing may be kept to a minimum so that only a little fettling is required, and when fired in a large reduction kiln the body may become attractive and richly coloured. The resulting ware can be sold at a relatively low price. For the city potter such a scheme would be foolhardy; the emphasis would need to be on a much smaller production of wares carefully thrown, probably with a turned foot and glazed all over. The higher selling price of the pots would reflect the greater amount of work involved and the demands of the firing process.

The choice of basic materials will also be deeply influenced by the types of production planned, the size and scope, as well as the space available. Without sufficient space in which to work it is very difficult to mix clay bodies, particularly if they are to be required in any quantity. Raw materials will need to be ordered in bulk if economies in cost are to be made which will require an adequate on-site storage area. Mixing clay body, a dusty operation, again needs suitable storage space so that the clay can be kept and allowed to age and sour. Potters who concentrate on making individual pots and

objects, where quantities are not important, may be quite content to mix bodies in small amounts, but potters with a production line to run will probably turn to ready-made commercial bodies and find ways of adapting or modifying them to suit their requirements. (The methods of developing attractive clay bodies is discussed in the chapter on clays.)

Costs, of course, cannot be totally ignored when making these decisions. Weight for weight, ready mixed plastic clay supplied by the factory will cost many times more than the equivalent made from raw materials. Not only are you buying the water, which is mixed with the clay, but you are also paying for other people's labour, the devising, mixing and packing as well as the cost of transport. To do this yourself, providing you have suitable mixing equipment, will cost only time. Against the time spent on this must be offest the fact that pots are not being made. There are many potters who prefer to devise and to make up their own clay bodies, seeing this as an essential part of the wholeness of pottery production. Such potters are also usually keen to build and fire their own kilns and the idea of using an electric kiln is not attractive. For such potters it is in one way a life-style involvement in production which includes the mixing of the clay, the making and the firing of the pots, which is as important as the end results. Other potters approach the craft differently and put the emphasis on the making rather than the mixing, and they are content to devise ways of

Caroline Whyman; thrown stoneware mugs with white slip and carved decoration, under clear glaze tinted with small amounts of copper carbonate and rutile

using materials which are available rather than starting from raw materials. They see the end product as being as important as the making of it.

The sort of production envisaged will also depend on the capacity of the kiln. A potter who wants to make individual one-off pieces will be unlikely to require a large kiln, which may also take a long time to fill, especially if much of the work is experimental. Yet the kiln must be of sufficient size to accommodate larger pots. For the production potter with a regular and systematic output the choice is likely to be between a large kiln fired less often, which allows a build-up of ware, or two or three small kilns fired more frequently. Kiln capacity can very much dictate the production rhythm. Some potteries with a huge kiln may only fire four to six times a year, with fairly set periods of time devoted to making, decorating, glazing, firing and dispatching. In other pottery workshops the firing room may contain five or six small electric kilns which are fired almost every day depending on the flow of orders. Such a system gives great flexibility and special orders can be produced quickly without upsetting daily routine. One of the pleasures of firing with electricity is the more frequent completion of the processes and the regular joy of peeping into the cooling kiln. When Harry Horlock Stringer first started potting in his own workshop he had a kiln of 0.03 cu m (1 cu ft) capacity which he fired every day. Results were quickly obtained and over the week he was able to produce 0.2 cu m (7 cu ft) of pots.

The method of firing, particularly if it is to be by electricity, will affect the design of the ware. As explained in Chapter 4 on clays, there is much less body-glaze interaction in electric kiln firing, and clay bodies do not automatically take on a rich, roasted effect. They are much more likely to be a dark, or a buff colour of no particular interest. Additions of red clay or iron oxide to the body will make it fire to a much darker colour but again it is unlikely to have the rich quality associated with reduction firing.

For this reason the surface of most oxidised pottery made for domestic use is covered with glaze so as to leave only the foot rims and gallery seatings where the body can be seen. Individual work, is of course, given quite separate consideration. Here I want to consider the production of functional wares. Potters who want to produce functional ware want it to be practical, to stand up to wear and tear and to be attractive to look at; part of the successful solutions to these problems depend on making full use of the qualities that are

David Morris; thrown stoneware teapot with white tin glaze and paint decoration

available rather than lamenting the absence of those which are not. With electric firing these qualities are clean, crisp firings, reliability and an emphasis on glaze rather than on body quality; edges that are rough, bottoms of pots that are not turned, chunky throwing rings and dry-looking clay bodies are difficult to handle well in electric kilns.

As a general rule the neater and more defined the form, the better it will succeed. Throwing rings need to be carefully controlled so they become an integral part of the overall design rather than evidence of vigorous throwing activity; edges need to be rounded either by compressing them by using the fingers or by wrapping over a piece of chamois leather. Sand in the body should, on the whole, be avoided as it can make it brittle and easy to chip. Fettling the body with a sponge should be kept to a minimum as far as possible as this brings out any grog or sand addition to leave an unpleasantly rough surface. During throwing it is particularly important to pay attention to compressing and smoothing over the insides of bowls, hollow ware and flat ware after sponging out the water. Ideally, the build-up of water should be avoided but this is not always possible. If care is taken when moving the fingers over the thrown, flat areas which have been sponged out, a smooth and strong surface will result.

Crispness and sharpness of forms can be greatly

helped by turning. Again, different potters choose different methods of making and some try to avoid turning the base of the pots; instead they concentrate on cleaning off the outside of the pot with a wooden tool and trimming the bottom of the pot using a metal point. A twisted wire is pulled under the base to separate the pot from the wheel head and the pot is then carefully lifted off. When leather-hard, the base is tapped in slightly to give a concave surface and this will prevent it from sagging during the firing. Any roughness on the edges is rubbed smooth either by rolling the pot on the edges of its base, or by smoothing it with the finger. For some pots this is an excellent method but can give a crude and unfinished appearance when fired in an electric kiln. It is often far better to spend some time in returning the pot to the wheel at the leather-hard stage and turning or trimming the base.

Turning, sometimes called shaving or skim-

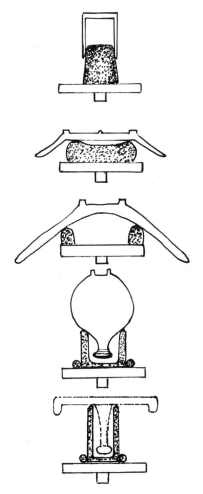

Methods of turning pots on chucks (or chums)

ming, involves removing unwanted clay from the bottom of a pot either to smooth it off or to create a foot rim of some sort by using a metal or wooden tool. Ideally, turning should be kept to a minimum as it does lengthen considerably the time spent in the making of a pot, but by employing a proper method of fixing the pot to the wheelhead this time can be kept very short. Various types of clay chuck, sometimes known as chums, which support the pot upside down from the inside, are best for holding pots on the wheel. No matter how large the pots are, the use of the chuck has many advantages for production potters over any other method; it allows pots to be placed and tapped quickly into position, and to be removed, whilst the wheel is in motion. This has the added advantage of speed and many chucks are almost self-centering, in that they help to bring the pot to a central position quickly; furthermore, they allow the entire profile of the pot to be seen and allow for the whole pot to be turned if this is decided.

Chucks are best used when leather hard and can be used many times. They can be kept and stored in polythene sheeting in between working sessions. Softer clay chucks tend to form grooves quickly and may also stick to the walls of the pot. The chuck is made by sticking the clay to the wheel head and turning it down to the required size. For turning cylindrical shapes a chuck which fits inside the pot is used; the sides of the chuck should be as vertical as possible as this gives a larger area to grip the pot and prevents the rim from pressing into the chuck and forming a groove which will subsequently cause the pot to wobble. If this happens the surface of the chuck has to be turned again to make it smooth. In order to centre the pot it is placed over the chuck and tapped into a central position as the wheel revolves. Some potters throw a new chuck after they have made the pots as it will then be ready to use when the pots are ready to turn.

All hollow ware can be turned by this method, with the exception of bottles which have narrow necks. These can be trimmed by fitting them into a hollow chuck which supports them on the shoulder. Flat ware is trimmed over a flattened chuck but is supported on the edges of the inside of the bottom.

Some potters throw chucks and then biscuit fire them as a means of preventing their destruction. It is much easier, however, to get the pot to stick to a leather hard chuck than to one which has been biscuit fired. Chucks, once made, can be fixed to the wheel head by means of rolls of clay pressed

Emmanuel Cooper; thrown teapot, stoneware, with matt dolomite glaze

firmly against the base. Many beginners find that the process of making chucks and centering the pot on it is difficult; yet once the skill has been acquired it is a much better method and far less likely to damage ware.

An alternative method of turning is to centre the pot on the wheel head and hold it in position with rolls of clay. This is a quick method for one or two pots, but may easily cause damage and distortion to the rim.

Whatever the method used, it is important to ensure that the turning should be clean and decisive. This is achieved by the use of a suitable metal tool (one which allows the clay to shoot free and is self sharpening) and by catching the clay at the right condition, i.e. between cheese and leather hard. If the clay is too soft the turnings will stick and not come away cleanly; too dry and 'chattering' will develop. Equally important is the decision about the turning and what you want it to achieve. A tall foot can be elegant and a positive part of the pot, serving not only to provide adequate areas for glazing but to lift the pot up and give a light and growing feeling. Balance between the rim or top of the pot and the width and size of the footring will also help determine these qualities.

Not all footrings need to be tall; a small, soft, rounded foot can be both gentle and flowing – maybe ideal for a salad bowl or plate. On some pots a footring may not be necessary; instead, a smooth skimmed base will be sufficient. This may be excellent for example, on small items such as coffee mugs, or egg cups.

Once turned, dried and biscuit fired, the pots are ready for glazing and glaze is usually applied over the entire inside, outside and base of the pot. Painting some sort of water resisting liquid such as hot paraffin wax or liquid wax emulsion onto foot rings, seating galleries and lid rims will help to give neat, precise edges. However, this is not essential as the usual wiping off of glaze together with sponge fettling will serve almost as well.

Not all pots and objects are thrown and there are many potters who use a wide and inventive range of making methods. Hand building methods such as pinching, slabbing, coiling or press moulding, are used in all sorts of ways by many well established potters. The ceramic industry makes most of its wares by either jiggering and jolleying the clay into moulds or by slip-casting in moulds, and fires practically all its pots in oxidising conditions. There is not the space in this book to go into the details of these more industrial making methods, each of which needs relatively complex equipment and different skills. Here I am concentrating on the methods usually used by

James Richardson; thrown stoneware teapot with fluted decoration, made from a clay body which contains 10% spodumene. The tenmoku glaze (the same as in his faceted bottle on p. 13) fires much redder

studio potters. Yet more and more potters are turning to more mechanical methods which if well used can give rich and interesting results.

Inlay and agate wares, which rely for their effect on the use of different coloured bodies and are usually fired without glaze, are ideally suited to oxidised firing methods. Under such conditions the colours tend to retain their brightness and retain their differences. When fired in a reducing atmosphere the effect of the iron content in many clays makes them look very much alike. Coloured slip decoration, painted or sprayed onto the body and fired without glaze, can give rich and varied colours. Glaze and body stains mixed into the slip will extend the range of colours available and all can be intermixed for subtle effects.

The use of slips has been known and practised for many hundreds of years but usually applied under the glaze and fired at earthenware temperatures; the traditional slip decorated red wares of America or the detailed trailed ware of Staffordshire are techniques which can be adopted for use in the electric kiln, either at earthenware or stoneware temperatures.

Whatever the method of making and whatever the function for which the work is intended, there is little that can be left to chance with an electric kiln firing. Without glaze or decoration the clay body by itself will tend to be dry and dull. In a reduction kiln such a body may spring to life in response to the flame atmosphere. A vigorously thrown and partially glazed pot, fired in a reduction kiln, can take on all the best qualities of traditional wares, having an attractive rustic and natural quality. If we want these qualities in an electric kiln we have to engineer them either by treating the surface of the pot or the glaze, with suitable materials. Whatever effect is required has to be put there; it will not happen merely in the firing.

6 Glazes in the electric kiln

All too often glazes fired in electric kilns are either too dry and matt with a surface very unsuitable for functional pots, or else they take on a hard shine which, though practical, lacks the subtlety and depth associated with studio pottery. Yet such glazes are only two types available for oxidising firings, and many potters achieve a wide range of attractive and functional glazes. The difference between 'a good' and a 'bad' glaze from either an aesthetic or a functional point of view may be slight, and quite a bit of experimenting will be required before a satisfactory surface is acquired. Judicious use of colouring oxides and a well fluxed glaze can be the positive features of an oxidised stoneware glaze. The composition of oxidised glazes are slightly different to those used for firing in a reduction atmosphere.

While the theory and chemistry of the glazes remains the same no matter what the atmosphere of the kiln, materials do behave differently according to the amount of oxygen in the chamber. This has to be taken into consideration. Many glazes, for instance, designed for the reduction kiln will be far from mature when fired in oxidation. Conversely, glazes which work well in oxidation may well be over fluxed in reduction. Materials behave differently in the different atmospheres principally because when there is a reduction in the amount of oxygen in the kiln, the materials become much more likely to combine with each other. The level of activity under these conditions is increased between the different ingredients in the glaze and also between the glaze and the body. A glaze that may be a deep, smooth, pale satin blue in a reduction firing may, when fired at the same temperature in an electric kiln, give a dry, underfired dull cream. Equally, a rich black-brown tenmoku glaze fired in reduction may give a pale treacle colour in oxidation. Conversely, an oatmeal white dolomite glaze in oxidation may give a dull grey surface in reduction. In other words, glazes are not automatically interchangeable; information about the behaviour of

materials and the make-up of glazes in particular kiln atmospheres must be taken into account. All too often such information is ignored, or glossed over as being unimportant.

I will not here go fully into the chemistry of glazes and how glaze formulae can be calculated; this is fully described in *Glazes for the Studio Potter* (Cooper and Royle). Here I want to discuss the practical aspects of making glazes for electric kilns, concentrating particularly on those fired to stoneware temperatures. First, it is necessary to briefly discuss the three different parts which go to make up the glaze. Chemists describe glaze as a glass-like layer which covers the surface of the pot and which is fused into place by reaction with the clay body. For functional pots this layer needs to be smooth – so that it can be cleaned easily – to be non-porous – so that it is hygienic in use, and well fitting – so that it strengthens the pot. Finally, the glaze must be safe in use; the glaze/body fit must not craze nor flake off rims or handles, and the fired glaze must not be soluble in use with liquids in which it may come into contact. In practical terms the solubility of glaze materials only applies to lead glazes or special glazes commercially manufactured, containing cadmium or selenium. Cadmium and selenium glazes, which are usually coloured bright red or yellow, must be mixed, applied and fired according to manufacturer's instructions and then they will be perfectly safe in use.

Glazes can be divided into three parts, which the Chinese imaginatively called the 'flesh', the 'bones' and the 'blood'. The bones are the glass-forming part of the glaze and is usually provided by silica, added in its 'pure' form of flint or quartz (SiO_2) or in combination with other materials such as in feldspar or china clay. Silica will fuse at $1710°C$ ($3110°F$) to form a transparent glass. Since this temperature is well above any normal firing temperature other materials have to be added to produce a melt at lower temperatures; these materials are known as the 'blood' of the glaze and serve as activators or fluxes. Glazes for higher temperatures will require proportionally more silica than those which mature at lower temperatures, though proportions will depend on whether the glaze is required to be shiny or matt and will also depend on the type of flux used. Boric oxide is the only other readily available substance which gives a similar result to silica, but will still require the presence of some silica to give a satisfactory glaze.

Much of the quality of the glaze depends on the fluxes chosen: there are, at first sight, an almost bewildering number from which to choose and each has its own particular quality. Again the firing temperature will indicate the fluxes that can be chosen (some only work at lower or higher temperatures) as well as the glaze quality required. Lead, for instance, starts to volatilize at around 1100–1150°C (2012–2102°F), while magnesia (MgO) only starts to become active around 1200°C (2192°F).

The major fluxes are:

		TYPICAL SOURCE
Lithia	Li_2O	Lithium carbonate (Li_2CO_3). Lepidolite. Petalite. Spodumene. Amblygonite.
Soda	Na_2O	Soda feldspar (Albite). Alkaline frit. Nepheline syenite.
Potash	K_2O	Potash feldspar (Orthoclase). Alkaline frit.
Magnesia	MgO	Magnesium carbonate ($MgCO_3$). Dolomite. Talc.
Calcia	CaO	Whiting ($CaCO_3$). Dolomite. Wollastonite.
Zinc Oxide	ZnO	Zinc Oxide. Frit.
Baria	BaO	Barium carbonate ($BaCO_3$).
Lead Oxide	PbO	Lead frit. (Lead bisilicate is recommended.)
Boric Oxide	B_2O_3	Borax Frit. Colemanite. Gerstley borate. Calcium borate frit.

Most glazes contain at least two or more fluxes (a major exception are the lead earthenware glazes) when various qualities from each can be combined. Equally important is the effect of one flux on the other; the fluxing action is usually increased. Not listed here, though certainly important and of great value in stoneware oxidised glazes, is wood ash, which acts as a flux. This will be discussed later.

As well as the glass formers and the fluxes, a third ingredient is necessary to act as a stabiliser to stiffen the glaze to prevent it running off the

Emmanuel Cooper; standard stoneware mugs with white dolomite glaze. The mug on the left has been fired 20°C (68°F) higher

surface of the pot. Technically they are referred to as amphoteric oxides and they serve as a bridge between the fluxes (which are alkaline) and the glass formers (which are acidic). Alumina is the major stabilizer used by the potter and this is present in clay as well as in feldspar. Only rarely is it added in the form of alumina hydrate. The presence of clay not only serves to stiffen the melting glaze but is also valuable in the glaze slop, where it helps to keep the heavier and coarser ingredients in suspension for longer periods. It also acts as a binder in the dried glaze, preventing it from being brushed off the surface of the pot when it is being handled and placed in position in the kiln. China clay, which contains both alumina and silica, is used in the glaze as an 'uncontaminated' source of these two materials.

Few materials used by the potter really fall into only one of these groups. Most materials are compounds and contain several different elements. For the potter anxious to know how each material behaves in the kiln a simple method is to mix each material with water and to paint it, to glaze thickness, onto a tile. When fired in the kiln these trials will indicate the materials that will melt (some will do so vigorously) or combine with the surface of the clay (fluxes will not melt to form a glass but will react with the clay surface). Other materials will melt to form a stiff, opaque glass, while others will hardly be affected by the firing. The materials can be considered under three broad headings:

Group I: Fluxes

Whiting. Dolomite. Barium carbonate. Wood ash. Talc. Cryolite. Lithium carbonate. Wollastonite. Calcium borate frit. Gerstley borate. Alkaline frit. Borax frit. Lead frit.

Group II: Stabilizers and stiffeners

Feldspar. Cornish stone. Petalite. Nepheline syenite. Basalt.

Group III: Glass formers and stiffeners

Quartz. Flint. China clay. Red clay. Local clay.

Fired on a tile, these materials will give visual evidence of how they each behave in the kiln and will help the potter understand how they will act in the glaze. Not mentioned so far are the colouring oxides; these not only colour the glaze but may also serve as fluxes, helping the glaze to melt or, conversely, may serve as stiffeners, making the glaze more refractory. In the case of glazes fired in the electric kiln it is through the addition of small amounts of metal oxides that many subtle and rich colours and textures will be obtained. They are added in the form of oxides, carbonates and pentoxides in quantities which are usually expressed as a percentage over and above the total weight of the glaze ingredients.

Approach to glazes

To many potters brought up on a tradition derived from oriental ceramics, the only true stoneware glaze is one with a 'reduced' appearance in which iron spots even if small, are present, and colours are muted and earthy, ranging from pale celadon blues and greens to dark blacks and browns. To such potters, glazes which fall outside these parameters are unsatisfactory. Faced with having to use an electric kiln they set out to make glazes which come as close in appearance to traditional glazes as possible. With a careful mixing of suitable fluxes and the sensitive use of colouring oxides such effects can be created; listed in the appendix are glazes which will do this. But the electric kiln does offer opportunities for other, equally rich, effects. Not everyone likes iron spots, not even potters who fire with reduction, and some of them go to great lengths to sieve out any iron specks from the glaze and body.

For other potters the creation of the reduced appearance in bodies and glazes is not sufficient and so they adapt their kiln and create a reducing atmosphere by dropping combustible material into it, or by burning a gas flame inside the chamber. In a recent edition of the American magazine *Studio Potter*, a potter in Japan described the construction of an electric kiln complete with a firebox for burning wood, so that the effects of a wood-burning kiln could be achieved. (Methods of reducing in the electric kiln are discussed later.)

Not all glazes need to be modelled on reduction effects; oxidising atmospheres can impart their own qualities to the glaze, and with the judicious selection of suitable raw materials these qualities can be both colourful and, if required, subtle. One approach is to start with a recipe which is at least near to what you want (my book, *The Potter's Book of Glaze Recipes*, lists over 500) and adapt it to your purpose. The first task, apart from deciding on the glaze description (i.e. transparent, matt, clear, coloured) is to find out what the chemical make up of the glaze is and how it will respond to colouring oxides and so on. This can be best deduced from the chemical formula of the glaze, but there are rule of thumb methods which can be applied based on the ingredients. The most useful classification of glaze types depends on identifying either the fluxes that are present or the main ingredient in the glaze; the major exception is glazes which are high in clay, sometimes called clay or raw glazes.

Classifications of glaze

Clay glazes

These usually have over 25% of plastic clay in the recipe and can be applied to the raw pot before it is biscuit fired. Some glazes, based on locally obtained clays, can have as much as 80% in the recipe. Such glazes cannot easily be applied to biscuit; one way around this problem is to replace some of the clay with calcined – that is, pre-fired – clay. Ground clay calcined to 960°C (1760°F) in the biscuit kiln is rendered non plastic and can be substituted for part of the plastic clay. Local clays are usually rich in iron and can give brown glazes which can be smooth and even or, depending on the flux, mottled and variegated.

Clay glazes have the advantage of having a wide maturing range, and melt over quite a long period. Only at very high temperatures do they become runny. The high alumina content of the glaze will have an affect on its appearance making it matt and opaque. If too much clay is present the glaze may be stiff and dry, with a rough and uneven surface. The behaviour of the metal oxides will also be affected by the clay and thus the range of colours that are available. On the whole it will make them lighter and reduce intensity. Crystalline glazes tend to be low in alumina as its presence tends to discourage the formation of crystals, although some potters have formulated high alumina crystalline recipes suitable for raw glazing.

Robert Fournier; handbuilt stoneware pebble pot with glaze and slip decoration

Feldspathic glazes

These are usually used on stoneware or porcelain and have as the primary, or major, flux a large proportion of feldspar $(R_2O,Al_2O_3,6SiO_2)$. Such a glaze may incorporate as much as 70–80% feldspar but usually contains a supplementary flux such as whiting. These glazes tend to be clear or semi-opaque, relatively stiff when fired, in the electric kiln, and without a great deal of character. Because of the high potassium and sodium content they may craze. They are excellent bases for the addition of iron oxide to give a good range of colours ranging from pale creamy to olive green, black, breaking brown and red. The addition of cobalt tends to give inky and dark colours whilst copper (in small quantities) gives green.

Magnesium glazes

These have as their major (or most influential) flux magnesia. This is introduced either as magnesium carbonate $(MgCO_3)$ which is slightly soluble in water and can cause crawling in the glaze or, more usually, in dolomite $(CaCO_3.MgCO_3)$, where it is combined with calcium, or as talc, $(3MgO.4SiO_2.H_2O)$ where it is combined with silica; neither of the latter materials is soluble in water. A typical magnesia glaze is a soft, satin, semi-opaque white matt over stoneware caused by the formation of tiny crystals in the cooling glaze. Depending on the amount of dolomite present (a glaze can contain from 10–30%) the surface of the glaze will vary according to thickness. With a relatively thin coat there can be an attractive body/glaze interaction giving rich oatmeal-coloured mottlings. Magnesia responds to the iron content of the body and can break up to give interesting surface qualities. A thicker layer of glaze will tend to disguise this reaction and may give a slightly rough, if very white surface, which, though still pleasant, will tend to stain in use. This is because the glaze is over-fluxed with magnesia, which crystallizes out to give the rough surface.

Magnesia glazes give particularly interesting responses to metal oxide additions. The magnesia has a bleaching effect on the iron and this combines with the opacity of the glaze to give lighter, more muted colours. This can be attractive or it can be crude. Additions of 2% iron oxide, for instance, can give a broken leopard-skin colour and texture with thinnish glaze layers; a thicker coating will give bright banana-skin yellows. Greater additions of iron oxide will give matt and dull tans rather than an increased density of colour. Cobalt in small quantities will give pale pinky-mauve; 1–2% of copper, pale orange salmon or dusky pinks. Very small quantities of manganese will respond in a similar way.

Calcium glazes

These have, as their principal flux whiting ($CaCO_3$) which, in combination with other fluxes, will give reliable glazes in the stoneware range. Other calcium bearing minerals are dolomite ($CaCO_3$ $MgCO_3$) and wollastonite ($CaSiO_3$). Added in excess, calcia can give smooth matt glazes as a result of the formation of calcium silicate crystals. Up to 30% of calcium in the recipe of the glaze may be required, but the result will depend on the other materials present; for example, china clay will aid the formation of these small crystals. Such a glaze will give good colour responses from copper and cobalt when typical bright and attractive shades of blue and turquoise will be formed. However, calcia (which is lime) does have a bleaching effect and will not encourage strong colours. This is particularly noticeable with iron oxide which, in a lime matt, will give pale shades of creams, yellows or greens, depending on the amount used. This is in contrast to glazes in which calcia is the secondary flux. In a transparent or semi-transparent glaze, such as one based on feldspar, the 8–10% iron oxide will go into solution, and will give rich and deep shades of browns and blacks. Calcium matt glazes can be silky and attractive in appearance but functional wares will stain easily and the slightly rough surface is not pleasant to use.

Barium glazes

These behave very much as calcium glazes and contain a percentage of barium carbonate ($BaCO_3$). This will only be effective in combination with other fluxes and only relatively small amounts are required to get the typical barium response. That is, rich alkaline shades from copper or cobalt. With iron oxide opaque indian red colours are possible. Too great a proportion of barium carbonate will give dry, pin-holed glazes for no added colour advantage. Other oxide colours can be equally exciting. In combination with nepheline syenite, the addition of 1–2% nickel can give purple whilst a combination of barium and zinc oxide with similar amounts of nickel will give bright blues, pinks and mauves.

Alkaline glazes

This is a broad classification used to signify mixtures which give marked alkaline responses, usually in clear transparent matrix. These are brought about by the presence of a high proportion of the more powerful alkalis such as lithia, soda, potash and baria introduced either through a mineral or as a prepared commercial frit. To encourage a good colour response from metal oxides the stabilizing or amphoteric oxide content of the glaze is kept low, which can result in a narrow maturing range and runny glazes.

Glazes high in soda and potassium will tend to craze but this can be partly overcome by the addition of small amounts of lithia (2–3%) or boric oxide. From a functional point of view alkaline glazes lack strength and give difficult glaze/body fit problems; their advantages lie in the colours that can be produced, the quality of the glazes (such as attractive crackles) and their use with other fluxes to lower firing temperatures.

Zinc glazes

Glazes which contain a large percentage of zinc oxide are principally used for special effect crystalline mixtures. As a powerful flux the zinc will cause the glaze to become molten and in the slow cooling period zinc silicate crystals may be formed. A zinc crystalline glaze may contain up to 30% zinc oxide. These are discussed more fully in

Chapter 10. In most glazes, however, zinc is used in much smaller amounts of about 5% to great benefit, where it acts either as a secondary flux or as an opacifier. Such small amounts of zinc will promote fusion of the glaze, reduce any tendency to craze (zinc oxide has a low degree of expansion) and will generally brighten colours, especially the blue of cobalt and the greens from copper. In zinc glazes chrome will give tans and browns. During the nineteenth century, potters started to use zinc oxide as an alternative flux to lead, which gave rise to the so-called Bristol glazes.

Opaque glazes

These have a smooth, clean surface brought about by an opacifier, a material which suspends itself in the glaze matrix to refract and reflect the light. The most common, and attractive, white opacifier is tin oxide (SnO_2) which, depending on the composition of the glaze, is added in amounts from 4–15%. It gives results ranging from a pale blue-white semi-opacity through to an attractive, completely opaque, snow white surface. For instance, an alkaline glaze may require the maximum amount of tin oxide (15%) but this will have the effect of increasing the viscosity of the glaze and cause crawling over the body. An addition of 2–4% tin oxide to the glaze will promote a body/glaze reaction which may cause

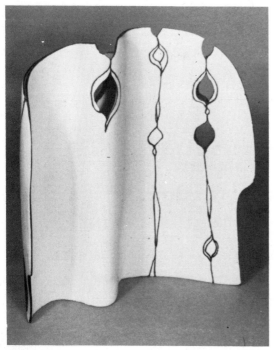

Sheila Fournier; a porcelain 'screen' pot with incised and carved decoration

the iron to 'bleed' into the glaze as well as developing a rich, orange mottled sparkle. In earthenware lead glazes an addition of 15–20% tin oxide can give attractive orange-tan colours when applied over a red body.

Zirconium oxide (ZrO_2) and zirconium silicate (Zircosil $ZrO_2.SiO_2$) can be used in much the same way as tin oxide, though they tend to promote creamy rather than blue shades. Zirconium is useful for producing an opaque green from chrome oxide. Unlike tin oxide, zirconium does not tend to make chrome oxide give pinks. Apart from zirconium's lower cost over tin oxide, it also has the advantage of increasing the strength of the glaze, making the surface more scratch resistant. Zirconium silicate is often given trade names such as 'Zircosil', 'Opax' or 'Disperson'. Other opacifiers include titania, usually used in the form of titanium dioxide (TiO_2). Amounts from 5–10% can produce a pleasant opacity with a crystalline soft matt surface. In some glazes soft white crystals can be formed in a cream base giving a chun-like (pale, translucent blue) quality. Nickel will give opaque lemon yellows with titania.

At earthenware temperatures relatively small amounts of titania will give typical semi-matt vellum surfaces, pale cream in colour and attractive to handle.

Borax glazes

These are fluxed by the presence of boron in combination with other elements. This is added to the glaze either as a borax frit for which a typical formula would be $Na_2O.2B_2O_3.3SiO_2$, or as a naturally occuring mineral, colemanite ($2CaO.3B_2O_3.5H_2O$), or gerstley borate, which is a form of colemanite which contains some soda and is more reliable in the glaze. Potters in the U.K. usually substitute weight for weight a calcium borate frit which has much the same effect as colemanite but with none of the disadvantages of 'spitting' or 'jumping' off the pot when water is liberated early in the firing.

Borax frit can form the major flux in the glaze (in combination with various clays a wide range of glazes can be formed) but the mineral is more often used as a secondary flux to balance the glaze and to add sparkle to the colours. In small quantities the addition of borate can lower the melting point without changing fundamentally the appearance of the glaze. At earthenware temperatures borax glazes lack the richness and lustre of lead glazes, but being cheaper to produce and perfectly safe to handle are widely used in the ceramic industry. In

Emmanuel Cooper; porcelain bowl, thrown, with glaze made up of wood ash

oxidised glazes, borates, because of their wide firing range, can be very useful and many of their benefits have still to be fully explored.

Lead glazes

These contain lead in some form as the major, or (in some cases) the only flux. Because lead begins to volatilise at around $1100-1150°C$ $(2012-2102°F)$ its use is restricted to earthenware glazes, where it gives bright, lustrous qualities which no other material will give. In the ceramic industry in the U.K. its use in any raw form is forbidden, as raw lead compounds are poisonous, and so it is prepared for use as a lead silicate frit. This makes the glaze perfectly safe to handle when it is being mixed or applied. The use of lead bisilicate does not particularly influence the solubility of the fired glaze layer. The dangers of the lead solubility of the fired glazed pottery is a different problem.

The usual lead frits are:

Lead monosilicate	$PbO.SiO_2$
Lead sesquisilicate	$2PbO.3SiO_2$
Lead bisilicate	$PbO.2SiO_2$

Any commercially supplied lead glaze will be safe to use if it is mixed, applied and fired according to any specified instructions; the additions of other materials may change the balance of the glaze and render it unsafe. An addition of copper is particularly dangerous in this respect, and as a general rule copper should not be used in, or in conjunction with lead glazes. Equally, a safe lead glaze, if applied over certain coloured slips, may be rendered poisonous in use if it comes into contact with food. Many potters give recipes for lead glazes which they have found safe and these can be used, but any workshop producing lead glazed wares should have the lead release of their fired glaze checked regularly by a reputable ceramic laboratory. There are government regulations (in the U.K. BS4860) which cover this. Potters who want to make lead glazes should be mindful of its dangers and be particularly aware of its use on domestic pots. It is worth noting that virtually all earthenware and bone china tableware is glazed in lead glazes and no one has ever been poisoned by commercially produced pottery.

Small quantities of lead frit are often incorporated into stoneware glazes where they help to cause early fusion of the glaze; some potters have found that lead can still be used in glazes fired at $1200°C$ $(2192°F)$ but this is relatively uncommon. The colour response from lead glazes tends to make cobalt inky blue, copper apple green, manganese a misty mauve brown, iron yellow and brown.

Wood ash

The rich variations and glaze textures makes wood ash a particularly useful material for the potter firing in an electric kiln. The use of wood and plant ash as a glaze ingredient dates far back in antiquity. It was probably the Chinese who first discovered and made use of the fact that at higher temperatures the ash from wood employed to fire the kiln settled on the surface of clays to form fairly simple, but often attractively mottled, glaze. Ashes contain, in a fine state of subdivision, large proportions of silica, salts of potassium and sodium alkaline earths, iron and often phosphate salts. The amounts and varieties of these minerals vary considerably from plant to plant, soil to soil and, with the same plant on the same ground, from season to season. The colour of unfired ashes, either before or after washing, varies from white to grey brown and black. While some of this colour is due to fine particles of charcoal (carbon), which burns out from the glaze, some is due to the presence of iron, which affects the colour of the glaze. Some potters think that small quantities of copper may be present in certain ashes; for example, those of the cupressus, and these can give soft colours.

When combined in simple mixtures with

feldspar or clay, wood or plant ash will form richly textured and coloured glazes at temperatures of 1250°C (2282°F) and above. The romantic appeal of using ash makes it a favourite material for the stoneware potter. Various analyses of ashes have been carried out and though they are relevant only for that particular batch, they do give some idea of the composition of that particular variety of wood. (See p. 136).

Ashes can be classified by several means. The most useful classification for the potter is hard, soft and medium ashes, which refers to the temperature at which the ash melts. A soft ash melts at 1250°C (2282°F) for instance. The iron content of the ash is also worth noting as this gives some indication of colour response. A more precise classification identifies each ash by its name. Generally speaking, the quicker the plant growth, the harder the ash, and the higher its silica content. The slower the growth, the softer the ash; consequently the hard woods, which have taken many years to grow, yield low silica and high flux content, such as potassium and calcium, and give soft, fusible ash. Quick grown plants, such as bracken, give a high silica content and a hard, infusible ash. However, the silica content of ash is often intimately combined with the other constituents and so does not necessarily act as a refractory material in the way that flint or quartz would act.

Classic combinations of materials to use with ash in glazes include feldspar, clay and flint. Small quantities of calcium carbonate (whiting) or dolomite are often added as a secondary flux. Ash is classified as a fluxing material and many ashes will give a glaze without the addition of other materials.

Ash can be collected from several sources, but tests are only economically worthwhile on sizeable batches. Ash burnt in the hearth, if collected over a period, can provide a good supply, as can bonfires. Wood and plants specially collected for burning to provide named species should be burnt on a firebrick base out in the open on a calm day; the bricks prevent contamination from iron (which is present in soil), ensure a good supply of oxygen, so that thorough burning can take place, and the lack of wind will help to prevent the fine ash particles from being blown away. The wood ash can be used as soon as it is cold, either as it is, complete with bits of grit and carbon, or it can be sieved to remove coarse particles and washed to remove soluble salts. This is done when the ashes are cold – which takes some time as ash is an efficient insulating material – by putting them into water, and the unburnt black carbon will float and can be removed. The soluble salts of sodium will begin to dissolve and as a result the water will be yellow and feel soapy to touch. The water should be changed several times until it stays clear and tasteless – about three changes are usually sufficient. The ash can now be passed through an 80 mesh sieve and allowed to dry. The method of preparation used for the ash should, as far as possible, be the same for all similar batches if the ash is to be used as a regular glaze material. Some potters prefer to use unwashed ash after passing it dry through a fairly coarse sieve. This will make the resulting glaze less reliable because it will gradually change as the soluble sodium salts are dissolved out of the ash.

Before using the ash a simple test to find out its fluxing power is to mix it with water, paint it onto a test tile and fire it. At 1250°C (2282°F) some ashes, particularly those rich in iron, will melt readily, while others will be much less fluid; some will be dark, while others will be white opaque. After this test, combinations with other materials can begin – either in line blends with feldspar, nepheline syenite or clay (because of their low alumina content ashes need stiffening), or in triaxial blends with such materials as feldspar and clay. Two traditional ash recipes which will need temperatures of at least 1260°C (2300°F) are:

ash 2, feldspar 2, china clay 1.
ash 2, feldspar 2, ball clay 1.

Useful line blends of ash with such things as feldspar, nepheline syenite, cornish stone or clay will yield interesting results, especially in the electric kiln. The difference between ash glazes fired in reduction and in oxidation is particularly noticeable. In the electric kiln a combination of 80% mixed ash with either 20% clay or feldspar will give a typical ash effect. Such a glaze will probably be too runny in a reduction kiln, where a 50/50 combination will give similar results. Different ashes will, of course, in similar combinations, give different results. Small amounts of flint added to the glaze will tend to make it more glassy.

Some ash glazes only develop their full qualities at higher temperatures than those which are reached in the average stoneware firing. Such glazes can be rendered more fusible, without greatly affecting the glaze composition, by the addition of 5% alkaline frit. Ash glazes respond very well to small additions of colouring oxides and painted oxide decoration. Iron oxide works particularly well on or in ash glazes, where it breaks and forms bright reds to dull yellows.

Local clays and earths

Generally speaking, clay only differs from soil in its lack of vegetable or organic materials. This causes soil to crumble rather than enabling it to be moulded and modelled. However, in the kiln, organic material burns away and the soil can be used as a substitute for clay for use in glazes. Soil usually contains iron in varying amounts and this will always have the effect of colouring the glaze.

Elisabeth Fritsch; handbuilt coil pots with painted slip decoration

Clay, as dug, varies enormously in composition from area to area. Outcrops of clay, which have a fairly consistent composition, are mined and sold commercially in the U.K. in Staffordshire, Devon and Cornwall. These clays, for the purpose of special effects in glazes, are usually too pure. Also, for special glaze effects, the finer the clay particles the more integrated they become in the glaze mix. Red, brown and yellow clays indicate varying amounts of iron (often in different forms) and/or manganese present in various combinations. Sometimes the lighter coloured clays contain the higher amounts of iron. London clay, found approximately at a depth of 60 cm (2 ft) in the London area, is yellow ochre in colour and can form the basis of many iron glazes. At stoneware temperatures it vitrifies to a dull brown or red colour. Another rich source of clay is a local brick works. Any local clay gives better results in a glaze if the particles are fine; in the case of U.S. materials, Albany and Barnard clays, present no problem. U.K. clays which are to be used in glazes are often very much improved if they are first milled for 2–4 hours in a ball mill.

Clay is best collected from a depth of at least 120 cm (4 ft) if possible, as this gives a more homogeneous mix as well as helping to eliminate vegetable matter and stones. The material is prepared by breaking the dried clay into small pieces and soaking it in plenty of water. Any floating material should be skimmed off and the clay passed through an 80 mesh sieve. Dry out the clay, stirring regularly to create a homogeneous mix and to prevent the larger particles from remaining at the bottom. Test fire the clay alone painted at various thicknesses on the tile. Depending upon the amount of vitrification that has occurred, use the clay in line blends (systematic blends of two materials) with such materials as whiting, ash, cryolite, dolomite. Tests can be made with mixtures of clay, ash and feldspar. Most glazes will give iron colours and further additions of iron oxide will give good results. Occasionally recipes call for quite large amounts of clay, up to and over 30% for example, and this presents certain problems of application. Such high proportions of raw clay may cause the glaze to crawl on biscuit fired ware. If raw glazing is impractical, a proportion of the clay to be used in the glaze can be crushed, calcined at ordinary biscuit temperature, crushed again and then added to the glaze mix. Most glazes benefit from the presence of a reasonable proportion of raw clay so a combination of calcined and raw clay will enable the glaze to be successfully applied to a biscuited pot.

Muds

The fine muds deposited in streams, rivers and ponds, will often make a good vitrified dark glaze used alone or in combination with other materials at high temperature. Famous examples are Albany slip and Barnard slip from the U.S.A. No direct equivalents are known in the U.K. except those which may be discovered locally. Line blends with feldspar, whiting and ash may again produce successful results. Red Fremington clay has an analysis which approximates nearest to Albany slip and can be used as the nearest British equivalent.

Granite and other rocks

Outcrops of granite which occur in the U.K. in Devon, Cornwall and Scotland (The Grampians) and in County Wicklow, Ireland, make interesting glaze materials. Granite varies in colour according to the amount of iron present. In polished granite the three main ingredients present can be recognized by their separate colour and shape – feldspar, mica and quartz. Granite dust will melt at stoneware temperature to form a stiff glass. In glazes, granite can be substituted for feldspar. Accessible sources are monumental masons, quarries and road building materials.

Some suppliers of raw materials supply granite dust and will provide analysis of named stones. Hornblende, a ferro-magnesium alumino-silicate rock, quarried at Helsbury Quarry, Camborne, Cornwall (U.K.), can be used in a glaze to replace some or all of the feldspar. It approximates to the formula $(MgFe)_2.SiO_4$. Other similar materials are the basalts, pumice and volcanic ash, all of which are general terms rather than specific types. All can be used in a glaze to replace feldspar. Some granites will form melts at lower temperatures if small amounts of alkaline or borax frits are included in the recipe. Pumice, which, like basalt, is a volcanic rock, has a similar composition and can be used in a similar way. It can be used in glazes as a substitute for feldspar. Its high iron content makes it unsuitable for transparent or white glazes. Analyses are given as follows:

Pumice

	European	American
SiO_2	55.28	72.51
Al_2O_3	21.90	11.55
Fe_2O_3	2.66	1.21
K_2O	6.21	7.84
Na_2O	5.10	1.79
TiO_2	0.28	0.54
CaO	1.88	0.68
MgO	0.37	0.07
H_2O	5.64	3.81
	99.32	100.00

Having the molecular formulae:

European

0.429 Na_2O		
0.346 K_2O	1.126 Al_2O_3	4.822 SiO_2
0.047 MgO	0.089 Fe_2O_3	
0.178 CaO		0.021 TiO_2

American

0.230 Na_2O		9.596 SiO_2
0.659 K_2O	0.897 Al_2O_3	
0.016 MgO	0.063 Fe_2O_3	
0.095 CaO		0.056 TiO_2

Basalt glazes

Natural glaze materials such as local clays, earths, river muds and wood ash are invaluable to the potter working with an electric kiln, for not only do they enable the rich deep qualities to be obtained which are associated with impure materials, but they can be a source of interest and stimulation in their own right. Basalt is one such material; it is a basic (alkaline) igneous rock which, when ground, is a dark grey colour and has a crystalline texture; it derives from the fine grained rock laid down as a lava and is hard and brittle. Igneous rocks are well known to potters throughout much of the world, but the ones in general use are usually those containing small amounts of iron minerals such as the granites, and their weathered derivatives, the feldspars. All iron-containing materials are regarded as impure by industrial and commerical potteries who want to control as precisely as possible the materials they use. Iron is particularly unwelcome in the production of white wares. For the studio potter this is far from the truth.

Materials like basalt which are rich in iron will give only dark glazes, but this is no disadvantage if this is what is required. Because basalt occurs naturally and is not carefully selected or finely blended, batches from the same supplier may vary and from different countries.

An average of 198 typical basalts gives the following composition:

SiO_2	49.06
Al_2O_3	15.70
Fe_2O_3	5.38
FeO	6.37
CaO	8.95

MgO	6.17	
Na_2O	3.17	Molecular weight 259.8
K_2O	1.51	
H_2O	1.62	
TiO_2	1.36	
P_2O_5	0.45	
MnO	0.31	

This has the Seger formula:

0.406 MgO	0.403 Al_2O_3	2.15 SiO_2
0.419 CaO	0.220 Fe_2O_3	
0.133 Na_2O		
0.042 K_2O		

Basalt will melt to form a dark smooth, opaque semi-matt glaze at around 1200°C (2192°F); this is chiefly due to the high calcium and iron content. For a more workable glaze an addition of free silica, in the form of flint, is required (about 15%), plus some clay to make the glaze easier to handle and apply. This could be red earthenware or ball clay. In recipes calling for Albany or Barnard slip, basalt plus red clay can be substituted. Ash given off in the St Helens volcanic explosions in the U.S.A. has been successfully incorporated into glazes by Val Prophet. These were fired to 1222°C (2231°F) and were made from combinations of the volcanic ash with wood ash or whiting and zinc oxide.

Other unusual materials

It is surprising how many materials can be used by the glaze maker, though most are either too expensive or too difficult to acquire for other than experimental purposes. Furnace slag has been used successfully in glazes. It melts at 1250°C (2282°F) to form a glaze. A similar material is basic slag (steelworks flue sweepings) which is often used as garden fertiliser, and can be obtained from a garden supplier. The material has a complex molecular formula $(Ca_3P_2O.CaSiO_2.C.Fe_2O_3)$ and is useful as a source of phosphorous. When basic slag is used adjustments to the alkaline earth content of any glaze must be made because of the high calcium content.

Iron rust scale can also be used as an impure iron pigment after grinding in a pestle and mortar. Coal and coke, when burnt, render an ash which seems to have a high portion of iron. Coal ash contains a large amount of silica and can be successfully introduced into the glaze by substituting it for flint as the analysis on p. 137 shows.

7 Colour in the pots and glazes

One of the most fascinating aspects of stoneware glazes fired in electric kilns is the subtlety and extent of colours that are available. The range is almost limitless and includes the elegant pale creamy whites to the full dark mystery of tenmokus. For the adventurous there are shocking pinks and blues as well as the deep turquoise and rich blues. Colour in glazes can be produced by the interaction that takes place with the body, a particularly interesting feature of dark stained clay or one which contains small additions of colouring metal oxides.

Supplied from the manufacturers as finely ground powders, metal oxides can be used in a wide variety of ways. They can be mixed into a slip or engobe which covers the body, or used under or on top of the unfired glaze or added to the slop glaze.

Metal oxides give their colours either by going into solution into the glaze – when they will give transparent effects – or by suspending themselves in the glaze – when they will be opaque. Generally speaking all oxides will to some extent go into solution, but with the refractory oxides such as nickel or chrome only a small amount will dissolve. By far the most important factor with regard to colour is the composition of the glaze, i.e. the proportion of clay present and the major fluxes used. Some indication of the colour response is given under the types of glaze, but it is worth considering each metal oxide separately.

The metal oxides

Iron oxide
Available in many forms, which includes black ferrous oxide (FeO), red ferric oxide (Fe_2O_3), ferric oxide, synthetic (Fe_3O_4), iron spangles (Fe_3O_4), yellow ochre (Fe_2O_3), crocus martis ($FeSO_4$) and iron chromate ($Fe_2O_3 . Cr_2O_3$). Most are naturally occuring and therefore contain many impurities; the synthetic iron oxide is prepared under strictly controlled conditions and is the most pure and reliable in composition.

Chemically any iron compound behaves in the glaze as an amphoteric and has a relatively low fluxing power in oxidized firings. Under reducing conditions, however, the iron behaves as a flux and may cause a glaze which is viscous in an oxidising fire to become fluid. The usual state of iron oxide is red iron oxide (Fe_2O_3) and in oxidised firings will give creams, yellows, olive greens, tans, blacks and reds when added in proportions in the glaze of 1–15%. This is in marked contrast to the effect of reduction firing in which the red iron oxide releases some of its oxygen to become black iron oxide (FeO) with colours which range from pale blues, celadon greens, browns, blacks and reds. At amounts over 8% the colours rendered by the iron in both oxidation and reduction conditions are very similar. The red iron has a tendency, even in an oxidised firing in amounts over 7–8%, to be reduced to black iron when it will act as a flux. As far as predicting colour response, it is the amount of iron present and the nature of the glaze that will determine the shades available. In a feldspathic transparent glaze iron, either black or red, will give the typical colour response outlined earlier. In the glaze matrix the iron goes into solution to give stained transparent shades which will depend to some extent on the colour of the body. In amounts below about 10% the iron will go into solution and remain in the solution as the glaze cools. Amounts from about 10–15% will go into solution in the molten glaze but during cooling some of this iron oxide will be precipitated to form small rust red crystals. This gives rise to a typical khaki or tea dust glaze which is reddish brown, semi-matt and opaque. Oxidation is necessary for this effect. The colour can be modified by the presence of other materials. With about 5% tin oxide the red becomes more Indian in colour and brighter, while with bone ash in amounts from 5–15% iron takes on a mottled red brown colour. Iron brushwork painted over such a glaze gives lustrous metallic effects.

In glazes fluxed with magnesium which are

semi-opaque and matt, the colour of the iron is muted and subdued. Amounts of 2% give banana yellows while larger quantities give dull, streaky tans. Lime matts will also give opaque matt results which can range from pleasant orange brown to a dull muted brown. In glazes containing zinc oxide the iron colours may tend towards greenish browns, while in those containing small quantities of titanium dioxide (TiO_2) the colour can be brightened to give orange reds.

Iron in its non-pure forms, such as crocus martis, iron spangles, and the iron ochres (yellow and orange) will all give similar results but the presence of other materials (impurities such as manganese and titanium) will all affect the colour and will all tend to act as fluxes in the glaze. Local clays, rich in iron, such as Albany, in the U.S.A., or Fremington in the U.K., can form the basis of iron rich glazes. Fluxed with alkaline frits or even nepheline syenite, mottled and attractive deep brown glazes can be achieved.

Copper

Copper is probably one of the richest sources of delicate colour available to the potter who fires in an electric kiln, especially when used on porcelain or light coloured stoneware bodies. Despite the fact that the colour is sometimes fugitive and precise quantities are required, the wide range of soft shades of blue-greens and orange pink-reds make copper a material well worth experimenting with. It is commonly available as either copper oxide (CuO) or copper carbonate, ($CuCO_3$), and both behave in a similar way. Copper oxide is black and, of all the available forms of copper, has the least fine particle size; weight for weight it contains the most metal and is therefore the most powerful in the glaze. Copper carbonate is pale green or mauve in colour and the fine particle size helps its even distribution in the glaze. It is less powerful than the oxide weight for weight but behaves in exactly the same way in the kiln. Cuprous oxide (Cu_2O), which is dark red in colour, is also available but has the disadvantage of not being so easy to disperse in the slop glaze.

In most transparent glazes copper in amounts form 1–3% will give various shades of green. In lead and feldspathic glazes this can range from apple to lime greens. In alkaline glazes a more turquoise blue green is obtained and this can be very attractive. (The use of copper in lead glazes has virtually ceased because of the effects of the copper on the lead; it can increase the solubility of the lead unless the glaze composition is very precisely balanced.) Colour response is very

dependent on the amount of copper used. In quantities much above 3–4% the copper will give metallic black pewter effects which, though attractive, should not be used on surfaces which may come into contact with food. Small amounts of copper of $\frac{1}{2}$–1% will give delicate shades of green or turquoise.

Some stoneware potters use copper as the basic colourant in a transparent glaze to give a shade and quality similar to that of a reduced celadon. Derek Emms gives a base recipe for a clear glaze to

Alan Heaps; handbuilt stoneware teapot

which is added either prepared stains or oxides in very small amounts. The American potter Debbie Shapiro advocates a similar celadon-style glaze, but she finds it is essential to modify the harshness of the copper green with a black pigment made up from a judicious mixture of oxides.

On its own copper begins to volatilize at around

David Greaves; slab pot, stoneware, built up from stained and stratified clay bodies

1050°C (1922°F) and will start to react with the clay body. This can be well demonstrated by rubbing a thin layer of copper oxide onto the surface of a pot which, after firing, will take on a metallic look tinged with green. When copper oxide is mixed with manganese oxide and painted onto clay, a bronze 'pigment' surface will be formed; this gets more molten with increased temperature.

Turquoise colours obtained from copper are at their richest in strongly alkaline, semi-opaque matt glazes; barium, sodium and potassium are excellent fluxes and can promote the formation of deep colours which range from a vivid blue green to a cerulean blue. A glaze rich in nepheline syenite fluxed with a small amount of dolomite and whiting plus china clay will, with 1 or 2% copper oxide, give a frail duck egg blue/green when applied over a white body or porcelain. A bright reflective body is essential to achieve the full delicacy of the colour.

In glazes fluxed by calcium or magnesium small proportions of copper can give salmon pinks. An excess of copper will give grey greens; smaller amounts will encourage the formation of orange spots. Such a glaze will tend to develop an attractive crackle surface. Quite why copper does this is not clear and it is not a reliably reproducible result, for it depends on the thickness of the glaze and the firing schedule; a long, slow soak towards the end of the firing encourages the development of both the colour and the crackle. In a quick firing the colour and texture tends to be less interesting. Mary Rogers has developed some rich salmon pinks in glazes fired to 1280°C (2336°F) on porcelain.

In reducing conditions and in certain glazes copper gives red colours known as *rouge flambé* or *sang de boeuf*. During the firing the copper is reduced from the black to the red state. These reduced red and lustrous colours of copper can be developed well in raku glazes containing copper. When the fired pot is removed from the kiln it is immediately buried in leaves, sawdust or similar material which 'reduces' the copper, which becomes a rich, variegated red with lustrous black.

Making a reducing atmosphere in the chamber of the electric kiln will enable similar effects to be obtained. However, the techniques are limited and present many problems. Alternatively, the colours of reduced copper can be produced in an oxidised firing by using a reducing agent in the glaze. Both these processes are fully explained in Chapter 10.

For soft colour effects with copper various transmutation effects can be explored. Briefly, this occurs when the colour of the glaze is changed or affected by materials which are separate from the glaze. A typical example is the way in which some glazes will attract and retain volatilized colour from an adjacent pot in the kiln. This sensitivity to colour can be also utilized by mixing small amounts of oxide into the clay body or into a clay slip coating the ware. During the firing the glaze picks up this colour and, depending on the amount of oxide present, delicate shades can be obtained. This method is particularly successful with copper under dolomite glazes.

Manganese
In most glazes manganese either as the black oxide (MnO) or the lighter coloured carbonate ($MnCO_3$) will act as a flux. This has to be taken into account when calculating the glaze recipe, especially if amounts over 5% are included in the recipe. When fired on its own manganese vitrifies to give a smooth, dark brown, glossy pigment at 1150°C (2102°F) and can, when mixed with red clay, be used at higher temperatures as a reliable black glaze.

When added to transparent glazes at about 4%,

John Loree; stoneware bottle with satin white glaze decorated with yellow iron, cobalt, copper and rutile mixture. Orton cone 8

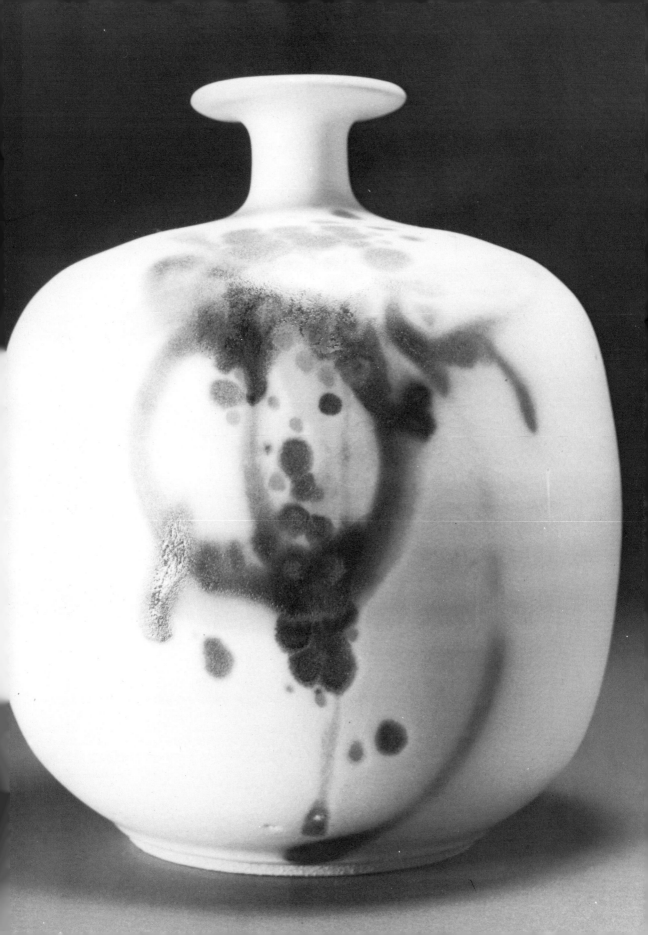

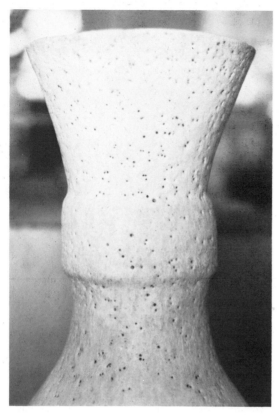

Lucie Rie; close-up of white matt glaze on a stoneware pot giving an idea of the textures she achieves.

manganese give brown-purple; in alkaline glazes this colour becomes more purplish. Larger amounts give darker, more opaque shades. Where a broken, slightly speckled colour is required, manganese dioxide (MnO_2) can be mixed in, but not sieved, to the slop glaze. Alternatively, the manganese dioxide can be added (but not sieved) to a prepared engobe and the specks will burn through the glaze.

Pale pinks can be obtained by adding small quantities of manganese to high alkali glazes provided they are low in alumina. A suitable base would be nepheline syenite fluxed with a small amount of barium carbonate and alkaline frit. The colour can be intensified by the addition of 0.5% cobalt carbonate. In crystalline glazes small amounts of manganese are often used to soften background colours and give shades of pale beige and fawn.

The ability of manganese to soften other colours, particularly copper and cobalt, has long been recognized. With iron oxide it is the major colourant in the Rockingham glaze; this is typically a dark, lustrous black/brown with a wide firing range and a trouble-free surface. In a transparent feldspathic glaze additions of 7% red iron oxide and 3% manganese dioxide give an attractive dark glaze. Variations in the proportions of these oxides will give different shades; for example, 7% manganese dioxide and 3% red iron oxide will result in a more reddish colour. Manganese is also used to produce a black glaze; a typical addition is iron oxide 4%, manganese dioxide 3% and cobalt oxide 3%.

Additions of manganese to the clay body can give a black or dark brown colour and will subsequently affect any glaze which is applied. These bodies can be particularly successful at earthenware temperatures, when dense black bodies can be produced. However, at higher temperatures the manganese will start to flux the body and unless a considerable amount of high temperature grog is included, bloating and distortion will result. Even with a grog addition, precise firing temperatures are essential. Glaze and body response will be greatly affected by such a reactive body and results can be very different to those normally experienced. Lucie Rie has made brilliant use of this technique on many of her individual pots.

Cobalt

As one of the potter's most powerful and reliable oxides, cobalt needs to be used sensitively. When the Chinese started using it for the blue and white wares, they could only obtain an impure native ore. A cobalt pigment Bernard Leach found in use in China some 50 years ago was prepared by hand grinding a dark olive pebble called asbolite; when spectroscopically examined, it was found that, besides 10–30% cobalt, 17 other elements were present, the most important of which was manganese. This cobalt gave anything but a pure cobalt blue and as a result was all the more attractive.

The oxide (CoO) and carbonate ($CoCO_3$) available today are almost 100% pure and will give, even in amounts of less than $\frac{1}{2}$ of 1%, a noticeable shade of blue. In high alumina glazes this colour will tend to be more greenish, but usually this will be the inky medium shade with which most potters are familiar. Such colours are easily obtained in transparent feldspathic glazes when only 1 or 2% of cobalt oxide is required. Specking may occur unless the oxide is thoroughly mixed into the slop, either by hand grinding it into a small amount of glaze before adding to the bulk or by ball milling. For this reason the carbonate is often preferred even though it is less powerful.

8 Above *Richard Zakin; pressmoulded platter with ash glaze fired to cone 6*

9 Right *Hans Coper; pot assembled from several thrown parts. (Courtesy of Sotheby's, Belgravia)*

10 Below *Val Barry; porcelain slab pots with matt dolomite glaze and small amounts of copper carbonate*

11 Below *David Morris; thrown stoneware jugs with opaque white tin glaze and painted inglaze decoration in blue pigment*

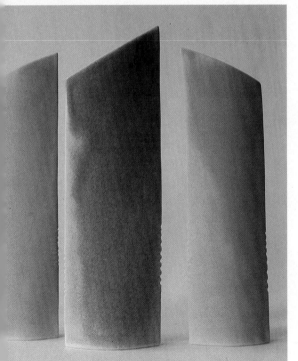

12 Left *Lucie Rie; bottle form with matt glaze made from sections thrown with coloured clays partly wedged together*

13 Below left *Sarah Bodine; thrown cream bowl and sugar basin glazed with Hatch Top and Randy's Red. Orton cone 6*

14 Below *Richard Shaw; ceramic objects. White clay with transfer decoration*

Because of its smaller particle size it spreads more evenly in the glaze. Some glazes will 'absorb' more than 2% cobalt, but usually 2% is sufficient to give a good midnight blue shade.

Most potters prefer to soften the blue with the addition of other colouring oxides. Iron and/or manganese will take away any harshness, while copper will make it slightly more green. Additions of 3–5% rutile, depending on the thickness of the glaze, will cause some break-up of the blue, while small amounts of zinc oxide will brighten the colour. Small quantities of chrome oxide will tend to give sea greens, although these may be opaque.

In alkaline glazes which are rich in magnesia, and low in alumina, small proportions of cobalt (less than 1%) will give soft mauves and greys and, depending on the type of glaze, an amount as small as 0.1% of cobalt may be all that is required. In barium glazes pinks from cobalt can also be obtained.

Chromium

Available either as chrome oxide (Cr_2O_3) or, in combination with iron, as iron chromate ($FeO.Cr_2O_3$), chromium is the most reliable source of green in the glaze. Like cobalt, chrome is immensely powerful and only small amounts of 1–2% are required to obtain the typical opaque, holly green glazes. Unlike most colouring oxides, only small amounts of chromium dissolve in the glaze melt, hence its ability to render glazes opaque. In the glaze chromium is amphoteric (a stabilizer) and, even in small quantities, will stiffen the glaze. At temperatures above 1200°C (2192°F) the oxide will start to volatilize, and though this will have little or no effect when an amount such as 1 or 2% is present, where much smaller amounts are used the colour can be fugitive.

Depending on the other constituents present in the glaze the colour which chromium gives will vary. A transparent feldspathic glaze with an addition of 2% chrome oxide will give the typical holly green, opaque and strong in colour. This drab colour can be enlivened by small amounts of cobalt to give peacock greens. With small amounts of boric oxide the colour is further brightened. However, in other glazes this colour will be modified, most notably with zinc oxide and tin oxide and lead. In glazes containing more than about 4% of zinc oxide, chrome oxide will give brown. These can range from pale yellow tans to dark tans and are well worth exploring.

One of the most dramatic colours for earthenware, stoneware and porcelain is chrome tin pink. Only tiny quantities of chrome are required (0.1%) and this amount goes into the melting glaze, where it combines with the tin oxide to give attractive and delicate pinks. About 4–10% tin oxide will give results in a feldspathic glaze fluxed by whiting and dolomite. At temperatures above 1250°C (2282°F) such a small amount of chrome is likely to burn away and, depending on the body, these pinks seem best at around 1200–1220°C (2192–2228°F). Industrial white earthenware bodies, for example, work very well at this temperature when they are strong and well vitrified. Most porcelain bodies require slightly higher temperatures. While the pinks work well on stoneware bodies the colour tends to be more muted.

The chrome can be applied as a thin slurry either under or on top of the glaze (a mixture of chrome and china clay serves well) or it can be mixed into the glaze. Larger amounts of chrome oxide will give darker, dusky pinks but these can go grey if slightly overfired. Because chrome volatilizes at stoneware temperatures, adjacent pots carrying tin glazes in the kiln may become flushed with pink. While this effect can be attractive, it may be unwelcome. A pot fired inside a saggar which is coated with chrome can be the basis for producing experimental pink flushes. For more delicate effects a soluble chromium salt can be used. Potassium dichromate ($K_2Cr_2O_7$), which can be dissolved in water, will be suitable for some effects. Increasing the amount of chrome oxide in the glaze will result in murky colours and not reds, though in some mixtures a dusky crimson will result.

A Chinese red colour with a crystalline texture can be obtained from chrome oxide in a high lead low alumina glaze fired to around 800–900°C (1472–1652°F). With large amounts of lead the chrome goes into solution and gives rich reds and oranges. However, with such small amounts of alumina present the glaze is fluid and will run off any vertical surface. For this reason such a glaze can only be used on tiles and the like, where attractive colours will result. Because of the high level of lead required these glazes are likely to be poisonous and are therefore never used on domestic wares.

Nickel

As one of the least explored of the colouring oxides, nickel oxide, (NiO or Ni_2O_3) remains both a mystery and a source of great excitement. Nickel oxide is rarely given much of a listing in glaze reference books. Few authors recognize nickel as having any particular quality to give to a

glaze other than in small quantities as a modifier of colour; for example, to soften strident cobalt blues or deepen iron reds, which it does very well. But nickel can give far more interesting and exciting effects that this, particularly in the electric kiln. Nickel is usually available in two forms, as nickelous oxide (NiO) and nickelic oxide (Ni_2O_3); the former is a greyish green and the latter black in colour. Both work well in the glaze without any noticeable difference between the two. Nickel oxide is a refractory oxide with a high melting point and only small quantities (0.5–2%) are required in the glaze to produce a wide range of colours. Such small quantities will go into solution in the glaze; larger amounts will give a refractory viscous mix.

However, far from the limited muted greys, greens and browns attributed to nickel, it is capable of giving a wide spectrum of colours which include lemon yellows, electric blues, shocking pinks, purples and pale greens, all at stoneware temperatures from about 1180–1260°C (2156–2300°F) in an electric kiln. The principal factors determining what colours will develop are the other materials in the glaze, the most important ones being zinc and barium, either used alone or in combination. In zinc glazes nickel gives steel blues, while with barium glazes the colour tends to be pink. This ability of nickel to give such a wide range of colours has long been known to many studio potters in Germany, who have experimented with zinc barium combinations in glazes containing feldspar with small amounts of whiting, china clay and flint. They report bright colours with attractive break-ups and textures. Zinc oxide, with flint, will under certain firing conditions, grow crystals of zinc silicate in a glaze (explained in Chapter 10), and these can be coloured by small amounts of nickel to give electric blue crystal formations. The problem with glazes which are balanced so sensitively is that they require a precise firing temperature; if the temperature is too low by 10°C (50°F) then the glaze is dull and undeveloped, too high by the same amount and the glaze will have run dramatically, often onto the kiln shelf. These glazes are not to be recommended, therefore, for functional wares, but the effects are well worth trying.

Lemon yellow colours from nickel are obtained

John Loree; thrown porcelain bottle with satin white and barium 29 glazes. Decorated with copper and cobalt, and rutile mixture. 43.2 cm (17 in) tall in combination with titanium dioxide (TiO_2). Titania serves as an opacifier in the glaze, where it forms small crystals and gives a pleasant matt surface. Small amounts of titania in the glaze can intensify and brighten colours, larger amounts can subdue the tones. With 1–2% nickel a slightly broken lemon yellow colour is obtained. Val Barry got a slightly crystalline yellow in a basic feldspathic glaze with 9% titanium dioxide and 2% nickel oxide.

Uranium

In many countries uranium is not available in any form; in the U.K. depleted uranium, that is, spent oxide which has only a low level of radioactivity, can be purchased direct from the United Kingdom Atomic Energy Authority (U.K.A.E.A.). Even such a low level of radioactivity can, if kept for long periods in constant contact with the body, be harmful to health and could cause burning of the skin. Strict recommendations are made for its storage in metal containers, but in small quantities it is an oxide which can be used to get attractive results. Because of the possible health risks involved with uranium it is not used by the ceramic industry nor marketed by the usual suppliers. Yet it is a material which can give rich reds in lead glazes at low temperatures and lemon to deep egg-yolk yellows at stoneware temperatures. The material available in the U.K. is uranium oxide (U_3O_8), a dark greenish black powder; this should be kept in a lidded metal container and stored away from working areas. Avoid touching the materials and do not ingest it or use it on domestic pottery, for the oxide retains its radioactivity even after being fired in the glaze. In high lead glazes with some zinc oxide and low alumina, but without lime or boric oxide, up to 10% of uranium oxide will give stable reds. These will withstand 1040°C (1904°F).

In stoneware glazes a wide range of yellow-greens can be produced in a variety of bases. A clear feldspathic glaze will give a clear yolk yellow with 2–5% uranium oxide. In barium glazes the colour will be greener; zinc oxide helps the colour. Tin oxide will make the colour opaque. Soda feldspar encourages greener yellows. In reducing conditions, uranium colours lose their brightness.

Vanadium

Usually available as a fairly coarse and expensive yellow green powder, vanadium pentoxide (V_2O_5) can give some surprising results. In low temperature glazes, such as those fluxed by lead, vanadium will give yellow colours; at higher

Harry Horlock Stringer; stoneware bottle thrown in sections and joined together, with sprigged decoration and matt nepheline syenite glaze

temperatures the yellow colour is lost and, depending on the type of glaze, shades of blue, yellow, grey or brown are achieved. In amounts over 5% the vanadium will give a matt, opaque cream-brown which can give mottled and attractive textures. A proportion of 10% vanadium in the glaze will give a matt brown. With a fluid gloss glaze containing either gerstley borate or a calcium borate frit the vanadium may go into solution in the firing and give broken mottled blues and yellows.

For most potters vanadium is best used in the form of a prepared glaze stain, the most common of which is a stable yellow. This is made by calcining at $1000°C$ ($1832°F$) a mixture of 95 parts tin oxide and 5 parts vanadium pentoxide. A blue coloured stain can be produced by calcining together vanadium and zirconium. Both the blue and yellow stains are refractory and of low colouring strength; for this reason the glaze usually has to be fluid to take up the additional material without becoming dry and unattractive.

Ilmenite

Ilmenite is a naturally occuring ore consisting mainly of ferrous titanate ($FeO\ TiO_2$). Ilmenite can vary from batch to batch and is supplied in various grain sizes ranging from coarse to fine. In the glaze fire ilmenite gives weak iron colours. Coarse ilmenite stirred into the glaze slip can give an interesting surface break-up made up of spots or specks, and when used in the granular form as an engobe, or mixed into the body, the specks will bleed into the glaze to give attractive effects.

Rutile

Like ilmenite, rutile (TiO_2) is an ore containing mainly titanium oxide with amounts of iron oxide, usually less than 15%; it is supplied as light, medium or dark, depending on the amount of iron it contains. Amounts up to 10% are used in the glaze to give pale creams to tans, and can give attractive break-ups of colour in an otherwise smooth glaze. Larger amounts can be used when a larger break-up is needed. The colours can range from pink orange colours in zinc silicate crystal glazes to blue/grey streaky colours in those containing calcium borate frit or gerstley borate. (This material has the ability to dissolve the rutile and hence the brightness of the colours.)

In association with other colouring oxides small amounts of rutile can soften and break up the colours to give pleasant textured effects. Rutile is often added in sizeable amounts to produce crystalline glazes where it helps in the formation of the crystals.

Body and glaze stains

Prepared industrially by calcining different materials and oxides together, glaze and body stains offer the potter a wide range of stable and reliable colours. Depending on the way in which they are prepared they can be mixed into the plastic clay body or added to the slop glaze. Some will withstand medium stoneware temperatures and others will go to higher temperatures. Some stains will give bright and intense colours, but these tend to be opaque and even, without any of the variations which occur when oxides are used. Their value lies in their reliability as well as the wide range of colours they offer. Often they are best used in small quantities to obtain pastel shades. Because the stains are inert in the glaze and give their colour by suspending themselves in the melted glass, there is a limit of about 10% that can be added without the glaze becoming too viscous or dry. Stains are particularly useful for obtaining pale blues and greens in transparent glazes, when amounts as low as 1–2% will give soft, muted shades. Usually they are added along with the other ingredients when the glaze is mixed and sieved. Some stains may need grinding in hot water or ball milling in order to prevent specking in the glaze.

Underglaze colours are similar to stains; they are prepared in much the same way but as they are intended to be applied under, or over, the raw (unfired) glaze they are mixed with a small amount of flux or glaze. Underglaze colours are usually more finely ground than body or glaze stains (and hence more expensive), but can be used in the glaze mix in the same way. From the wide range of colours that are available most are intermixable; some will withstand a high stoneware temperature, others will work only at lower temperatures.

8 Making, formulating, correcting and applying the glaze

There are three major methods of evolving glazes; they can be purchased as ready-made mixtures, they can be prepared from known recipes, or they can be compounded from your own formulae. For good results, whichever method, or combination of methods used, all depend on some understanding of the glaze and how it works, as well as the method of application and the particular firing atmosphere. At the end of the potting process it is the finished pot which will testify to your success, and where the glaze came from will be of secondary importance. One of the highest compliments we potters can receive is to be praised for the pot as a whole, for its form, its glaze and for its completeness and unity. Such success is often only achieved by much knowedge and experience.

Lucie Rie; weights and scales for measuring glazes and slips

Ready made glazes are relatively straightforward. Manufacturers give instructions regarding thickness of application and details of firing temperatures and these should be followed if exact results are required. Methods of application are similar for any slop glaze. However, many potters find prepared glazes are best when modified and, as such, can save time and trouble over having to mix up complex recipes. One potter found that a prepared transparent stoneware glaze with an addition of 10% red iron oxide gave a rich tenmoku glaze. Another potter blends together a clear glaze and a tin glaze to give a deep, opaque mottled-white mixture. The disadvantage of this system is that without knowing what ingredients are present in the glaze it is difficult to modify, but the basic rules described in this chapter still apply.

For most potters the starting point for their glazes are recipes culled from books, magazines,

schools, teachers and so on. You will rarely get good results at first and you will need time to work out the handling qualtities; to decide, for example, on the best thickness, temperature and clay body. All will have an effect on the result, and the glaze may also need modifying to suit personal taste. Once some understanding has been gained of how materials act in the glaze, the recipe can then be understood and consequently some idea obtained of how it will perform. The contents of the glaze will also indicate to some extent how it will respond to additions of colouring oxides: this, of course, can only be proved as a result of trials. It is always a wise precaution, before putting it onto a pot, to test any glaze, whether it be ready mixed or prepared from a recipe; the result may not be quite as it has been described.

Compounding your own glazes can be approached in two ways, either empirically or by calculation. Both methods will depend on a thorough knowledge of the materials. The first method is a practical approach which involves mixing materials according to some understanding of how they behave. The other method is more scientific and needs a familiarity with glaze chemistry. There is not the space here to describe this in detail but this method is explained in *Glazes for the Studio Potter* (Cooper & Royle). Whichever method is followed, the first step is to test all the individual glaze materials separately; this is done by simply mixing each material with water, painting it onto a tile and firing this to your usual temperature. From this test the materials can be classified into groups of fluxed, vitrified and unaltered. Tests of mixtures of materials from the different groups will begin to suggest possible different glazes. (This empirical test-and-see approach is also fully detailed in *Glazes for the Studio Potter*.)

Developing the glaze

A balanced glaze could be said to be one in which all the ingredients are in suitable proportions to give a smooth, well-fitting surface, which may be clear, coloured or opaque. Such a glaze may in theory be perfect, that is, with a practical surface, easily cleaned, resistant to staining, and so on. For most potters such a glaze is likely to lack visual interest; the effective surface may not heighten the form and may not be immediately attractive to touch. As potters we want, perhaps, the glaze to be matt, coloured or have textural break-up, to take on a quality and depth of its own. Making glazes our own is as much a part of the job of being a

Bowl with crawled glaze

potter as making the shapes we like.

Once we have a basic glaze it can be adapted to suit our requirements. A transparent glaze can be made opaque by the addition of tin oxide or zirconium silicate; it can be made matt by increasing the clay and flint content or by adding a material such as titanium dioxide. Attractive satin surfaces can be made by adding up to 15% dolomite or talc to the glaze. Glazes that are too fluid can be stiffened by increasing the amount of clay or flint while, conversely, the fluidity can be increased by the addition of a flux; for glazes fired in the electric kiln 10% of an alkaline or borax frit will help promote fusion. The other fluxes worth adding in small amounts are zinc oxide (5%) whiting (up to 10%) or lithium carbonate (2–3%). The latter also has the advantage of promoting surface break-up and adding visual interest.

To lower the melting point of a glaze a direct substitution of nepheline syenite for feldspar, can be tried, but this can render a clear glaze opaque; the melting point can be raised by the opposite move. Depending on the fluxes present in the glaze, the amount of feldspar can be adjusted to raise or lower the firing temperature. Generally speaking, an increase in the amount of feldspar in the recipe will raise the melting point; less will lower it.

The range of colours available in the oxidised atmospheres of electric kilns have already been indicated and only a series of trials will indicate what the spectrum can be. Amounts of oxides added to the glaze can range from as little as 0.1% to as much as 15%, though the colours obtained will depend on temperature and the other ingredients in the glaze. Careful tests on blends of colours are well worth trying.

Mixing the glaze

A reliable, personal glaze recipe book, with notes on results obtained and so on, is essential; the loss of a favourite recipe is upsetting and irritating. Preferably the batch recipes should be kept separate from records of glaze tests. Most of the glaze recipes in this book are listed as totalling 100 parts by weight with colouring oxides expressed as an additional percentage over and above this. The chief value of this system is that quantities of materials in one glaze can easily be compared with another. When materials are added to modify or change the glaze the ingredients should be recalculated to total 100. This is simply done by dividing the amount of each individual material by the total amount of all the materials and multiplying by 100. Except for oxide additions, figures can usually be rounded up or down to the nearest whole number.

Example
A basic semi-matt pale celadon coloured glaze. 1260°C (2300°F)

Soda feldspar	25
Dolomite	15
China clay	25
Bone ash	10
Flint	25
	100

+copper carbonate 1.5

This proved to be a smoother, more fat glaze with the addition of 25 parts soda feldspar, which brings the total to 125. To express this as a percentage recipe each ingredient has now to be divided by the total of all the ingredients (125) and multiplied by 100. This gives the revised recipe:

Soda feldspar	40
Dolomite	12
China clay	20
Bone ash	8
Flint	20
	100

+Copper carbonate 1.5

Bowl, porcelain, with bloated surface

Recipes, unless specified otherwise, are expressed as parts by weight and can be read as grams, ounces, pounds, kilos or even tons. 100 grams of a glaze will give a cupful, which is an excellent amount for a glaze test. Translated into 100 ounces it will give a half a bucket-full: amounts multiplied by 10 to give 1000 grams will give a small barrel-full. Example using the above glaze:

		bucket amount			barrel amount		
	%	grams	lb	oz	grams	lb	oz
Soda feldspar	40	200	2	8	400	5	0
Dolomite	12	60		12	120	1	8
China clay	20	100	1	4	200	2	8
Bone ash	8	40		8	80	1	0
Flint	20	100	1	4	200	2	8
Copper carbonate	1.5	7.5		1½	15		3

Measured amounts of glaze materials, once weighed, should be lowered gently into water; adding water to them can cause lumping; this method also avoids raising glaze dust. Add the plastic material in the middle of the batch to serve as a 'sandwich' and to aid mixing. Be generous with water and leave the glaze to slake for an hour or so before mixing; hot water speeds up the action and can make mixing easier. Stir the slop up well and pass the glaze twice through a sieve of say 80 mesh and this will usually break up the ingredients to give a smooth, homogeneous mix. Some potters prefer to use a finer sieve, whilst some prefer a coarser sieve. Once the glaze has settled, the layer of clear water can be removed from the top and the mixture checked for thickness. This is determined by experience and on how the glaze behaves on the pot; some are better when thinner rather than thicker. Once the correct thickenss has been found, (described by different potters as 'like single cream' or 'a good hand coating') the use of a simple hydrometer can record this. A length of wood with a weight on the end of it can be inserted in the glaze and the depth to which the hydrometer sinks can be marked on it. Subsequent batches can then be checked against this; if the mark is above the surface the glaze is too dense or too thick and more water is required. If the mark is below the surface then the glaze is too thin; the glaze has to be allowed to settle in order that water can be removed from the top of the glaze. With glaze batches it is always a good rule of thumb to take water away first and then carefully put back sufficient to make the glaze workable. Once the glaze is stirred, water cannot be removed until the slop has had time to settle again.

Glaze should preferably be stored in lidded polythene buckets or barrels and the inside should be wiped with a sponge after each time the batch has been used in order to prevent bits of dried glaze falling into the mixture and making it lumpy. Most of the materials used by the potter are not soluble, or only slightly soluble in water, and can be stored wet without unduly affecting the glaze. Exceptions are vanadium pentoxide, which can cause sedimentation in the glaze, and wood ash which, even if washed, still leaches soluble salts of sodium and potassium over a period of time. Borax compounds and frits can cause the glaze batch to form large, hexagonal-shaped crystals. Glaze is best stored dry if it is expected to be stored over a long period of time. To dry, remove the water layer from the settled glaze slop, mix up the slurry and then leave to dry out.

Glaze faults

No matter how good or reliable a recipe is, it can go wrong. Equally, tests can give what look like interesting results but require some change to make them practical. For example, a glaze is easier to apply if it contains about 10% clay; this helps to suspend the glaze in the slop, it helps to stop the glaze ingredients settling in to a hard layer at the bottom of the barrel and it binds the glaze onto the surface of the pot so that it does not brush off easily. Some glazes which are low in alumina contain very little clay or even none at all, and the substitution of 2–3% bentonite for any clay

present can make such a glaze more workable. When clay is not included it is worth trying a test with 2% bentonite to see if it makes the glaze more workable. Alternatively a flocculent can be added. These include materials (usually soluble) such as Epsom salts (magnesium sulphate) or calcium chloride which will help suspension in amounts of approximately 0.1%.

There are some glaze faults which are instantly recognisable – a runny glaze for instance – but others are neither easy to diagnose nor cure. Crazing can be classified as an attractive crackle or as unwanted and unhygienic craze lines. Boiling or pimpling of the glaze can be due to over fluxing or over firing, or both. There are one or two basic rules to the correction of faults.

1 Do not change more than one ingredient at a time unless you are sure this will give you the result you want.
2 Stick to the same temperature and firing programme, unless you definitely want to change; make your glazes work for this temperature. In other words, keep constant whatever you can.
3 Limit your materials so that you find out what they do; a suggested list of materials for stoneware temperatures is:

potash feldspar, soda feldspar, nepheline syenite, whiting, dolomite, barium carbonate, calcium borate frit (or gerstley borate), alkaline frit, bone ash, flint, china clay, bentonite, talc. (Lead frit can be added for eathenware temperatures.)
To this list can be added: borax frit, ball clay, wollastonite, lithium carbonate, petalite, cryolite, spodumene, volcanic ash.
Useful local materials: local clay, wood ash, red clay.
The various glaze faults detailed here are indications of what can happen to the glaze, and suggested ways of correcting them are listed.

Pinholed dry-glaze surface
When a glaze melts it goes through many changes, which vary according to the type and the content of the glaze. Shiny glazes, high in fluxes, melt and form a glass early in the firing, some as low as 100°C (212°F) below the final maturing temperature. They go through dramatic changes and bubble before evening out to form a clear glass. In contrast, glazes which are more matt and opaque are often high in china clay and flint, both of which stabilize the glaze. In these glazes the melting and maturing process takes place over a longer period and over a wider temperature range. Bubbles are slow to clear. If temperature has been too low or

Bowl with a runny glaze which stuck the foot to the kiln shelf. Beware of this happening

reached too rapidly such glazes may be dry with pinholes; here the remedy is simply to fire to a slightly higher temperature or have a longer soak at top temperature. Some glazes only develop smooth surfaces when fully matured.

If the temperature cannot be reached, then the glaze may benefit from a slightly increased amount of flux (the material that makes the glaze melt). This may be done either by reducing slightly the amounts of china clay and flint or increasing the fluxes, such as whiting or dolomite, in the recipe. Alternatively, small amounts (3–4%) of a secondary flux such as alkaline frit or calcium borate frit may be introduced. Gerstley borate may be substituted weight for weight for the frit. In these quantities the glaze temperature is effectively lowered without the quality of the glaze being drastically affected. Some pots on which the glaze has not reached the correct temperature can be fired again, but this refiring may result in a different glaze surface, particularly with ash glazes.

Runny glaze

A glaze which runs freely down the side of the vessel and causes the pot to adhere to the kiln shelf has either simply been fired to too high a temperature or been applied too thickly, or soaked for too long at top temperature. Alternatively, the glaze must be stiffened, or made more viscous by the addition of equal parts of china clay and flint to the glaze recipe; a starting point would be 4–6%

by weight of each of these materials. This may of course affect the appearance of the glaze, and is a factor which must be borne in mind, especially in the case of crystalline or special effect glazes, where movement of the liquid glaze is essential if the effects are to be created. This is often achieved by having a low alumina content. In this case it may be better to reduce the thickness of the glaze layer and to slightly lower the firing temperature. Pots on which glazes which have run freely can be reprieved by grinding off the surplus glaze, reglazing and refiring to a lower temperature.

Bubbled and cratered glaze

As already described, glazes during firing go through a series of complex changes and reactions which are not necessarily brought to a stop when the temperature is reached or when the glaze is said to be matured; the surface may continue to even out and smooth over and, depending on the rate of cooling, may form crystals. However, if the temperature is increased further then the ingredients continue to react much more violently; just as, for example, when a syrup solution is overheated it boils and burns, so can a glaze boil and bubble. This process may be so violent that part of the glaze is given off as vapour and the glaze will not settle down; the result is a rough surface often displaying craters with jagged edges. (Incidentally, this sort of glaze surface must not be confused with crater glazes which are produced intentionally. In this case, the craters are smooth and not jagged.)

Bubbled and cratered glaze surfaces can be

avoided by firing to a lower temperature or by having a shorter soak period. Alternatively, additions of china clay and flint to the glaze will increase its maturing temperature. Pots which have been overfired and where the surface has bubbled can sometimes be successfully refired. This is best done by rubbing over the surface with a carborundum stone and a further layer of glaze applied to the warmed pot and then refiring.

Crazing

The reaction and balance between the glaze layer and the body of the pot is crucial to a well fitting and strong glaze. In the latter part of the firing the glaze slowly melts and reacts with the surface of the pot to form an interfacial layer of interaction between the glaze and the clay. Depending on the glaze ingredients this layer is either diffuse (as for example in an ash glaze) or the glaze and body are two fairly recognisable layers as in glassy glazes. In this sort of glaze the expansion of the glaze and the body should be more or less equal if a well fitting glaze is to be achieved. If the glaze has a large proportion of high expansion fluxes, such as sodium and potassium, then the glaze will have a high thermal expansion; subsequently, as the glaze cools, these fluxes cause it to have a relatively high contraction, often more than the body of the pot. When this happens the glaze develops fine, hair-line cracks or crazes over its surface which effectively allow the glaze to contract. This is a particularly bad fault on earthenware pots which are not vitrified as these craze lines allow moisture to be absorbed through the glaze surface into the pot. On domestic pots it may also be unhygienic. The remedy here is to biscuit fire the pot to a higher temperature to make the pot less porous.

On stoneware pots where the body is vitrified, crazing is not so important from the hygienic point of view, but it does make the pot physically less strong. A comparison is with plywood where three layers give strength to the other. If one layer cracks and breaks up the other layer is drastically weakened. On functional pots which are handled frequently, crazing is a physical weakness.

On pots which are more decorative, such an effect can be very attractive and is known as crackle. The Chinese potters were excellent at obtaining this effect. Depending on the glaze and position in the kiln, various crackle effects can be achieved, ranging from long, slender-lined crackles to tiny angular islands. Finely ground colouring oxides or inks can be rubbed into the surface to heighten the crackle effect. To connoisseurs the crackle is a vital aspect of the pot.

When crazing is a problem the glaze has to be stiffened to stop it melting so freely and to produce a lower expansion. Either the high expansion alkaline fluxes have to be replaced by those of lower expansion, such as magnesia or lithium, or the amount of flint has to be increased. A practical suggestion is to add small amounts of talc (a mineral consisting of magnesia and silica) to the glaze.

Other remedies are to fire the glaze to a different temperature, or to add small amounts of boron to the glaze in the form of calcium borate or gerstley borate. Zinc oxide will also help to correct this.

Shelling, shivering or peeling

The opposite problem to crazing is a condition where glaze flakes off the pot at the rims, on the edge of handles, or on raised decoration, and this is known as shelling, shivering or peeling. This fault occurs during the cooling period when the body contracts more than the glaze, putting it under slight compression, a condition which gives the pot greater strength. For all practical purposes this is the ideal situation. However, when this compression becomes too great the glaze is literally forced off the rims of the pot or edges of the handles as flakes or slivers of glaze. This may not happen at once, but may develop over a period of days or weeks. It is dangerous, for the glaze slivers may fall into food, and it is also unsightly. In extreme cases the compression may literally cause the pot to split into long spiral rings and give rise to the condition known as spiral cracking.

The cure is the opposite of that suggested for crazing and is aimed at making the glaze contract more on cooling. This is achieved by substituting high expansion fluxes for those with lower expansion and/or by reducing the amount of flint. In practice, the flint can be replaced by feldspar or by alkaline fluxes. I have found that lowering the firing temperature also helps to correct this maddening fault; particularly irritating in this respect are some glazes high in iron oxide.

Crawling

Crawling, which is the way the fired glaze forms rolls and lumps, leaving bare patches on the surface of the clay, has two basic causes – dust on the pot surface or excessive shrinkage of the glaze. Some glazes, particularly those containing tin oxide, if applied too thickly or over a dusty surface, will crawl up into large fat lumps. The remedy here is to ensure that the pots are dust free by wet-sponging the surface. Avoid blowing off the dust unless this is done in a dust extraction booth, as it should not be inhaled. If the glaze needs a thick application a small percentage of gum arabic can be added to the glaze mixture. This sort of crawling can also occur over painted or sprayed underglaze decoration which may act like dust under the glaze. In this case a small amount of glaze or gum arabic needs to be mixed into the underglaze powder in order to bind it onto the pot.

The second major cause is a glaze which is too high in plastic ingredients; during drying the glaze contracts and forms small craze lines which break up the surface. During the firing these glaze islands do not melt to form an allover covering but go into lumps; this usually happens on biscuit fired pots. Such glazes can usually be successfully applied raw, that is, directly onto unfired or green ware; they can be adapted for use on biscuit fired work by substituting non-plastic clay such as a calcined clay, either molochite (china clay) or calcined ball clay (marketed in the U.K. as Kalbrite, available in various grades) weight for weight for plastic clay. Gently rubbing the dry surface of the glaze with the finger to smooth over and fill in any cracks can also help.

Rapidly heating the glaze before it has dried out will also cause islands to form.

Freshly glazed pots, fired too quickly whilst the glaze is damp, may also crawl. The glaze contracts rapidly and again divides into islands which do not heal over. Allow pots to dry before firing them or allow a slow drying period in the kiln.

Bloating

Bubbles or lumps which occur in the body of the fired body of the pot which, when broken, show no evidence of contamination, are known as bloats. They usually only occur at high temperature, in which case the body is overfired (when there are many smaller lumps) or when carbon is trapped in the body. Carbon from the remains of plants and rotting vegetation is present in all clay bodies to a greater or lesser extent. During the biscuit or first firing the carbon burns away as carbon dioxide or carbon monoxide from $500\,°C$ ($932\,°F$) to $900\,°C$ ($1652\,°F$). During this period the firing must be sufficiently slow and in the presence of enough oxygen to allow for complete combustion of the carbon to take place; this process is slower on pots with thicker walls. If the firing is too rapid then the surface of the pot will begin to vitrify and prevent the carbon gases from escaping, and the heat will also not penetrate sufficiently into the thickness of the wall. During the subsequent glaze firing the trapped carbon converts by oxidation into gas, expands and, as the body softens, causes a bloat or bubble to form. In extreme cases the surface of the pot may split.

The remedy here is to fire the body to a lower temperature or, more practically, slow down the speed of the biscuit firing so that the carbon can be burnt off. Some clays have a higher carbon content than others, and kilns during firing of these can emit quite thick clouds of slighlty blue and acrid smoke. To remove these gases ventilation is essential, as in too large quantities they are quite dangerous and a build up of the gas can occur if sufficient precautions are not taken.

Dunting or spiral cracking

Pots can crack in the glaze firing for two main reasons. The first reason, shivering, has already been dealt with. The second fault, commonly called dunting, occurs when a pot is cooled too quickly either by a draught of cool air or because the door of the kiln has been opened too soon. Dunting rarely occurs in electric kilns, which have no strong through draughts, but it is more common in flame burning kilns. The crack often takes the form of a sharp line down the pot, usually seeking a point of weakness such as where the wall of the pot is slightly thinner or where the base and sides join. Too great a glaze compression will also encourage this to happen.

Dunting as opposed to other forms of cracking can be recognised by the characteristics of the crack: if it is a clean, sharp split showing clear distinctions between body and glaze layer then the crack has occurred during cooling and after the glaze has matured. Cracks which were already present before glazing and firing will show smoother edges where the matured glaze has healed over. These cracks can result from the use of a soft biscuit which has not been taken to a high enough temperature.

Draughts must be avoided. For safety, kilns should not be 'cracked' or opened until $200\,°C$ ($392\,°F$), and kiln doors not disturbed until $100\,°C$ ($212\,°F$). The top damper can safely be opened at $400\,°C$ ($752\,°F$), never earlier. Spyholes should remain firmly shut so as not to create through draughts. A further precaution is to ensure that the pot is glazed on both the inside and the outside so that the glaze compression on both sides of the wall is equal.

Spitting

Spitting of the glaze off the pot and onto the kiln shelf can occur with some glaze materials which contain large amounts of combined water. Some varieties of colemanite are particularly prone to spitting off the pot as the water turns into steam (a particularly violent reaction). For this reason potters in the U.K. substitute, weight for weight, calcium borate frit, which gives no trouble, while those in the U.S.A. use gerstley borate, described as a well-behaved form of colemanite. The calcining or roasting of colemanite to dull red heat, 600–700°C (1112–1292°F) will remove the water without causing the material to fuse. This can then be used safely in the glaze.

Glazing the ware

Applying liquid glaze to ware fired to 950–1000°C (1742–1832°F) can be done by dipping, pouring, spraying or painting. Stoneware and earthenware clays fired to a biscuit temperature of 950°C (1742°F) are sufficiently porous to absorb the glaze and strong enough to handle comfortably. Porcelain fired to this temperature is porous but not as strong. The high porosity can be reduced using a higher biscuit temperature or, if this is not possible, partially nullified by quenching or wetting the ware in clean water before glazing. The raw glazing of pots which have not been biscuit fired needs suitable glazes and methods: these are described in Chapter 12.

Dipping

By far the most popular method of glazing is dipping, a technique used by most studio potters engaged in making repetition wares; it requires no special equipment, is quick and efficient. All that is required is a sufficient volume of glaze contained in a large enough barrel so that the object to be dipped can be completely immersed and agitated. Too small an amount of glaze or too small a barrel makes it a very difficult method. Depending upon the shape and size of the object to be glazed, it is normal practice to grip an open pot by its rim and foot and immerse it completely, ensuring that the inside is totally filled with glaze. Leave the pot immersed in the glaze for only a brief moment, gently agitating it all the time; lift out the pot, shake off the surplus liquid, and place the pot to dry. A glazed pot can be handled when the glaze has lost its shine, which usually occurs within a minute or two. Other shapes are handled according to their needs. Leaving the pot in the glaze for longer than a few seconds will not necessarily cause a thicker glaze layer to form on the pot, for once the walls of the pot become saturated the outer layer of glaze will not adhere and will be washed off. A thick glaze layer can be obtained by allowing the pot to dry until the glaze has lost its shine and then dipping it again. This may be repeated several times. During glazing keep the glaze well stirred to prevent the settling of the materials. It is not always possible to dip thin walled pots because of the speed at which the walls become saturated. In such instances the inside is swilled with glaze first and allowed to dry and then the outside is glazed separately.

Pouring

Pouring is a glazing method for large pots, for certain intricate shapes and for special decorative and 'accidental' effects. With large pots, the inside is first swilled with glaze and drained. The pot is then supported on struts across a bowl and glaze poured over the outside. If a sufficiently large volume of glaze is used, and the pot slowly revolved on a turntable, an even coating can be achieved. However, some shapes need to be supported by hand whilst the glaze is poured and this makes an even coating more difficult to obtain. Many potters prefer poured glaze effects because the fired results are often more in character with the properties of liquid glaze. Overlapping, running and dribbling, which arise as part of the glazing process, are enjoyed, and their effects often deliberately incorporated. This is in marked contrast to the attitude of the purists who argue that glaze serves only a secondary function, and its ability to create dramatic effects should not be allowed to detract from the form of the pot. Pouring can be used as a more formal decorative technique. Glaze can be poured onto the walls of a pot to form apron-shaped areas depending upon the angle which the pot is held. Overlapping the aprons will introduce further variations.

Spraying

Glaze can be sprayed and this is an ideal method to use for large or awkwardly shaped objects and has the advantage that only small quantities of glaze are required. It enables very thick or very thin layers of glaze to be built up and it is an efficient method for the glazing of vitrified pots. The fired appearance of sprayed glaze tends to have its own particular qualities; glazes containing colouring oxides tend to develop a more speckled appearance, and if the glaze has been applied thinly the speckling effect is heightened.

The disadvantage of spraying is that sophisticated and expensive electrical equipment is essential. This will include a compressor, a spray gun and a spray booth fitted with a powerful

Jane Osborn Smith; porcelain potion bottles and boxes with matt white glaze and enamel decoration. Approximately 8 cm (3 in) tall

extractor fan which should be sufficiently power-ful to remove the unwanted fine glaze mist which forms inside the booth. This glaze dust is dangerous if inhaled. A wise precaution, when spraying, is to wear a face mask fitted with replaceable gauze inserts. Certain shapes are difficult to spray successfully; a cup, for example, where the glaze spray often misses the underside of the handle and the very bottom of the inside. Short bursts of glaze sprayed onto the slowly revolving pot enables an even glaze layer to be built up. Spraying too long on one area will saturate the surface and the glaze will then run or be blown off.

Glaze to be used for spraying needs to be thoroughly sieved to remove any small lumps which would quickly clog the nozzle of the spray gun. Some glazes may even need to be ball milled for two hours to make them finer. If a mill is not available the glaze can be ground with a pestle and mortar. A turntable inside the spray booth enables the pot to be rotated while being sprayed. The spray gun is best held 30–40 cm (12–16 in) away from the pot. Pots with a non-porous surface, such as some industrial biscuit or fired glazed pots, are more successfully glazed if they are heated prior to spraying either in an oven or special heating cabinet, otherwise the glaze takes too long to dry to the condition in which it can be handled.

Painting

To achieve certain decorative effects glaze can be painted on to the biscuit and the advantage of this method is that only a small amount of glaze is required, and drips, runs and overlapped areas of glaze can be avoided. A binder such as gum arabic or tragacanth should be added to the glaze to prevent the brush from sticking and lifting the glaze off the pot. Used thicker than usual, the glaze can either be applied in thin layers, with each coat being allowed to dry before the next is painted or, with practice, applied as a single coat. One glaze can be applied on top of another and thicknesses can be varied with this method.

Preparing glazed wares for the kiln

Once glazed the pots must be fettled ready for placing in the kiln; this will include gently rubbing down any large runs or dribbles of glaze, and touching up any bare or thin patches of glaze with a glaze mop (a large, rounded, soft-haired brush). Goat's hair is often used for these mops. A small jar of glaze kept for touching-up avoids the necessity of agitating a large barrel or bucket of glaze merely to obtain a small quantity. These jars of glaze, suitably labelled, are also handy when kept near to the kiln to repair damage due to accidental chipping of the glaze. In the case of stoneware pots the foot of the pot must be wiped clean of glaze using a small wet sponge, a job made easier if the foot has been painted or banded with either molten paraffin wax or a wax emulsion before glazing. Waxing is almost essential when pots are fired with their lids placed in position; both surfaces are waxed before, and then cleaned after glazing. A thin layer of alumina and china clay may then be painted or dabbed onto the two surfaces to prevent sticking in the firing. To prevent a messy effect the covering over of finger marks by dabbing or painting on glaze must be done carefully. Glazes with a high clay content are best left to dry before retouching, whilst those with a low plastic content need to be touched up as soon as the glaze has lost its shine. In the firing all stoneware and porcelain pots soften slightly and become pyroplastic. For this reason they are fired sitting directly on the kiln shelf without the use of the stilts and spurs which are employed when placing low temperature earthenwares. The use of spurs enables the pot to be glazed all over, completely sealing the surface, and eliminating the foot-cleaning procedure. When spurs are used for supporting earthenware pots the glaze should not be applied too thickly or the points of the spur will become deeply embedded in the glaze and, after firing, will be difficult to remove.

Incidentally, the grinding over of the spur points, using a carborundum stone, should be done as soon as ware is unpacked from the kiln as these points and the thin slivers of glaze on the base of the pot are razor sharp and can cause deep cuts. In the pottery industry these points and slivers are referred to as glaze daggers. Rubbing the base of pots with a carborundum stone will also remove any roughness caused by sand or grog.

9 Decoration

Unlike pots fired in a reduction atmosphere, those fired in an oxidising kiln have to be much more carefully decorated; painted oxides can look crude and garish in the absence of the softening effect of the reduction atmosphere on the iron oxide, and the iron oxide in turn tends to make any other oxides more subtle. This means that pots fired in the electric kiln have to be more carefully considered, both in terms of the oxides or glazes which are to be used and in the *sort* of decoration planned. Few potters would consider the shape and the decoration of the pot separately but would think of them together as part of the unity of the form, the one dependent on the other.

However, for the sake of simplicity it is easier to look at all the aspects of decoration under one heading, even if this is a slightly artificial convention. Traditionally, decoration is thought of in terms of some sort of design or pattern which is applied under, in or on the glaze by such methods as painting or spraying, but this is really only one type of decoration. The other major approach to decoration is through the body of the pot as opposed to its surface. Obvious examples are modelled relief or incised and inlaid designs; another is the use of coloured bodies. These can either be left raw, that is, unglazed, or can be covered with a glaze which reacts with the oxide in the clay to give many shades and tones of colour.

Body colour

Bodies fired in oxidation unlike those fired in reduction kilns, do not get blackened and darkened by the firing process. Oxidation can result in useful neutral-coloured clay bodies, and by the clever use of body stains or metal oxide additions it can give attractive colours, which range from rich blues to pale salmon pinks and olive yellows.

This use of body colour was used by early slipware potters who added a coloured layer to the body surface, and it was also developed by Josiah Wedgwood for his unique coloured bodies. His Jasper ware was a rich cobalt blue while Basalt was deep black. More rarely he produced browns and mauves. These bodies fired to this colour without the use of coloured glaze or coloured slip and were produced by adding either prepared body stain or metal oxides to the body from which the pot was made. Either method is suitable for the studio potter firing with electric kilns and both can be adapted to give a wide range of effects.

Manufacturers supply ready-made body stains in a wide variety of colours. These are made from such materials as oxides, fluxes, flints and so on, which are mixed together and calcined to around 800–1000°C (1472–1832°F) to produce a stable colour. Amounts of 2–15% added to a light coloured clay body will give it colour. Some stains will fire to a higher temperature without colour

Ruth King; handbuilt coil pot, with green matt glaze with brush painted decoration, 1260°C (2300°F)

change while others will loose their colour at stoneware temperatures, but as a means of colouring bodies at low to medium temperatures, body stains are excellent. Their colour is often heightened by the wetting action of a transparent glaze, but this can detract from the sculptural qualities of the pot or object.

Alternatively, to produce colour, metal oxides can be added to the clay, though this is unlikely to give such a wide range of shades. This does have the advantage over body stains in that a far smaller addition is needed to produce an effect. With both methods the easiest way to prepare the coloured body is to knead together measured amounts of plastic clay and stain. The ideal method is to mix the dry clay and stain together and then add water to make the mixture plastic, but this is unnecessarily complicated unless precise effects are required. Amounts as low as 2–3% of oxide added to the clay will produce colour in the fired body, though this may only be noticeable as a darkening effect until covered with a glaze. A transparent coating of glaze will 'wet' and to some extent absorb the colour, while a matt opaque glaze may produce some subtle and attractive effects.

There are two major aspects when colouring clay which have to be considered: one is the fluxing effect of the oxides or stains on the body, and the other is the necessity to start with a light firing body. Dark bodies contain iron in some form and this will tend to obscure the effect of the colour addition, and in some cases will totally cover it. Even light-firing stonewares contain some iron and will dull the colour to some extent, but these can still work well for the dark shades. Many potters use porcelain as the base to which colours are added. They may open up the dense body by the addition of white grog; molochite is ideal but suitable alternatives are silver sand and alumina hydrate or a mixture of zircon sand and alumina hydrate. All these materials will render the porcelain more opaque and in fact produce a white proto-porcelain body which can be attractive on its own terms, and is excellent for the additions of colour.

The fluxing effect which additions of colouring oxides and stains have on the body can cause bloating or distortion. This is particularly noticeable with such oxides as manganese, iron, copper and cobalt, which will all act as fluxes in the body causing vitrification at temperatures much lower than normal. Chrome oxide or stains are more refractory and will have a less pronounced effect. Nickel oxide, even in small amounts, blackens the body considerably. Body stains generally tend to have less effect, but again this depends on the particular colour. Black, for instance, which is so rich in oxides, has a greater reaction with the body and again may lower its vitrification point. Other stains will remain almost inert in the body. One way round the fluxing of the body is to include some high temperature grog or blend in china clay to counteract the flux.

Coloured bodies are ideal for decorative pieces but for the domestic potter making large quantities of work present problems, as firing temperature and quantities of added stain often have to be precise. For potters interested in more decorative pieces there is a wide variety of ways in which coloured bodies can be used. When laminated with other coloured bodies they form the basis of agate ware, which derives its name from the semi-precious stone called agate. Such clays can be prepared as slabs and laid inside or over in moulds; they can be built up as slabs or they can be thrown on the wheel. Two lumps of clay of contrasting colour are knocked together and thrown on the wheel. A random spiral effect will be formed though with experience the position of the spiral and its position on the pot can to some extent be determined by the size of the

Michael Bayley; press moulded dish made up from different coloured clays, stoneware

clay lump and the throwing movements.

With any throwing technique there is a certain amount of slurry build-up on the surface of the pot and this may mask the contrasting clays. For this reason this surface slurry on the pot may have to be lightly trimmed off during the turning operation. With mould-formed work no slurry build-up will occur but the surface pattern may get slightly messed up in the handling process. Wet-wiping with a sponge will not remove this; it is best cleaned when the pot is bone dry by gently rubbing the surface with fine wire wool or sand paper. Unfortunately, this process gives rise to a fine dust which should not be inhaled; wear a dust mask, rub gently, rather than vigorously, and let the dust fall into a bowl of water.

Coloured clays can also be inlaid into the body. A design can be cut or pressed into the clay and this can be filled with clay of a contrasting colour; when it is leather hard the surface can be levelled off and smoothed over when dry. On fine designs it may be easier to build up the inlay using coloured slips, applying them in several layers. Again the surface can be rubbed smooth once it is dry. The dangers of inhaling clay dust are explained elsewhere in this chapter.

Agate or inlay decoration can often be left unglazed to give attractive effects. A transparent glaze will deepen the colour but this may also pick up some of the colour, which 'bleeds' into the glaze; this may or may not be desirable. Matt glazes which respond to body (or slip) colour, sometimes called transmutation glazes, will pick up the colour in an attractive way. Dolomite glazes, for instance, over bodies containing copper, may give pinks and greens. Experiments with other oxides may give a surprisingly wide range of colours.

Decorating slip

Made by mixing colouring oxides or prepared commercial stains with clay slip into a smooth creamy mixture, decorating slips (sometimes called engobes) are used to cover completely or partially the surface of objects. Decorating slip (engobe) should not be confused with casting slip which is deflocculated and is used to make pots by casting in plaster moulds. The use of coloured decorating slips goes back many hundreds of years and they were traditionally made with naturally occuring clays of contrasting colour. It was, for example, a method employed by the slipware potters of Staffordshire of the seventeenth and early eighteenth centuries to produce richly decorated wares which were covered with a transparent glaze, and which represent some of the finest of Britain's folk art. The use of slip decoration on stoneware has been, relatively speaking, unexplored, principally because it has been so successful at earthenware temperatures. Potters in the Far East have painted thick white slips under glazes in the 'hakame' technique to give soft effects in which the brush strokes can still be seen. The use of slips under glazes can give unique results, particularly if there is a reaction between slip and glaze – such slips are called reactive or vitreous slip. John Lawrie, a potter in the U.S.A., uses a slip of Barnard clay 85 and whiting 15 under glazes to get some rich effects. Potters in the U.K. could substitute Fremington clay or any local clay.

Slips which provide a layer between clay body and glaze can be used to mask the colour of the body as those for example which are rich in iron bearing clays. It can also be used to provide a coloured layer which, on the whole, has little reaction with the glaze. Here the problem is to achieve a good fit between body and slip. Shrinkage has to be much the same and a good bond has to form between body and slip. The simplest way of doing this is to use the same clay body from which the pot is made as the basis for the slip to which colour is added; this system is excellent for colours which are darker than the body but will not work for lighter colours. For lighter colours a slip has to be made up which will bond with the body. Usually a single white firing ball clay will work, but blends of ball clay, china clay and feldspar will also give good results. The U.K. ball clay HVAR is white firing and can be used by itself.

If the slip flakes off edges and rims then it is not contracting sufficiently; additions of small amounts of feldspar or even alkaline frit to the slip will correct this. The opacity of the slip can be increased by the addition of tin oxide or zirconium silicate; the latter has the advantage of being very much cheaper and just as effective.

Slips covering all or most of the surface of a pot can be applied like glaze by dipping, pouring, painting or spraying. Dipping or pouring is best done when the pot is leather hard, but allow one side to dry before coating the other side. Spraying can be done when the pot is dry as layers can be built up slowly. Slip applied by painting will need an addition of a gum binder to stop it lifting off the surface, and will have to be built up slowly. Some clays are different and can best take slip when they are leather hard, whilst others are best coated when they are dry. Trial and error will determine

Chris Jenkins; thrown porcelain bowl with resist decoration, matt and shiny black pigment

Lucie Rie; a group of stoneware and porcelain bottles, in her studio, all thrown in two sections and joined together at the leather hard stage

the best condition of each clay.

Reactive slips can be regarded as glazes with a high clay content. On their own they will, depending on the amount of flux present, form a vitrified layer; some will be matt and some have a dull sheen. None will be sufficiently glassy to form a glaze. A reactive slip is one which gives a specific response under a glaze, usually one which is specially formulated. A simple example would be a slip made from a mixture of ball clay and iron oxide used under a glaze which contains feldspar and whiting. The highly fluxed glaze will 'eat' into the slip and, depending on the amount of iron oxide in the slip, will give rich mottled shades of green and brown. Many variations can be tried; for example, by changing the fluxes and by substituting alkaline frit for the whiting different colour responses will be achieved. The addition of small amounts of bone ash or an addition of titanium dioxide to the glaze will also change the colour, as will substituting other sorts of iron, such as crocus martis. Coarse ilmenite in the slip will break through the glaze to give a speckled effect.

Vitrified slips are made up from various sorts of clay such as red clay or ball clay; some such as Albany slip or Fremington clay, give a vitrified surface on their own, but most others will need to be loaded with oxides which act as fluxes; under a stiff glaze the slip bursts through giving attractive mottled effects depending on the oxides present in the slip. Naturally occuring materials which contain small amounts of many different types of oxides give the most interesting effects. Apart from Albany slip, already mentioned, such materials as yellow ochre, basalt, and various sorts of granite will give colours which range from opalescent blues to yellows, oranges, tans and browns.

Special effect slips, which do not, in themselves, have to be interesting but which have to carry small amounts of material are also worth mentioning. Such slips can be made out of specially compounded mixtures if, for example, a white base is required, or be simply made from the clay body. These slips are ideal for use with such materials as coarse ilmenite which will bleed into the glaze to give specks, or with small amounts of fine silicon carbide which will give local reduction effects under suitably prepared glaze containing $\frac{1}{2}$–1% copper oxide. (Recipes are listed at the end of the book.) Experiments with ground-up colours and slip loaded with oxide which will bleed into the glaze are also a possible source of good colour.

It is also worth pointing out that trailed slip decoration can be used under a glaze. The clay slip is prepared to a thicker consistency than usual and piped or trailed onto the leather hard pot, where it sits proud of the surface. Under a suitable glaze attractive results can be achieved.

Underglaze decoration

Just as colours can be added to the glaze, so they can be applied under the glaze and are picked up during the firing. Again, metal oxides and specially prepared underglaze powders can be used, the oxides being much stronger in colour and much more ready to dissolve into the glaze. Underglaze powders are prepared in a similar manner to body stains except that they are usually much more finely ground and have an addition of a small amount of flux or glaze. Both are normally applied to the biscuit fired pot, but they can equally be put onto the unfired pot and then covered with glaze. They can be applied by a wide variety of methods: painting, stippling, sponging, dabbing, stencilling, splashing or spraying. Colour response will be determined by the ingredients in the glaze.

Any design or pattern applied under the glaze will tend to run and lose its definition as it is attacked by and absorbed into the glaze, but this can be an attractive quality. Colours, depending on the glaze composition, can be bright or muted. Often the nicest colours are obtained from the smallest amounts of oxide and for this reason they are best prepared as pigments. Small percentages combined in a base of china clay will make a mixture which handles well and can be applied thinly. The following mixtures give soft colours:

1 Cobalt oxide 1   China clay 99
2 Chrome oxide 1.   China clay 99.
3 Copper carbonate 4.   China clay 96.
4 Manganese carbonate 5. China clay 95.

All can be mixed together and stronger colours obtained by increasing the amount of oxide. Too thick a layer of paint can cause the glaze to crawl during the firing; this can be avoided by adding a small amount of a binder, such as gum arabic, to the underglaze colour.

In-glaze decoration

Underglaze colours are painted onto the pot before the glaze is applied, whereas in-glaze colours are painted on the surface of the unfired glaze and sink into it during the firing. This technique is the basis of the colourful and lively earthenware maiolica decoration used by Spanish and Italian potters who paint onto a white opaque tin glaze though it can equally well be used at higher temperatures. To avoid lifting of the powdered glaze surface when oxides are painted on it, the glaze can be hardened on to the pot by firing to a temperature of around 600°C (1112°F). At higher stoneware temperatures the colours, whether applied as oxides or as underglaze powders, although they take on their own quality which can be of interest, tend to be less bright.

All of the pigments previously described in the section on underglaze decoration can be used on

David Morris; carved sponge for stamping on oxide decoration

The pattern being stamped on

Dish with the stamped pattern

top of glaze providing that they are thinly applied. Thick applications may give rise to dry surfaces as a result of the glaze being overloaded with pigment. Some of the most interesting effects can be achieved by painting mixtures of oxides onto a coloured glaze. A good example of this is to use a tenmoku type black-brown glaze which contains 8–10% iron oxide. Iron oxide mixed with water when painted in a broad design or pattern onto the surface of the tenmoku glaze can give splendid gold red colours formed as a result of the glaze becoming saturated with the pigment. An iron rich slip under such a glaze will give similar effects.

Some glazes will take painted designs without problems, but some will bleb up and air bubbles form under the glaze. This may either be because the glaze is too dry or because it is too wet; some glazes are too low in clay, which binds the glaze. An addition of 3% of bentonite will improve the binding qualities of the glaze. Spraying or splashing colours onto the surface will often get around this problem though this will, of course, give different effects. Pigment sprayed with a hand spray can give a soft build up of colours.

Stamps, cut from dense sponge or even made from rubber, can be used to apply designs either on top of or underneath the glaze. Here the pigment needs to be prepared in a clay or gum base.

On-glaze decoration

Once the glaze has been fired it can be further decorated by painting on top of it and firing in a third (or second) firing. Sometimes referred to as enamels or lustres, these colours are best purchased direct from the pottery suppliers. Enamel or on-glaze colours are made up from finely ground, prepared pigments combined with a low temperature flux. They are mixed with a suitable medium which is usually oil based, and applied by any of the usual methods to the surface of the glaze. During the firing they flux onto and are absorbed by the softening glaze. Different colours may require different temperatures but the range is usually between 600–800°C (1112–1472°F). The chief advantage of enamels is the bright range of colours they offer and the precise sorts of decorations and patterns to which they lend themselves. They are often used in combination with other decoration to add a high note of colour and contrast.

Lustres are supplied in a liquid form and are applied onto the fired glaze, usually by painting. They are simple to use and can be thinned with a suitable medium. During the firing they reduce to leave a metal deposit on the surface of the glaze. Precious metals, such as gold, silver and platinum are used, which makes them expensive; on dark glazes their effect is subtle, rather than gaudy, and to bring them out at their best they need sensitive use.

Wax and paper resist

Although wax resist is a technique rather than a decorative process, it has so many uses for the potter and it is worth explaining. In brief, the method is to treat areas so that they resist or reject slip, pigment or glaze. Various methods of producing a resist are used but the commonest are with painted hot paraffin wax, often diluted with paraffin, with water based wax emulsion, which becomes waterproof on drying, or with the use of paper. Hot wax is the most efficient resist medium, even if the most cumbersome to prepare. It can be banded onto foot rings or inside lid gallerys or on lid edges; it can also be painted to give delicate brush resist marks. The use of emulsion has none of the handling complications associated with hot wax and can be freely brushed on the surface of the pot, but does not give such an efficient waterproof layer. Yet the ease with which it can be used makes it an excellent substitute for wax.

Paper resist is best used for decoration on flat surfaces. Cut or torn thin paper (newsprint and duplicating paper are excellent) can be laid, wet, onto the surface of unfired clay, where it will resist slip and glaze. Almost any soft absorbent paper works well and will cling firmly, and though it cannot be used more than once it gives good sharp edges. The covering has to be left to become leather hard before the paper can be lifted off. Making the paper adhere to biscuited surfaces is difficult but it can be made to work using small pieces.

Some potters have successfully used rubber-based glues, such as Copydex and masking tape. All can be used to build up areas of pattern, overlaying one slip or a glaze on another.

Decorative use of the glaze

Some glazes are of sufficient interest in their own right and need little done to them. Much of the quality of the glaze will depend on the thickness of the glaze and this can make a significant difference to the appearance. This is basically because of the amount of reaction between the body and the glaze; a thin coat of a matt glaze will have more of the qualities of a pigment, while a thin coat of a

Mal Magson; agate ware press moulded pot, stoneware

shiny glaze will be rough and mean. Thicker coats of these glazes will bring out more of the quality of the glaze and will form a distinctive layer on the body. This ability of the glaze to give different results can be made a positive feature of the object.

Double glazing

Double glazing is another decorating method which can give distinctive if slightly unpredictable results, mainly because it depends for its repeated success on having the glazes and pots with walls at the same thickness each time. Briefly, the technique consists of applying one glaze over another in thicknesses which depend upon the glazes used and the effects required. A stiff white glaze and a runny dark glaze are often used together. Sometimes a white opaque glaze is applied over a dark slip glaze which has been applied onto the green unfired pot; this also eliminates the physical problems which can arise when double glazing biscuited ware. With double dipping it is usual to immerse the pot in a slightly thinner mix of glaze; this layer is allowed to lose its shine before the pot is dipped in the slightly thinner than usual mixture of the second glaze. If the first glaze is allowed to dry out completely then, when the second glaze is applied, the first glaze will often bubble and blob up resulting in an uneven coating. Occasionally the glaze will even fall off the surface as it dries.

Spraying on succeeding layers of glaze will eliminate many of these problems. Glaze layers can easily be tested for thickness, and spraying also eliminates the saturation of the first layer which occurs when dipping techniques are used.

In addition to the useful, as opposed to the decorative, aspect of double glazing, the technique is used for the reclaiming of fired pieces which have been accidently glazed too thinly. Applying glaze to fired surfaces is, as has been explained earlier, greatly helped by using a thicker glaze slip to which a binder such as gum arabic has been added. Heating the pot beforehand also helps.

The double glazing technique can be extended to include wax and paper resist as well as accidental double glazing such as splashed, flicked, and dropped glaze. Whichever technique is used, the only precautions which need to be followed are those explained earlier in this chapter.

Trailing

Trailing, which is the technique of piping on lines of glaze, primarily associated with coloured clay slips, can be used equally well with glaze providing that the glaze has been thickened by the addition of a gum. Trailing glaze by using a rubber bulb type of trailer is the most efficient method of application. The glaze must be trailed on top of the first glaze before the first glaze dries in order to prevent the applied lines from lifting off as they dry.

10 Unusual glazes

Glazes for use on domestic pots have to fulfil certain basic criteria which include practical surface quality, attractiveness, ease of application and reliability, wide firing range and so on. With electric kilns there are, however, possibilities and opportunities which provide the potter with unique effects. An amazing range of colour and glaze surfaces can be obtained, which include such special glazes as copper reds, iron blues and crystalline glazes as well as the possibility of carrying out reducing and reduction effects in the electric kiln.

Reduction atmospheres in the electric kiln

For those potters interested in glazing and who are working with electric kilns, one of the biggest challenges is to produce the elusive and highly

Marianne de Trey; coffee pot and jugs, standard domestic ware, 1260°C (2300°F). The brown glaze is applied as a slip on the raw pot, the white tin glaze on the biscuit fired work

regarded colours and shades of reduction glazes, particularly the pinks and purples of reduced copper or the rich effects of reduced iron oxide. Much research has been done in this area. There are two main ways of achieving the necessary reduction: it can be induced either by burning a flame inside the placing chamber of the kiln, or by bringing about reduction within the glaze itself. Although bringing about an evenly reduced atmosphere in the electric kiln is tricky because there is very little air movement in the chamber and, more important, although reduction can cause excess wear upon the exposed wire elements, there are ways of achieving this which do work.

Potters have devised various methods of reducing the atmosphere in the kiln which affect both body and glaze; most are achieved by the introduction of highly combustible organic materials such as slivers of wood, moth balls and charcoal which are fed into the chamber at regular intervals over 1000°C (1832°F). These will smoulder and burn in the chamber causing a smoky reducing atmosphere.

The size of the kiln and the inlet ports will determine the amount of material required. To keep in the smoke all cracks which create ventilation, ports, spyholes and around the door must be sealed with a mixture of clay and sand.

Needless to say the introduction of any material into an electric kiln is potentially dangerous. Materials must not be allowed to touch or fall onto the elements. When stoking takes place the hot air emitted from any spyholes may be harmful. Attention should also be paid to the electric wire elements which will be attacked by the smoke; as a result their working life is considerably shortened. At least three ordinary oxidising firings should be carried out between reduction firings to allow the elements to re-establish a protective oxidised layer. Attention, too, should be paid to the ventilation of the room in which the kiln is situated. Electric kilns are not fitted with chimneys and few potters will have a hood installed over the kiln fitted with an air extraction outlet, although this is a good idea if regular reduction firings are planned. A powerful extractor fan coupled to the outside should be sufficient to keep a small kiln clear and a build up of fumes should be avoided.

Silicon carbide rod elements are affected only very slightly by a reducing atmosphere and some kilns on the market are specially designed for reduction firings. They have gas inlets for the injection of natural or liquid propane gas in the kiln chamber. Combustible gases can be introduced into the kiln without risk of explosion if the temperature of the kiln is above the ignition point of the gas. Usually reducing conditions are not required until 1000°C (1832°F), which is a safe temperature for most gases. One of the problems with these kilns, which again must be situated in a well-ventilated room or fitted with an extraction hood, is that the gas tends to move and collect at the top of the kiln, leaving the bottom unaffected. Consequently reduction tends to be heavy at the top and light at the bottom. This can, to some extent, be remedied by denser packing at the top.

Experiments with the introduction of other gases – such as carbon dioxide – into the kiln have given good results without damage to the wire elements. In kilns not fitted with special inlet nozzles, gas can be inserted by the use of a poker fitter with a heat resistant nozzle. This needs to go into the spyhole and project 5–8 cm (2–3 in) inside the kiln, ensuring that it is clear of any element. The gas can be dispersed in the chamber by the staggered placing of shelves, so that some movement of atmosphere is allowed. The kiln chamber will fill up with smoke and the use of a dial or a flowmeter will indicate how much gas is consumed. A thin plume of black smoke emitted from the kiln will indicate that a good reducing atmosphere has been achieved. At this stage all bungs and outlets should be sealed as tightly as possible.

A typical firing schedule is:

1 Fire normally until 1050°C (1922°F).
2 Insert poker (or turn on gas) until the chamber is filled with smoke, then turn down gas supply to a level sufficient to maintain the atmosphere.
3 Reduce until required firing temperature (or just below) is reached, turn off gas and then soak or 'purge' the kiln for 30–50 minutes.
4 Switch off and cool.

Alternatively, some potters find they can reduce the kiln while it is cooling and get good results.

The dangers when using gas are explosions (which can be prevented by using gas only above 1000°C, 1832°F) and poisoning from inhaled carbon monoxide or sulphur dioxide. Carbon monoxide is produced during reduction and because it is odourless and tasteless can be a danger in confined spaces. Good ventilation is therefore essential. Carbon monoxide detectors are available. Sulphur dioxide has a pungent smell and its presence will be noticed at once.

Glazes and bodies fired in a reducing atmosphere will behave differently, although most of those mentioned in this book will give good results.

All the methods described earlier are complicated ways of producing effects which are much more easily obtained in a flame burning kiln; for the potter working with the electric kilns it may be more worthwhile to explore the use of materials which give their particular qualities in oxidized firing. Another aspect of these methods is that they do make use of the qualities that are available in the electric kiln.

Reduction glaze effects

The main alternative to creating a reducing atmosphere in the kiln is to add reducing materials to the glaze. Several materials are available but by far the most useful and one with which I have experimented is silicon carbide (SiC) better known

Sally Dawson; porcelain lidded bowl with crackle glaze stained with a brown pigment made up from iron oxide and household oil

95

as carborundum. This material is manufactured in an electric arc process and is extremely hard and refractory and from which, amongst other things, kiln shelves and props are made. When a tiny amount of finely ground silicon carbide powder is fired in a suitable glaze it breaks down to form the gas carbon and cristobalite (SiO_2) which goes into solution in the glaze; the carbon draws oxygen from its surroundings to form carbon monoxide and ultimately carbon dioxide, both of which are released as a gas. This reducing effect is particularly active with any copper present. Being one of the least stable oxides present in the glaze, copper is the first to lose its oxygen and converts to either the colloidal or cuprous state. Only small quantities of copper and silicon carbide are necessary to achieve a satisfactory effect. Too large a quantity of silicon carbide results in a rough sandpaper texture glaze which both looks and feels unpleasant. The fact that silicon carbide could act on copper to produce reds was discovered accidentally in the early 1930s by Littlefield and Baggs, who were working at Ohio State University. During a glaze firing a copper bearing glaze ran onto a silicon carbide shelf and the drippings showed a brilliant copper red colour.

In the glaze the silicon carbide acts in the following manner. In a suitable fluxed glaze the material is broken down by the molten glaze into silicon and carbon in the following equation: $SiC + heat = Si + C$, giving free silicon atoms and free carbon atoms in the glaze. Both materials, hungry for oxygen to make them stable, seek out available oxygen. The silicon picks up oxygen to form silica (SiO_2) and becomes a normal part of the glaze. The carbon is equally greedy for oxygen so that it can form either carbon monoxide or dioxide – both gases which are released in the reaction and which may leave the glaze looking frothy and bubbly. When this occurs, it indicates that either the firing temperature is not high enough or that the glaze is too viscous and needs a slight increase of the flux to lower the melting point.

In percentage terms, weight for weight equal parts of silicon carbide and copper carbonate, usually in amounts of 0.2%–0.5% added to the glaze, give strong colours. Much lower quantities of copper is used than is usually associated with copper colours. Amounts of copper above 0.5% give darker and liverish colours. Equally, too large a presence of silicon carbide will cause too great a release of carbon gas, which will leave a bubbled glaze. A small amount of tin oxide, 1–2%, present also seems to help in obtaining the colour. Such

Emmanuel Cooper; thrown stoneware bowl with oil spot glaze applied thickly

tiny proportions of the tin oxide will go into solution in the glaze and do not make it opaque.

However, as well as the colour of the clay body it is the other ingredients in the glaze which will determine whether the colour will be achieved. While any clear glaze base can form the basis for experiments only a few will actually work; most will not become sufficiently molten to attack and break down the silicon carbide, which will remain unaffected and give a rough surface.

Glazes which are highly alkaline seem to work best, so soda feldspar is preferred to potash feldspar. Calcium borate frit or gerstley borate helps to make the glaze fluid and seems to assist in the breakdown of the silicon carbide, but too much will adversely affect the colour and make the glaze run excessively. Whiting is a useful flux which does not harm the colour. The clay content must be kept to a minimum – about 5% – and this can usefully be satisfied partly if not totally by bentonite, which also makes the glaze easier to apply and keeps it suspended in the glaze slop.

Results cannot easily be predicted. One glaze will give a beautiful blood red on one pot, yet the same batch will yield a clear pale green glaze on another pot; equally, it is rare to get an even colour all over, as the reduction tends to act in small areas giving mottled effects; such glazes are sensitive to glaze thickness. All these variations are affected by the body (i.e. stoneware or porcelain), by the firing temperature and by the thickness of the glaze application.

Experiments with five ingredients, calcium borate frit (or gerstley borate), soda feldspar, whiting, china clay and flint as the base glaze, have given good results. In one series the whiting (15%), china clay (5%) and calcium borate frit (10%) were kept the same and the amounts of soda feldspar and flint were varied. Two combinations which work well are:

	1	2
Soda feldspar	50	35
Calcium borate frit (gerstley borate)	10	10
Whiting	15	15
China clay	5	5
Flint	20	35
Tin oxide	1	1
Copper carbonate	0.5	0.5
Silicon carbide	0.5	0.5
	A slightly runny mix, deep red in colour; do not overfire.	A slightly frothy mix, with good colour. Settles down at higher temperature.

Other variations in the proportions of feldspar and flint would give ranges between these two glazes. Experiments replacing the copper with other materials have had mixed results. The substitution of 1–2% iron oxide for the copper carbonate can give pale celadon greens or grey blues in conjunction with 2% bone ash and is worth investigating. No successes have been achieved with additions of rutile or titanium dioxide, both of which resulted in excessively rough lava-type glazes.

These glazes without the silicon carbide could also form the basis of tests over an engobe containing a small amount of silicon carbide, which could give interesting results; in the absence of silicon carbide the glaze fires to a pale green. It is essential, however, that the silicon carbide be ground as finely as possible (300 mesh) otherwise it does not dissolve in the glaze. Another variation is to leave the copper oxide out of the glaze then to paint the oxide over, or under, the glaze.

Carbon in the glaze

Materials other than silicon carbide will cause local reduction in the glaze mix and, being much more ready to go into reduction, do not present the same problems of glaze handling. Equally, they do not give such dramatic results. A typical example of this is the use of partly burnt wood ash which contains charcoal. During the firing this can give typical reduced effects in the glaze.

The result of additions of any reducing material to the glaze will depend upon the amount added and upon the composition of the glaze. Coal dust, coke, graphite, coal ash and partially burnt wood ash and charcoals are all useful sources of carbon. Graphite has a lower level of reactivity and less need be used. Ideally all the materials should be ground fairly finely and treated as ordinary glaze ingredients. Graphite, charcoal and coal dust can be classified as additions over and above the other ingredients in the glaze but wood ash and coal ash, as well as being reducing agents, have their own effect on the mixture. Any carbon powder needs to be added to the basic glaze composition in amounts of 10%, the whole passed through a 60 mesh sieve to ensure it is evenly distributed. Carbon works best in iron bearing glazes to give shades of green and brown depending on the amount and the form of iron present.

As mentioned in Chapter 6, wood ash varies greatly in composition, depending on the type of wood and the place in which it grew. Hard ash, rich in silica for instance, behaves very differently in the glaze to a soft ash rich in fluxes and low in silica. Tests with each batch of ash will be necessary in order to establish how it acts. Coal ash tends to be regular in its composition and is very similar to clay in its behaviour. Analysis of coal ash can be found on p. 137.

Crackle glazes

The development of craze lines in the glaze which are recognised as a decorative feature are known as crackle glazes – mentioned earlier in Chapter 8. On pots intended for functional use such a crackle creates both a poor bond between body and glaze, which makes it physically weak, and a trap which can hold food and make it unhygienic. For these reasons crackle glazes are best reserved for use on decorative pieces. A crackle develops because the glaze contracts when cooling more than the body, and this can happen with shiny or matt, coloured or clear glazes. Some glazes will develop a crackle which is clear and distinctive. On other glazes the crackle is at its most handsome when rubbed with a finely ground liquid pigment while the pot is still hot from the kiln. This pigment is drawn into the crackle and is relatively firmly sealed as the pot cools, although some of it can be washed out over periods of time.

Sometimes the pattern of the lines formed are squarish, sometimes long and thin, at other times small and dense. Thickness of glaze application and rate of cooling seem to determine the size of the crackle, with rapid cooling giving a finer network. For a glaze to crackle it has to contain

Christine Ann Richards; thrown porcelain vase with semi-matt high feldspathic glaze with stained crackle. About 15 cm (6 in) tall

dolomite 20, soda feldspar 50, whiting 5, china clay 25, the addition of 1% copper carbonate will give a naturally occuring crackle.

Shiny glazes, applied fairly thickly, have a tendency to form deep crackle patterns, though these usually need to be picked out by pigment. Firing temperature and thickness of application are critical for good results and potters often find these glazes only work in some parts of the kiln and at higher stoneware temperatures of around 1270°C (2318°F). Porcelain gives the best results but needs to be low in silica for a firm crackle to develop in the glaze. A glaze made of 85% soda feldspar with 15% whiting fired to 1260°C (2300°F) will often give a transparent crackle and is a good starting point for tests. Experiments with the addition of a high expansion frit may increase the crackle.

Saggar firing

Saggars, or lidded ceramic boxes, have been used in the pottery industry to protect the wares from the flames and dust of the coal burning kilns for several hundred years. Pots fired in electric kilns do not need such protection; however, for potters interested in special effects the saggars can also serve as small firing chambers, trapping in any local atmosphere. The saggar can be used to create local areas of reduction or for the volatilization of materials such as salt, or colouring oxides. Saggars can be made in the ordinary clay body, with additions of grog to make them more robust, either by throwing or hand-building; they can be so designed to sit snugly on top of each other to form a pile, or bung, with the saggar top given a well-fitting lid. A reduction atmosphere inside the saggar can be brought about by the inclusion of slow burning carbon materials which will last throughout the heating and maturing cycle and the kiln, which is fired in the normal way. Suitable materials are charcoal, coke, coal, graphite, wood and sawdust, although some potters have experimented successfully with various sorts of dried beans. The reduction agent is placed in the floor of the saggar to a depth of about 2.5 cm (1 in) or more depending on the size of the container. Some pots, if left unglazed, can be buried in the reducing material which, as it burns down, leaves decorative markings on the pot.

Whatever material is used the saggar must be effectively sealed to prevent the smoke leaking out before the end of the firing. It is unlikely that the reduction will be heavy. A plastic mixture of fine ball clay placed round the lid will serve as a seal

fluxes that have the highest level of expansion; these are the alkalis, soda and potash, which need to be present in large quantities. Nepheline syenite and soda feldspar are sources of these alkalis with the alumina and silica tending to provide much of the remainder of the glaze. Used individually both minerals will give a viscous, crackle glaze. With a small addition of a high expansion frit plus a small amount of clay they can be made to work well as glazes. The silica content of the glaze needs to be kept low as does the presence of such fluxes as boron, magnesia and zinc oxide.

For a porcelain glaze which will crackle in many sorts of patterns depending on the thickness of application, a useful starting point is nepheline syenite 80, china clay 10, and whiting 10. When stained with small amounts of copper carbonate a dark crackle in a pale green matt glaze develops. Even tiny amounts of copper in the glaze will cause interesting effects. In a dolomite glaze made up of but it must have a low firing contraction otherwise it will crack and let air in, or smoke out. A mixture of plastic clay and graphite with starch, to serve as a binder, is said to be efficient. A blend of charcoal and coal in the saggar works well. Even the most securely sealed saggars are likely to leak slightly and this can cause strong and unpleasant smells to be emitted from the kiln. Adequate room ventilation is needed in the kiln room to keep the atmosphere clear. One potter found the pungent smell from the burning beans permeated the whole of the pottery.

As well as being used for creating reduction atmosphere, saggars can also be used to catch volatilized gases. A thin layer of salt painted around the inside of the saggar combined with a reducing material will produce a mild saltglaze on the pot. Salt when vapourised attacks and eats into the clay surface on which it is painted and so only a very thin layer can be applied. Oxides such as copper and chrome, painted onto the inside of the saggar, will cause flashings of colour on appropriate glazes. Glazes containing, for instance, tin, will pick up chrome to give pinks, while dolomite glazes will tend to respond to the copper.

Crystalline glazes

Because of the ability to control relatively precisely the temperature of electric kilns, they are ideally suited for the production of crystalline glazes. Many glazes form crystals but these are usually too small to be seen separately; a crystalline glaze, with macro- as opposed to micro-crystals, is one which contains crystals which are large enough to produce a decorative effect. Macro-crystalline glazes have well developed individual or clusters of crystals either fully or partly immersed in a glassy matrix. They are considered as suitable for decorative rather than functional pots. Textural qualities can vary from matt, semi-matt to shiny, and the crystals can be formed in a variety of shapes which includes stars and needle-like forms. They may be coloured by absorbing small amounts of colouring oxides which have previously been added to the glaze. The background may be colourless or tinted.

Crystalline glazes depend for their development on the nature of the glaze, the firing temperature and firing programme, particularly the rate of cooling. Perhaps the most important criterion is what basic oxides are present in the glaze to form the silicates which saturate the glaze and which on cooling devitrifies to form crystals. The formation of silicates which crystallize as the glaze cools depend on the nature of the glaze, which must act as a solvent, possessing a low viscosity to encourage the growth of crystals. During the firing a fluid liquid must be formed in which oxides present in the glaze can move freely. When cooling starts, motion within the glaze slows down and in this slowing down period bonds form as perfect unit cells or crystallites which serve as nuclei around which larger crystals may form. The slower the cooling rate of the glaze, the larger will be the crystals. Some oxides are more conducive to the formation of crystals than others; zinc for example, in a suitable base glaze, will combine with silica to form large crystals of willemite. Smaller, secondary crystals of a different shape, may occur in the same glaze.

Like all dramatic glazes, crystalline effects are not predictable; crystals vary in shape and size, even in the same firing. Equally mysterious can be the absence of crystals in a glaze which seems to conform to the correct conditions. At too low a temperature the glaze will not melt sufficiently and the crystals are not formed; too high a temperature will cause the glaze to run excessively. It is worth refiring glazes which have not formed crystals and to add a mixture of 70% zinc oxide and 30% flint spotted onto the glaze.

Successful crystalline glazes must at top temperature become fluid and molten with the crystal

Eileen Lewenstein; thrown and modelled porcelain pots with crystalline glazes

forming oxides at saturation point. A comparison can be made between sugar dissolved in water until no more will go into solution. As the liquid evaporates the sugar forms crystals. To achieve this fluidity the glaze must be rich in alkalis such as potash and soda which, being soluble in water, can only be introduced in the fritted form. A wide range of commercial frits are available. While frits can be made in the workshop to suit particular requirements, without the necessary equipment the process is long and tedious. It involves devising suitable mixtures which then have to be fired to form a liquid frit; ideally this must be cooled rapdily and ground up to form a glaze powder. The wide range of commercially available alkaline and borax frits serve the studio potter well which, in combinations with small amounts of feldspar, flint and calcium, make useful base glaze. Additions of zinc oxide and a small amount of rutile or titanium dioxide, to act as a 'seeder', will help crystals to form. Without any colouring oxides such a glaze will be white with small white crystals on porcelain or pale yellow cream with tan crystals on stoneware.

Such glazes can be coloured by the restrained additions of oxides. Colour is an important part of the crystalline glaze because, when added in suitable proportions, it will be preferentially absorbed by the crystals in different combinations to appear in contrast against a coloured or clear background. Not all glazes respond in the same way; some will colour the crystals intensely and the background lightly, and so on. Cobalt gives shades of blue, copper gives greens, while manganese gives pale brownish mauve.

It is, however, the firing procedure which will determine the size of the crystals. Some kilns, which cool slowly, allow crystals to grow, but this is unusual; for the formation of large crystals the glaze needs to have a slow cooling period or, for stoneware glazes, be allowed to cool to $1100°C$ ($2012°F$) and then maintained at this temperature for up to two hours before allowing cooling to continue. Soaking at top temperatures is more likely to result in a boiled rather than a crystalline glaze.

Because of the fluid nature of crystalline glazes certain precautions during firing need to be made, otherwise the molten liquid glaze runs off the pot onto the kiln shelf. One safeguard is to leave a good sized area unglazed at the bottom of the side of the pot; alternatively, this space can be covered with a matt, non-runny glaze. However, the safest method is to stand the pots on either a setter or a pad of clay painted with alumina so that if the glaze does run, neither the shelf nor the pot is ruined. Any rough edges left can be ground smooth with carborundum stone. Another factor with crystalline glazes worth bearing in mind is that the highly compressed glaze puts the pot under severe stress and can, in extreme cases, cause the pot to crack. Evenly made thick-walled pots are a wise precaution and the glaze should be applied both on the inside and the outside so that, as far as possible, the stresses are equal.

Crystalline glazes are specifically those in which large crystals form in a shiny matrix. There are, however, many other sorts of glazes which rely for their effect on the existence of small crystals. Aventurine glazes, for example, named after aventurine, a feldspar containing tiny haematite crystals that catch the light and give a sparkle, rely on the formation of small crystals of iron. They are produced in feldspathic glazes by saturating it with iron (though other oxides can be used) which dissolves in the glaze during the firing. During cooling the iron produces small crystals. Depending on the composition of the glaze, amounts of iron over 12% are required, though some can take as much as 30% iron. Aventurine effects can be obtained at both earthenware and stoneware temperatures; a special firing procedure is not needed and the crystals seem able to form in a steadily cooling kiln.

11 Medium temperature stonewares

Traditionally one common classification of ceramics is to divide it into two main groups – earthenware and stoneware – the former being fired in the range 1050–1100°C (1922–2012°F) and the latter in the range 1250–1280°C (2282–2336°F). The qualities of earthenware are associated with red porous clays, bright glossy colours and shiny glazes. In contrast stoneware is assumed to be made from vitrified dark firing bodies with glazes which may be shiny, matt or opaque, speckled, spotted and generally dark or more muted in colour. Only rarely do potters consider the sort of qualities that can be obtained in the so-called middle ground between earthenware and stoneware. Here it is possible to get many of the bright qualities of earthenware with the strength, hardness and gentler tones of stonewares. It is this medium range of temperatures which is ideally suited to the electric kiln.

As we become more and more aware of the excellent qualities that can be obtained in electric kiln firings we can stand back and consider the best ways of developing and using them. When fuel was cheap and apparently readily available it was not necessary to think of economies or to set about cutting costs. Today the situation has changed. Fossil fuels are limited in supply and costs of providing them continue to rise. From both an economic and an ecological point of view it is necessary to assess the ways in which we work as potters and possibly discover better ways of making and firing pots. One of the chief users of energy is the kiln and we have to take great care to ensure it is operated as efficiently as possible; insulation has to be adequate and the most efficient we can devise. Equally, firing schedules are planned to make full use of any low-priced or off-peak tariffs. We can also look at the firing temperatures to which we take our work.

This is where the electric kiln is so excellent, for with such a precise control over the speed of firing, the soak period and the switch off point, we are in a unique position to decide exactly what we want.

Sarah Bodine; thrown stoneware teabowls, Orton cone 6

Eileen Lewenstein; press moulded stoneware dish with
slip painted decoration under a crystalline glaze

Many potters are used to the idea that most stoneware in reduction firings is taken to 1260–1280°C (2300–2336°F) or even, in some kilns, to 1300°C (2372°F) or higher. It is a reasonable assumption to think that this is the stoneware temperature and to aim for it in electric kilns. Yet, despite the technical advantages of more sophisticated kilns and different types of element wire which are available for firing over 1260°C (2300°F), these sorts of temperatures subject the kiln fabric to terrific wear and tear. Even a drop of 20°C (68°F) to 1240°C (2264°F) represents an enormous saving on the fabric of the kiln and a reduction in firing costs.

Yet at this lower temperature the glazes and to some extent the bodies, when compared with work fired to the higher temperature, will tend to look dry and underfired. It would seem they are only at their best, visually, with the greater heat. Yet, with only slight adjustments to the glazes and to the bodies a fully mature look can be achieved and true stonewares can be made. It is a lesson the ceramic industry has learnt very quickly. One large manufacturing firm has devised a clay body which becomes completely vitrified at 1000°C (1832°F); when this is covered with carefully worked out glazes, the resulting wares have a quality very similar to those obtained at high temperatures. Such a clay body can be made by blending either a suitable commercial frit or some body flux like nepheline syenite with clay, but the resulting body is likely to have a low level of plasticity. While few studio potters are interested in such dramatic measures, there is much we can learn.

Most potters, unless working with slipwares, will agree that whatever firing temperature they choose, they will want the clay body to have a low level of porosity and have all the qualities of high-fired stoneware; they also want to allow opportunity for interaction between body and glaze and full maturation of the glaze. Any suggestion that the work is underfired will not be satisfactory. The first step is to decide on the firing temperature at which you want to work and stick to it. Ideally, this should be done after some initial experiments, but potters with large kilns may find this a problem, so a choice may have to be made without much experience. Most potters agree that the range of 1200–1240°C (2192–2264°F) present opportunities for the best compromise; that is, lower firing temperatures plus all the qualities of higher fired wares.

The clay body

Most commercially mixed stoneware bodies that are on the market are claimed to have a wide firing temperature which may be as low as 1200°C (2192°F) and as high as 1290°C (2336°F). The chances are that at either end of this range they are slightly under- or over-fired, with the optimum temperature somewhere in the middle. Such bodies are liable to bloat and distort at top temperature and become very brittle. At the lower end they may be slightly porous but with most clay bodies this is insignificant.

The first test, then, with existing clay bodies is to see if they have a reasonable colour, are hard at the chosen temperature and so on. If the body looks dry and lacks density, the easiest remedy is to blend into it a lower firing clay such as a red earthenware. Additions of 10–20% will usually darken the colour and aid vitrification. Small amounts of grog or sand will help to open up the clay and make it more workable. Red earthenware clays are usually very fine grained and dense and they need an opener of some sort. The use of a low temperature clay, such as Fremington in the U.K. or Barnard in U.S.A. will give a much darker firing body, and if iron effects are sought it is well worth trying.

The blending in of other materials to prepared clay body can be done by simply wedging the dry or moistened powder into it. Nepheline syenite is one of the cheapest and most accessible materials that act as a flux in the clay. It is a non-plastic material and therefore cannot be added in great amounts. For the production of white firing bodies it is excellent, and amounts of 5–20% can be tried.

Other suitable fluxing materials are feldspar, talc, calcium borate frit (or gerstley borate) and wollastonite. All should be properly blended in and thoroughly tested before large batches are prepared. Very dark stoneware bodies can be made by adding manganese oxide, iron oxide or crocus martis, all of which will have a strong colouring effect on both the body and glaze.

For the higher earthenware temperatures of 1100–1200°C (2012–2192°F) the basis of the body can be an oridnary red earthenware clay to which a higher firing clay can be added. Flint blended into the body will raise its firing temperature, and this can be added either as a powder or as a fine sand. However, such bodies will be dark red, almost black when fired, which will have a considerable effect on any glazes as the bodies will bleed iron onto the glaze. This can be avoided either by covering the body with a light firing slip or by basing the body on a whiter firing body. Some ball clays which mature at lower temperatures are available, as are some white firing commercial earthenware bodies. These prepared commercial bodies, as they are not intended for throwing, often have a low level of plasticity, so check this before ordering large amounts. China clay is, of course, excellent for use in a white firing body but lacks plasticity and will need to be mixed with a white ball clay. To make it vitrify at the medium range temperature an addition of flux may be necessary.

Clay slips

Just as the clay body needs adjusting to make it workable at medium range temperatures, so slips can be similarly altered. The range and different types of slips are discussed in Chapter 9; it is only necessary here to point out how the basic slip can be adjusted. For slips which are meant to serve as a covering rather than become an active part of the glaze, the basic slip must become vitrified and have the same shrinkage as the clay body. A white firing ball clay makes a simple but excellent base for light coloured slips, and an addition of china clay will make it more opaque. For darker coloured slips the body clay can be used. Slips which are to be in some sense reactive and work under the glaze to give interesting effects may need an increase in the amount of flux. This can be in the form of nepheline syenite or a frit, though only small amounts will be required. The colouring oxides of iron and manganese will act as fluxes in the slip and their presence can be made more effective by an increase or addition of other fluxes such as a frit, whiting or nepheline syenite.

Glazes

In addition to the high temperature fluxes, there are also the low temperature ones such as lead, which are available in the medium range. While it is not possible to get the oranges and reds of selenium and cadmium at temperatures above 1050°C (1922°F), or the rich red from chrome in a lead glaze, most of the other colours associated with earthenware are available. For stoneware potters it is feldspar which is the basis of most of their glazes; at temperatures over 1250°C (2282°F) it is an active flux and, by itself, melts to form a stiff, if bubbly, glass. Below this temperature it is dry and underfired. However, nepheline syenite, though similar to feldspar, melts at 1200°C (2192°F). A direct substitution of nepheline for feldspar can be tried and this will lower the firing temperature of glazes by as much as 50°C (122°F), depending on the amount present in the glaze.

Another relatively simple way to lower the effective firing temperature of the glaze is to reduce the amount of feldspar. Again, this depends on the quantity present in the recipe. Equally helpful will be reductions in the amount of flint and clay in the recipe. For example, a 5% decrease will make a significant difference to the maturing qualities of the glaze. What such adjustments do in effect is to increase the amounts of flux in the glaze and this can give good results. However, this is not always satisfactory as they lessen the amount of glass former present (the silica) and changes in the amount of clay may render the glaze difficult to handle.

In this case the fluxes present have either to be substituted for ones which are more active at the lower temperature, or a particularly active flux such as lithia has to be added. Dolomite, whiting and talc are more active at the higher and less at the lower temperatures: frits such as alkaline and borax are active over a wide range of temperatures as are materials like calcium borate frit or gerstley borate and (in small quantities) zinc oxide. Lithia, either in the form of lithium carbonate or cryolite, even in amounts below 5%, has a powerful effect in glazes; as well as effectively lowering the maturing temperature, it is a flux which gives its own quality to the glaze.

Additions of any of these materials, in amounts from 3–10%, will have the effect of lowering the temperature range of the glaze, often without changing significantly its quality. The most efficient procedure to find the correct amount is to do a line blend, with the glaze, without addition at one end, and the glaze with the added flux of, say, 20%. The range of possibilities will then be found.

Glazes for intermediate firings need not be complicated. A blend of almost any clay and any borax or alkaline frit will give simple, workable and attractive glazes. For instance, 50% red clay and 50% borax frit will give a mottled brown glaze at 1200°C (2192°F), but other clays and other sorts of frits can be tried.

Lead, a traditional earthenware glaze flux, is one which can be used at around 1200°C (2192°F). At this temperature it begins to volatilize, so its use is limited, but it still serves as an active and powerful flux adding its own qualities and affecting colour in its unique way.

While there has been much public and private concern about the use of lead in glazes it is perfectly safe in use provided the potter understands the theory. Basically, this means using lead in one of its fritted forms when it is combined with silica; these frits are all safe to handle.

Lead, which is fully discussed in Chapter 6, can be safely added to any glazes which do not come into contact with food, but such mixtures need to be properly labelled. The advantages of lead glazes are many: they melt slowly over a wide temperature range, and they give smooth deep glazes as well as particular colour responses. Cobalt becomes inky in colour, copper a rich emerald green and manganese a brown purple. Lead glazes are also excellent for the production of aventurine iron glazes.

Almost any of the effects of high temperature firings in the electric kilns can be obtained at medium temperatures without loss of quality, and this includes iron tenmokus (with the use of a borax frit), crystalline glazes as well as matt white magnesium glazes.

12 Raw glazing

The term 'raw glaze' requires definition; to some potters, particularly in the U.S.A., and in the pottery industry, it refers to a glaze made up of raw, that is, non-fritted materials. Such a glaze may still be called raw even though some fritted materials are included. If all the ingredients in the glaze have been fritted together this is called a fully fritted glaze. Essentially, it is a term handed on to us from the ceramic industry where most glazes are prepared by fritting and grinding before being applied onto the pots. Such a process helps to eliminate some glaze faults and to achieve regular predictable results. Few studio potters require, or desire, this degree of reliability, and very few have the facilities for fritting their own glazes. In this book the term 'raw glaze' is used throughout to refer to glazes which are applied onto raw, or unfired ware, whether they contain fritted or non-fritted material; the term 'raw glazing' describes the process of preparing, mixing, applying and firing the raw glazed ware.

The separation of the firing processes into biscuit and glaze was first used extensively by maiolica potters in Spain and Italy. They found they could not apply the liquid tin glaze evenly and decorate it on unfired pots. Before then pots produced in the U.K. (and in the U.S.A.) were raw glazed. That is, the glaze was applied either in a dry form, as a dust, or as a liquid slop to the pot when it was leather hard or bone dry, and before it was fired. Only one firing was needed to mature both body and glaze. With the advent of more sophisticated shapes and with the greater refinement of clay bodies, the common practice of two firings became widespread. However, with the need for economies both in the speed of working and in the cost of kiln firing, more and more potters are returning to raw glazing as a workable and efficient method of production.

Mediaeval earthenwares were glazed by dusting a raw and fairly crude lead ore onto the sloping surface of the pots whilst they were leather hard. The results, though attractive, have little to offer us except for the idea of using a soft wood ash which can be dusted on in much the same way. At stoneware temperatures the wood ash will fuse with the clay surface to give a mottled if sometimes slightly rough covering. In later periods glazes in liquid slip form were applied to the pots. The attractive red wares produced in North America and the slipwares of Staffordshire were glazed with a liquid mixture of lead ore and clay. Visitors to China some 200 years ago record seeing Chinese potters at Ching-tê-Chên glazing fine porcelain ware by carefully lowering them, before they had been fired, into a liquid slip glaze. Some of the delicate porcelain bowls were supported by threads of string. Today many studio potters, often working in the country with large kilns, raw glaze all their work; their whole production including the design of shapes and the formulation of clay bodies and glazes is specially designed for this process. Potters working with electric kilns and in smaller potteries have been slower to take advantage of the technique, though there are many gains to be made. The first and most important consideration is that of economy. By eliminating the biscuit firing their electricity costs are much reduced (maybe by a quarter to a third), as is kiln wear and tear. Production can be speeded up giving much greater use of capital equipment. As far as workshop production is concerned there will also be savings in shelf space, as a result of the pots moving through the system at a much quicker pace.

The technical advantages of raw glazing are also worth considering, although they are less clearly understood. By applying the liquid glaze to the clay before it has been fired the possibility of a more intimate body/glaze reaction is increased. Val Barry, a potter working at $1250°C$ ($2282°F$) with both stoneware clay and porcelain, found when she stopped biscuit firing and started raw glazing that some glazes which had been adapted for use on the raw fired pots were much richer and more interesting. The basic dolomite/feldspar/clay glaze I use in my workshop works well on both biscuit and raw clay, but the texture and quality is improved when the pots are raw glazed. On ware fired to earthenware temperatures, where the body/glaze interaction is much more limited, raw glazing should give identical results to glazing on biscuit fired wares.

Aesthetically, the process of raw glazing has other attractions. By omitting the biscuit stage you also leave out the point at which the pot is at its least interesting stage; the body, matt, absorbent and underfired, lacks both visual and tactile attractions. It is at this point that the skills of the glazer have to be at their most acute to transform this bland and ordinary object into something of interest and life. For some potters this is a daunting task. Any vision of the finished pot conceived when the form was either freshly thrown on the wheel, taken from the mould or newly handbuilt, is hard to recreate on the dull biscuit ware.

The chance therefore, of removing this stage altogether, of moving direct from clay to finished object is one which will, for many potters, aid the creative spirit. Equally satisfying can be the linking together of the making and glazing processes, with the direct effect both in construction and application which they will have on each other. Instead of being considered as two separate and relatively unrelated processes, they now have to be intimately linked together at this stage as they will become a part of one another when fired. The one existing for the other; form and surface together making the whole.

Raw glazing does present particular production problems and though these can be overcome by invention and adaption they are worth discussing in some detail. The first consideration is the technical matching of clay and glaze. Clays vary widely in strength both in their green (dry but unfired) state and in their leather hard state, and some can only be raw glazed at particular times. This will mean testing out the body you use and this is discussed later in this chapter. Finding glazes to fit unfired clays is also a question of trial and error; whether, for example, the glazes can be adapted for raw glaze application (most glazes can be modified relatively easily) or whether it will be better to devise a series of new glazes based on established raw glaze practice. These are all problems which need to be considered before any decisions are made, especially as they will involve the way the glaze is to be applied.

For most potters, however, it is not only the technical difficulties which deter them from raw glazing but the problems of handling leather hard or dry pots and applying an even coat of glaze. The practical skills involved in putting glazes onto unfired wares are far greater than those required for glazing biscuit ware. An unfired pot will absorb water from the glaze and will soften; speed is essential and the pot must be handled carefully. The softening of the pots as they absorb moisture will also seek out any weaknesses incurred in throwing. Areas in which the clay has been stretched rather than thrown will tend to split, as the body is less compressed. Variations in thickness of the walls will result in different absorbtion rates which will result in uneven coatings of glaze. Very thin walls will also have a tendency to split in a spiral fashion. All the faults which are the result of bad throwing can in fact usually be avoided if the ware is biscuit fired first; raw glazing will soon pick out any weaknesses, and though a row of splitting pots can be annoying it is an excellent, if unwelcome, reminder of the need for good, even throwing.

Other disadvantages of raw glazing involve shapes; some are much easier to handle than others, especially if an even coating is needed. Control over thickness of application is less easy; even when the glaze has dried, raw glazed pots are not strong and need careful handling. Glazing mistakes are difficult and sometimes impossible to correct. The glaze cannot be washed off, nor can runs onto unglazed surfaces be easily removed. Again, careful glazing and detailed planning will avoid the need for such corrections and various methods are discussed later in this chapter.

Clay bodies for raw glazing

What makes one body suitable for raw glazing and another less so is still an area into which a great deal of research needs to be done. It depends in the main on the fineness of the particles and the density of the clay. A body which is based on fine ball clays will usually have fine particle sizes; it will tend to be plastic, to be strong when throwing, to resist the absorption of water and be slow to dry out. Such a body will also be prone to warping. These bodies, whether they are mixed in the workshop or used very much as dug, present little trouble to the raw glazer. The fine grained, highly plastic tough stoneware clays which occur in the La Borne district of France, for example, take several days to dry out and, once hard, can withstand severe knocks without breaking. They can be raw glazed at either the leather hard or dry state.

For most potters, however, the choice of bodies is between those they mix themselves from dry ingredients or those they buy ready prepared. Local clays and body mixtures need careful preparation, which in turn needs space and time. Potters firing by electrictiy tend to be makers rather than mixers, and will happily use commercially available bodies to which they can add other ingredients, or else blend various bodies together. Open bodies, made with the coarser fireclays or with additions of sand or grog, will absorb moisture much more quickly. They will usually be chosen for their fired appearance. These bodies will usually be glazed better when they are bone dry.

The stoneware body in regular use in my own workshop over the past ten years is made up from a basic commercial mixture with the addition of 10% medium size grog. It stands up reasonably well to throwing and turns and handles well. However, if there is a hint of moisture in the body after it has been glazed, then blebs or bloats appear in the body which do not disappear when it dries or when it is fired. When bone dry the body can be raw glazed without any problem. Other potters report different results with their clays; what is true for one body will not necessarily apply to another.

Glazes

To fit well, both before, during and after firing, body and glaze must expand and contract at much the same rate and to much the same extent. While most, though by no means all, glazes will stick adequately to a biscuit fired pot, making glazes adhere to a raw pot is more difficult. The chief difficulty lies in the fact that when the glaze is applied to the unfired pot, the clay absorbs moisture and expands. As glaze and body dry out, unless the contraction rates are similar, the body contracts more than the glaze and is literally pushed from the surface and flakes off. The simplest way around this problem is to add a material to the glaze which will make it expand and contract at much the same rate as the body. For some glazes, the addition of 5% bentonite to the basic glaze mixture will make it suitable for raw glazing without significantly changing its appearance. Bentonite is a fine, absorbent clay which has the equivalent effect, in terms of plasticity, of 20 times that of ball clay. Its fine particle size and its ability to absorb and hold water makes it an ideal natural plasticizer both in clay bodies and in glazes. It also has the advantage

over ball clays in that only very small percentages need be added.

In glazes which already contain clay the bentonite can be a further addition and should not upset the glaze; some potters substitute the bentonite weight for weight for clay already included in the recipe. In glazes which do not contain any clay, not only will their working qualities be very much improved by the addition of bentonite but, again, the low percentage required will make little difference to the composition. With highly specialised glazes this is of course a risk that has to be taken, and if the addition of bentonite does change the glaze in an unacceptable way then alternative methods of making it adhere to the pot can be tried. Some of these methods are discussed later in the chapter.

Many potters base their raw glazes on a high clay content and, depending on the clays that are available and the temperature at which the ware is to be fired, this can range from 90–30%. Local clays which are often rich in iron, or river muds, will on their own often give vitrified surfaces at 1250°C (2282°F). Only small additions of a fluxing agent are required to turn them into attractive, reliable glazes. Ball clays which are available from the ceramic suppliers vitrify at various temperatures and most suppliers will provide a percentage chemical analysis which will give some indication of vitrification points. Ball clays which are high in alumina will usually require higher temperatures; high silica ball clays usually work best in stoneware glazes. China clays, because of their relatively low level of plasticity, do not give glazes which can easily be applied raw. Either part, or all, of the china clay in a recipe can be substituted by ball clay, or bentonite.

Blends of different clays and frits will give simple and effective raw glazes. Frits, supplied commercially, are produced so that soluble or potentially poisonous glaze material (usually a flux) can be easily and safely incorporated into a glaze. Briefly the reasons for fritting are:

1 To make harmless any substance which can be considered a poison. The most dangerous material is lead which, in its raw (i.e. unfritted) state can be absorbed into the body through the lungs by breathing in dust, through the mouth by ingestion, and through open cuts on the hands. By heating a mixture of lead and silica until they fuse into a glass and then grinding it down to a fine powder, a safe and easily used glaze material is formed. Known as the lead silicates, they are prepared in the form of the monosilicate, sesquasilicate, or

Split lines in a raw glazed pot which can happen if the inside is not properly dry when the outside is glazed

bisilicate. Though lead, when incorporated in a silicate, is safe to handle, it must still be incorporated into a correctly balanced glaze. That is, a glaze which does not give lead release when exposed to a weak acid solution. If properly prepared, lead glazes are perfectly safe to use on pots made for domestic use, but to be sure the glazes should be tested by a reputable ceramic chemist. Glazes which are not tested or fail the test are best kept for surfaces which do not come into contact with food or drink. Most countries including the U.K. and U.S.A. have specific regulations regarding metal release from glazes.

It is worth noting here that other materials are poisonous and care should be taken in handling them. Barium, manganese, zinc, uranium, vanadium and nickel, for example, should not be ingested. Silica, in the form of flint or quartz, is also a dangerous material. When inhaled it settles in the lungs and can cause silicosis. To prevent generation of dust, flint and quartz as supplied will contain a small moisture content of about 13%.

2 Many glaze materials are soluble; they can be made insoluble by preparing them as a frit. Examples are boric oxide, soda and borax, all of which are highly soluble in water. If added to the glaze slop they would dissolve and be absorbed into the body of the pot; some would, in drying, crystallize out on the surface. This absorbtion would also upset the balance of the glaze, as a result of the soluble material being taken up more quickly by the pot.

3 To remove unwanted materials such as carbon, sulphur and fluorine from the glaze material. Such materials will normally cause the glaze to boil and bubble as they are given off.

4 Glaze materials, when prepared in a fritted form, enter more rapidly into fusion with the other materials in the glaze. A glaze in which all the glaze ingredients have been fritted together will give a smoother and more predictable result. For the studio potter such a glaze presents problems of application since, lacking plastic content, the glaze will not remain long in suspension and will settle out very quickly. When dry it will also lack strength, be dusty and will easily brush off the surface of the ware. Without the addition of a plasticizer, such as bentonite, such glazes cannot be used for raw glazing.

5 The use of frits enables specialist glazes to be made, such as those which require high levels of flux or special colours.

With their high levels of clay glazes rich in alumina have many advantages for the raw glazer. They will be relatively easy to apply as they will expand and contract with the clay and will usually give a good body/glaze fit in the fired glaze. Alumina glazes have other advantages for the production potter, for they have a wide maturing range. They start to fire slowly and do not undergo dramatic changes either by suddenly becoming runny or bubbling violently. An ideal method of glaze formulation is to blend clay with a suitable frit.

At earthenware temperatures any frit will work well when combined with almost any ball clay or any clay dug locally. A useful transparent glaze for 1050°C (1922°F) is approximately lead bisilicate 70 plus clay 30. Some potters use ball clay, others use body clay. Blends of red clay and borax frit will give attractive brown mottled glazes from 1200––1260°C (2192–2300°F), in the approximate ratio of 50–50. Small additions of iron oxide or manganese oxide will intensify the colour. Alkaline frits, rich in sodium and potassium, will also give good raw glazes, and experiments with various clays will prove worthwhile.

Applying the glaze

Unlike glazes which are applied to biscuit-fired ware, raw glazes need much more care in their handling, but once the principles of the process have been understood then suitable methods and processes can be devised. The first thing to discover is how your clay body responds to raw glaze, whether, for instance, it can be glazed at the leather hard or at the dry stage without causing bloats, blebs or deformation. Very few bodies can be glazed on both sides at once. Most pots are glazed on either the inside or the outside first, which is then allowed to dry before the others side is glazed. For some potters the rule is to glaze the inside first but others do it in the reverse order. Some forms, such as bowls, may need to be glazed on the inside before the outside is turned as when the bowl soaks up the moisture it may sag and deform. Too thick a mixture of glaze can also cause bloating or blebbing of the body.

Application of the glaze can be done by the usual methods though it is more important to ensure that the slop is properly and thoroughly mixed so all lumps are removed, as these can give an unsightly and uneven covering. It is also vital that the glaze is at the correct thickness as mistakes are very difficult to correct once the glaze has been applied. There are various ways of checking glaze thickness and most potters evolve their own method. Some can tell by feeling the glaze and by the way it adheres to the hand but it is most accurately measured by use of the pint weight. That is, one pint of glaze slop is weighed and the result is expressed in ounces. This is a measure of the density of the glaze slop; the higher the weight the denser or thicker is the glaze mixture. Once the correct weight has been established, then each succeeding batch can be checked against this. To reduce the thickness more water is added, to increase the thickness the glaze slip is allowed to settle and surplus water is removed. If there is any doubt about the pint weight the usual practice is to remove any water from the slop while the glaze is settled and before it is mixed up. If required, additional water can then be returned to the glaze until the required thickness is achieved.

If a glaze is specified for use at a particular pint weight care must be taken to determine whether the pint refers to the British (Imperial) measure or the American measure. One U.S. pint = 0.83 Imperial pint; 1 Imperial pint = 1.205 U.S. pints. Most glazes are used in the region of 29–32 oz pt, Imperial measure (roughly the thickness of single cream), which is the same density as 24.07–26.56 oz pt in the U.S.A. However, for raw glazing this is usually a little too thick and more water is required.

Pouring and swilling

This is done in the usual manner and most potters glaze the inside before the outside. Speed and rhythm of carrying out the process will be established with practice, but a smooth continuous action will work better than a jerky, hurried movement. The glazing of the insides of vessels is relatively straightforward. Less easy are the outsides. On no account must a pot be stood on its rim when glaze is poured over the outside since it is the rim which will soften first and become damaged. The pot must be held either by the foot or be supported on the inside by a suitable container. A sturdy foot ring is a great help in holding the pot for this operation.

With all raw glazing, the chief skill lies in the handling of the pot so that it does not become damaged by erosion of the edges by too much poured or swilled glaze. A suitable glaze resist applied to those areas where glaze is not required, such as foot rings, will help. Hot candle wax, which is the most efficient but messiest method, a wax water emulsion or a rubber based adhesive (Copydex) can be painted onto foot rings, lid galleries, edges of lids, etc. Any droplets of glaze which stick can then be wiped off with a sponge. Glaze which runs onto areas which need to be kept clean but which are not waxed can be removed immediately by wiping most of the wet glaze off with the finger. When the pot has dried, the rest of the glaze can be removed, as mentioned earlier, by careful light sponging or by gently rubbing with fine wire wool. This latter method does give rise to clay dust and is best kept to a minimum, and then carried out over a bowl of water into which the dust will fall. Care must be taken not to damage the surface of the clay as excessive sponging or fettling will leave a rough, unpleasant surface.

Dipping

Dipping is by far the easiest method of glazing but has a limited use for raw glazing. Very few clay bodies can be completely immersed in glaze without distorting, sagging or bloating. Once the insides have been glazed and the pot allowed to dry out, the outside can be glazed by lowering the pot into the glaze and allowing an air trap to form to keep the glaze from entering the inside.

Spraying

Spraying on the glaze will avoid any of the difficult handling problems which arise from pouring or swilling. This method, which must be done in a spray booth fitted with adequate ventilation, is discussed more fully in the chapter on glazes.

Painting

Painting raw glaze is a method which, for small areas or individual pots, has much to recommend it. Only small amounts of glaze are required and, by applying two or three coats, the thickness and evenness of the glaze layer can be controlled. Since only small amounts of water are involved, the dangers of softening and distortion are removed. One of the disadvantages of painting is the length of time the process takes. Usually, several coats are required to obtain an even covering, and these must be allowed to dry between each application. However, this technique of building up of one layer over another allows for experiments with layers of different glazes and also allows for glazes to be applied in thicker layers than by other methods.

Few glazes can, however, be painted directly on the pot without the addition of a binder to make them stick. The easiest and cheapest binders to use are the natural glues, such as gum arabic, which burn away during the firing. Gum arabic can either be bought in the form of a white powder or as brown lumps which need soaking for several hours. Both are dissolved in water and small amounts added to the glaze slop. A fairly thick glue-like mixture is produced and this is painted on the pot in even strokes. If stored the gum will start to ferment and go mouldy, especially if kept in a warm place such as by the kiln, but this will not affect the firing properties of the glaze. Alternatives to the natural gums are the recently introduced plastic based agents.

Applying glazes by painting is a particularly useful method for special effect glazes when no additions (such as bentonite or ball clay) can be made which will affect its fired qualities. A crystalline glaze which contains no plastic clay, for example, can be made to stick on the pot with gum arabic.

Potters who plan to incorporate raw glazing as a regular part of their production technique usually bear this in mind when they are designing shapes.

For instance, they avoid as far as possible making pots which cannot be held firmly at the foot. A large foot ring helps solve this problem. Teapots often present glazing difficulties; spouts may have to be glazed on the inside before they are stuck into position, and so on. An unglazed area at the bottom of the pot will provide a space where a firm grip can be made so the pot can be dipped easily. Problems may arise over glazing handles of items such as casseroles, jugs or mugs, because they are glazed on both sides. They may bloat or bleb, or may soften and distort. The answer here may be to glaze one side (say the underside) first, by painting, to allow this to dry and the paint on a coat of wax, or other glaze resister, before dipping or painting. The use of a thinner glaze mixture will also help.

Firing the ware

Raw glazed wares, as far as the firing schedule is concerned, must be treated like biscuit fired ware but packed like a glaze kiln. As no changes have yet taken place in the clay body the unwanted gases and vapours must be given time to be liberated. Suggested firing schedules are listed in the chapter on firing. As far as placing the pots in the kiln is concerned, the raw glazed ware must be packed in the same way as for a glaze firing. That is, the foot rings must be carefully kept free of glaze, as must any galleries and lid edges which are being fired in position. Any heavy runs of glaze may need to be rubbed over with the finger and any thin patches or finger marks touched up with a loaded brush, just as for any glaze firing. The arrangement of the pots on the shelves must allow space for the pots to expand, and pots cannot be packed so they touch each other.

13 A touch of genius - potters who fire with electric kilns

Despite the relatively short period in which potters have been firing pots in stoneware and porcelain at high temperatures with electric kilns, a rich variety of work has been produced. This has been achieved both in the types of ware made, which range from domestic tablewares to highly individual pieces, as well as sculptural objects of many sorts. Potters who have found themselves working with electric kilns have had to find out a great deal of information for themselves, often by trial and error, but many have happily adopted different making methods, glazes and slips to provide the effects they want. When Lucie Rie arrived in Britain at the end of 1938 from Austria the first pieces she made were medium temperature earthenware fired in an electric kiln to 1050°C (1922°F). In some kilns, thin slivers of wood or a mixture of sawdust and crushed moth balls were introduced into the placing chamber of the kiln towards the end of the firing to give a reducing atmosphere. When kilns fitted with elements which would withstand higher temperatures came onto the market ten years later she turned to stoneware, but this she fired, and still does fire, without a reducing atmosphere.

Lucie Rie was informed at the time that the elements in her kiln would fire only to 1250°C (2282°F) and this was the temperature to which she took the kiln; she still fires to the same point. Glazes which matured adequately and gave interesting results all had to be worked out; tests with recipes listed in Bernard Leach's *A Potters Book* (then recently published) failed to mature at this temperature in her kiln and experiments to adapt them as well as evolve new glazes have been going on ever since. Most of her kiln firings contain a test of some sort.

Finding a suitable clay body for the domestic ware was another problem, but a suitable commercial mixture was found. Lucie Rie found that by adding to it 10% Grolleg china clay a workable preparation was obtained which could be raw glazed without trouble. Unlike most studio

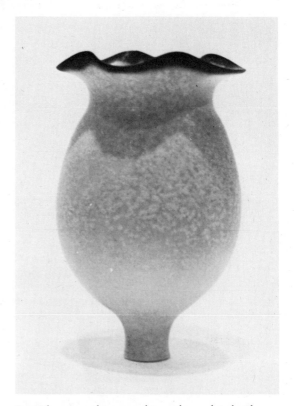

Ray Silverman; thrown and turned porcelain bottle

potters firing with electric kilns, Lucie Rie raw glazes all the work she makes, whether it is the individual pieces or the finely potted domestic tableware. Again there was little information available on how this could best be achieved, but she knew that by adding gum arabic to the glaze the slop could be painted onto the dry clay without undue bother. It is the glazing method she still uses and finds very suitable for the pots she makes. Applying glaze with a brush also has the advantage for her that accidental streaks and overlapping areas of glaze can be avoided.

Never having worked with reduction fired stoneware, Lucie Rie was not in the position of looking over her shoulder at what she should be

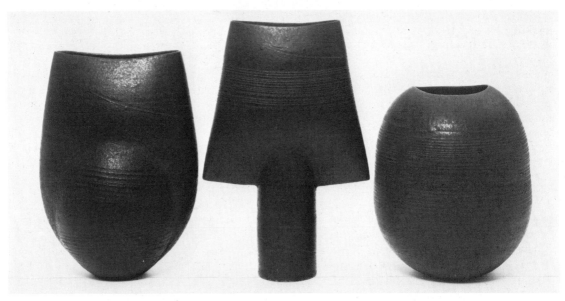

Hans Coper; three pots with incised decoration and matt black glaze; stoneware. (Courtesy Sotheby's, Belgravia)

doing, but was able to concentrate on discovering what effects could be obtained in the electric kiln. Instead of aiming for typical reduction appearances, particularly those obtained with iron oxide such as the celadons and tenmoku range of colours, she moved in the opposite direction, both in the design of tableware and in the individual pots and bowls. For the tablewares, thrown in simple shapes, she favoured a white, smooth opaque glaze containing tin oxide. This was often combined with a matt black brown pigment made up of manganese dioxide on parts of the pots which did not come into contact with food or drink, which gave the forms a sophistication and elegance and was quite unlike traditional country wares. It spoke eloquently of refinement and careful planned design. Nothing was left to chance or fortunate kiln happenings. These pots combine the finest skills of the potter with their associations of warmth and the individual hand with a bright and intelligent mind. We can respond with both the heart and the intellect.

Much the same can be said for Lucie Rie's individual pieces. Rarely is brown used; instead these are glazed with the cool, matt creams or luminous whites. Porcelains glow with egg yolk colour obtained from uranium oxide, or deep blue-greens from copper on the stoneware; glaze and body are often so devised that they react to give gritty, textured lava-like surfaces striated with subtle shades of greys, greens or pinks, with much of the colour coming from small quantities of oxides mixed into the clay. None of the work bears any relationship to the products of the reduction kiln; it is very different and by introducing the possibilities of coloured bodies which can influence the body and the glaze the range of work with which the potter can be concerned is extended. These pots are very much more to do with sculpture than with useful items (though Lucie Rie thinks all can serve as containers for such things as flowers or fruit). These pots relate to the whole history of ceramics and not just to the classical traditions of the Far East.

While some of the shapes of the pots may recall the classic forms of the Sung Dynasty of China or reflect some particular Japanese shape, the glazes and the clay bodies, though relating to geological formations, are products almost unique to the electric kiln; they are about the effects of heat rather than the results of the reduction atmosphere. Other shapes echo the strong forms of the Near East and the purity of classical Greek forms.

A potter whose work has been closely linked with that of Lucie Rie is the late Hans Coper. During the 40s and 50s he worked in Lucie Rie's studio in London, and much of their domestic ware was produced jointly and bears a double seal. As well as making these tablewares he developed his own style and later concentrated on individual pieces. Many of these were made from separate thrown components assembled into 'double-sided' pots and so on. Though definitely sculptural in feel all still remain pots and can serve as containers for cut flowers and the like. Like

Lucie Rie, Hans Coper made full use of the qualities that could be obtained in the electric kiln. He limited the effects he used to a small range of colours – black, browns and creams, and achieved these with matt vitreous slips. These were applied to the surface of the pots, rubbed, and further overlaid with other slips. Much work was done on the surfaces of the pots so that a slow build-up of texture was achieved. One of the reasons that these textured surfaces work so well is that they highlight and complement the crisp forms of the pots, which are precisely balanced. Some, set on very narrow tapering bases, recall the shapes of ritual pots from Cyprus and ancient Egypt, but happily translated into modern times.

Potters who have tackled the problems of producing domestic tablewares in electric kilns have had to consider clay, shape, glazes and decoration very much to suit the kiln. Robert and Sheila Fournier who fire to 1250–1260°C (2282–2300°F) have devised a general body based on commercially available plastic clays. In their kiln it is fired to a hard chip-resistant material which stands up well to daily use. All the shapes are turned to give neat outlines, precise footrings, and so on. A soft creamy-white glaze is used which is decorated with a delicate brushwork motif. Both Robert and Sheila Fournier have worked mainly with electric kilns and they like the control that this method of firing gives. They also like the fact that they can check temperature and the firing speed and, despite having carried out some 3000 firings, still cannot wait to unpack the kiln. In the individual work he makes, Robert Fournier likes to be as free and experimental as possible. On the 'pebble pots' and water bowls, unlikely materials such as copper shavings or iron filings are added to the body or pressed onto the surface. Sometimes two or three glazes are poured over each other so

Alex Leff; thrown stoneware platter with ash glaze and painted decoration, 40.6 cm (16 in) diameter

that rich reactions will result. This is 'putting into' the kiln rather than leaving it to the reduction atmosphere. Sheila Fournier works in a different way. For her it is the precision and sharpness of shape and decoration which is particular to the electric kiln that she likes to make full use of. Her recent work with porcelain decorated with carefully drawn incised patterns inlaid with colour requires a particularly precise glaze and firing with careful control of the temperature. In her earlier work she used the deep rich turquoise greens which copper can give in alkaline glazes in the atmosphere of the electric kiln, but her more recent work has explored the creamy white glazes on porcelain, some with neat and well placed incised and inlaid decoration.

David Morris is a potter who has produced an attractive range of tablewares by considering the qualities of oxidation firing and making full use of them. All this work is thrown using a commercially available speckle body. All larger shapes are made on batts and, after a twisted wire is passed underneath them, they are left to stiffen before being removed. This eliminates the need for lifting the soft pot, which avoids distortion, and also reduces turning to a minimum. Handles are extruded to give a ridged cross-section and, when placed on the pots, gives them a lively, skipping quality. David Morris's glaze is made up from a combination of two commercially supplied glaze mixtures, one of which contains tin. This is decorated with a flower design, stamped onto the unfired glaze surface with a piece of foam cut to the required pattern. A precise firing temperature is needed so that the speckle in the body breaks through the glaze sufficiently to give a pleasant soft texture. Too high a temperature gives too many speckles, too low and the glaze is an unrelieved white. This precision presents no problems in David Morris's 0.34 cu m (12 cu ft) electric kiln, the control of which he now fully understands. When it is packed in a particular way with the same number of kiln shelves with similar spaces between them consistent results are obtained.

Precision and control in the production of a standard range of tableware is the hallmark of Marianne de Trey's domestic pots. All are thrown on the wheel except for the plates, which are jolleyed. A matt brown slip glaze is applied to parts of the pots before they are biscuit fired, and this is complimented by a smooth white opaque glaze. The combination of warm, round forms with the brown and white glazes is both attractive and functional.

Not all potters have found working with electric

Karin Buser; press moulded lidded pot with painted and drawn decoration

kilns so amenable or satisfactory results so easy to obtain. For some it is a stepping stone, a period before the reduction kiln is acquired, though potters such as Michael Casson, Robin Welch and Janice Tchalenko produced some lively work with electric kilns. Gwyn Hanssen, who trained in a workshop which fired with large reduction kilns, found that when she began working with electric kilns the effects she liked and wanted to achieve were based on those obtained in the reducing atmosphere. She devised a dark buff/brown body and concentrated on the use of iron oxides in the glazes. A semi-matt brown and a grey/blue speckle became the preferred glazes. Though quiet, their subtle surfaces with incised 'comb' or neat fluted decoration again established the possibility of these sorts of wares being made. Over iron bearing slips they gave typical bird's-egg speckled effects.

Sally Dawson, a London based potter, aims for simplicity and clarity both in the shapes of her rounded bowls and teapots and in the glazes. In her glazes she seeks to combine quiet visual interest with a particular attractive surface quality which will enhance the forms of the work. On the porcelain wares she used a basic clear glaze which, if applied thickly, crackles to give a rich, deep

Eileen Nisbet; porcelain structure 30.5 cm (12 in) long

surface. Some of these pots are lifted from the kiln while still hot and rubbed with a mixture of iron oxide and ordinary household oil which stains the crackle. This is particularly effective on glazes lightly tinted with tiny amounts of colouring oxides. Sometimes the oxides are used directly, but with a powerful oxide like cobalt Sally Dawson uses the cobalt mix recommended by Katharine Pleydell-Bouverie. This is made up of ten parts china clay and one part cobalt well ground with a pestle and mortar.

Other potters too have found that some effects are particularly successful in the electric kiln and work well on shapes based on the classic Chinese forms. Christine Ann Richards, who makes only porcelain, uses several rich and successful glazes in this way, which include a pleasant mottled chun-type which can be coloured either with oxides or small amounts of glaze stain, and a smooth and silky matt glaze which crackles very well. This glaze she stains with Chinese ink which, she finds, is the only pigment ground sufficiently fine to stain the crackle. Recently she has produced a subtle red-green *sang de boeuf* semi-matt glaze with the use of small amounts of silicon carbide in the glaze.

Other typical oxidised effects are the soft colours of porcelain and stoneware glazes explored so well in the glazes devised by the American potter Richard Zakin. He has worked out many glazes and body recipes which will mature at medium temperatures which look and feel properly mature. Dramatic crystalline glaze effects which can be encouraged to grow in the controlled temperatures of the electric kiln have also been successfully developed by potters on both sides of the Atlantic. Glazes rich in zinc oxide, for instance, will yield large formations of zinc silicate crystals if the temperature of the kiln is held to around 1100°C (2012°F) for periods of an hour or longer. These glazes are seeded by some material such as rutile, which acts as a nucleus around which the crystals form. Any colouring oxide in the glaze is picked up by the crystals and often coloured crystals can be encouraged to form in a neutral or contrasting shaded background. Notable is the work of Phyllis Irman who has devised a range of single-fire glazes.

Glazes which have all the richness of iron bearing mixtures fired in a reduction atmosphere have been devised by Harry Horlock Stringer. Over the last few years he has worked out a series of so-called reactive glazes based on the use of a

Ruth Franklin; two handbuilt slab pots with painted
decoration based on the London Underground

slip and a transparent glaze. Originally he set out
to produce a chun, but his results led him in the
direction of iron reds and greens as well as ash-
type effects. In his glazes, which are marketed in
the U.K. by a pottery supplier, various effects
depend on the thickness of the application and on
the precise firing temperature. But, as he points
out, it is not the glaze, or glazes, which produce
pots which are interesting, it is the way in which
they are used.

Not all potters want to follow the traditions,
which many potters have established; they see
themselves and their work outside any usual
aesthetic considerations associated with either the
ceramics of the Far East or of the work of the
country potter. For these potters the electric kiln is
a method of breaking away from such traditions
for it demands a complete re-evaluation of the
work produced and the methods used.

Ruth Franklin makes pots and objects out of
porcelain which are glazed with cream coloured
shiny or matt glazes. All the pots are thrown,
turned and carved. After biscuit firing these are
decorated with underglaze colours or pencils and
incorporate such things as drawings of animals,
washing lines and televisions. In *Ceramic Review*
Ruth Franklin wrote that she uses some of her pots
as a camera for drawings of people in different
situations such as dog shows, on the London
Underground, sitting in cafes or drinking in pubs.

Recently she has started modelling flat silhouette-
like figure shapes and decorating them with details
of the character.

Alison Britton is another potter who has broken
away from the traditional household forms. On
her jug shapes, for instance, which are built up
from slabs of clay, she curves and moulds them
into twisting forms which, though they are still
jugs and can be used, are sculptural objects in their
own right. Once they are fired the forms are
decorated, either with underglaze colours or
crayons, and covered with a semi-matt glaze.
Firings are taken to 1180°C (2156°F) so that the
light, buff-coloured body is well vitrified. The
imagery Alison Britton uses on her work is rich
and varied. Some is based on mythical scenes and
characters, some shows animals, while other
decoration is much more surface patterning.

Forms which have no specific use but which still
serve as containers are typical of Jacqueline
Poncelet's work. The most recent pieces are very
concerned with surface treatment. Some have
abstract swirls and twirls or the semi-formal criss-
cross patterns of the abstract expressionist
painters. Forms, some of which are like clogs,
others like half-covered bowls, are abstract in feel.
It is, however, the bright overall colours which

Mary Rogers; stoneware 'Prow Form', 25 cm (10 in) tall

give the pieces their specific attraction and, in theory, all could be used. Even though the objects relate only obliquely to use or function, Jacqueline Poncelet still defines herself very much as a potter.

Tradition can never be totally rejected, however different the working methods or the objects produced. Methods of making, for instance, still have to be learnt and skills acquired, and often the traditional ways are the best. Potters may use the electric wheel in preference to the hard work of the kick wheel, but the actual throwing skills remain exactly the same.

Pinching or squeezing a lump of clay to make a pot is one of the simplest, and one of the most difficult methods of potting. It is one which Mary Rogers has brought to perfection. Her method is to work on several pots at once, moving from one to the other, allowing time for drying and resting of the form before more work is done squeezing it into the desired shape. Most of the shapes are based directly or indirectly on those found in nature, such as simple opening buds, rock formations or flower forms, but all are highly finished with thin-walled forms combining finesse and elegance. Glazes such as dolomite, silky-matt, creamy whites are kept plain, though some have been decorated with designs made up of tiny dots

or small strokes. Copper oxide is used which gives delicate salmon pinks or apple green colours.

Elizabeth Fritsch is a potter who uses coiling, one of the oldest, if not the oldest, methods of building pots. The asymmetrical shapes are built up coil by coil and the surface is then smoothed down with a hacksaw blade or serrated edged tool, until there is no trace of the coils and only the shape remains. Onto this is painted mixtures of various coloured slips or underglaze colours in patterns which are often based on music rhythms. No glaze is used, so both the surface of the unpainted areas and the decoration remain matt. Carefully selected colours, sometimes complementary, sometimes in slight tonal contrast, such as orange and pink and in pattern sequences which relate to the form of the pot, give these wares a superbly satisfying sculptural dimension. We can respond to all the warmth they have as pots built by hand, to their tactile quality and to their precise and logical intellectualism, the one in perfect balance with the other.

Elizabeth Fritsch uses mixtures of commercially available clays, aiming for a body which has a pleasant – though not overpowering – fired colour, as well as suitable working qualities. On some of the pots the surface is rubbed with a thin layer of manganese oxide. This has the effect of breaking through the colours with tiny specks and speckles of oxide which are picked up by the painted patterns and give soft colouring effects. Both metal oxides and underglaze colours are mixed with clay to give pigments which Elizabeth Fritsch paints onto the surface of the pots.

Oxides and body stains added to the clay to give either a muted or a brilliant range of colours can be developed to their full in the oxidised atmosphere of the electric kiln. Many potters have found delight in producing various sorts of agate wares. If the oxides are added to the basic clay body then usually only darker shades result. This technique has been used by, among others, Val Barry to produce wares which recall the strength of geological outcrops or the delicate striations of rock formations.

Other potters use the agate technique to obtain more precise effects, both in the patterns they create and in the colours used. A porcelain body or a white firing stoneware is used as a base and to this various colours are added. This can result in strong shades, particularly with browns and blues, as well as the softer pastel yellows and pinks which are usually obtained from body stain. Dorothy Feibleman has developed a particular attractive range of coloured clays which she uses on her tiny

asymmetrical forms. These she makes into thin sections and builds up shapes inside plaster of Paris or biscuit moulds. Light filigree patterns are created by carefully laying one colour next to the other. The effect is only revealed when the pot is taken from the mould and the surface gently rubbed down with fine wire wool to remove any smudged or smeared clay. No glaze is used but the pots, often fired in protective saggars, are taken to the vitrification point.

Ruth Duckworth, a potter who has a studio in Chicago, works mostly with electric kilns and makes sculptural forms from porcelain and stoneware. Simple glazes made from combinations of wood ash with either feldspar or clay enhance the form with slightly textured, semi-matt surfaces. Recently she has incorporated various coloured clays on some pots, either added onto or inlaid into the surface to great effect. Like all the most successful pots and sculptural forms, it is Ruth Duckworth's concept which is far more important than the firing method, though the need to define, simplify and control is as much a result of the oxidised firing as the positive decisions taken about the effects required.

The specific qualities of oxidised firing, such as clean, bright colours, or soft pinks and pale blues, matt pale or dark glazes, are all qualities which potters such as Gordon Baldwin and Eileen Lewenstein have developed fully. Gordon

Val Barry; slab built stoneware pots with inlaid decoration of clay of a different colour

Baldwin's sculptural forms still relate to the ceramic container but are so altered in the way they hold volume or relate to surrounding space that any possible functional qualities are secondary. Glazed with matt dolomite tin glaze "to serve as a good quality cartridge paper", this is decorated with carefully and precisely applied abstract patterns and designs, mostly derived from geometrical shapes. Use is made of soft chrome pinks, or the rich greens from copper glazes applied to the fired stoneware and refired at a lower temperature.

For Eileen Lewenstein it is the fascination of the slow build up of gentle shades of blues, greys, mauves and creams, only possible with an electric kiln, which has caught her attention. Full use of this technique has been made on simple press-mould shallow dishes. Wavy patterns, recalling the movement of the sea, have been overlapped and built up and the use of a particularly reactive glaze picks up the colour and gives an added dimension of depth. Finding out what the kiln will do and making full use of the qualities that can be obtained have been used by Eileen Lewenstein on box and vase forms. A relatively simple glaze, semi-matt, with a high calcium and clay content which will form small crystals in a slow firing, has

Dorothy Feibleman; agate ware porcelain pots

proved particularly successful. When small quantities of oxides are added to the glaze contrasting crystal and background colours are produced which, according to the position of the pot in the kiln, can vary from one side of the pot to the other.

Some decoration requires an oxidised atmosphere to bring out the subtlety of colour; enamels or on-glaze, as well as many of the underglaze colours only reveal their tones in the electric kiln. Jane Osborn-Smith's finely painted porcelain pieces rely entirely on oxidised firings. Recent work by Geoffrey Swindell on small pots uses commercially supplied lustres to obtain the effects.

Geoffrey Swindell throws his shapes in porcelain and turns them when leather hard to get the wall thinness and the precision of the shape that he requires. These are then glazed chiefly with matt white dolomite mixtures lightly sprayed with copper oxide to produce pinks and greens. Various coloured and metallic lustres are applied to the pieces when they have been glaze fired and are sprayed with spirit, which causes them to separate and break up into streaky and random patterns. When fired to a low temperature in a third firing the lustre patterns become totally

integrated into the form of the pot but give a jewel-like intensity of colour.

All the potters I have talked to while writing this book have all agreed on two points: one is that working with an electric kiln is more difficult than with a reduction kiln. The other point was that, though more difficult, it could be done. Nothing, they point out, is given by the kiln itself except the heat. With the reduction kiln, the lack of oxygen, the movement of air, even the lick of the flame, will have an effect. Yet pots from the reduction kiln can be dull and lifeless. Is this the fault of the kiln? Most studio potters brought up on an aesthetic based on reduction fired stoneware find the challenge of the electric kiln hard and apparently ungiving. Yet the criterion for a pot to be satisfying is to do with the form as a whole, in which shape, glaze and decoration feel happily part of it. For potters electric energy is comparatively new; it has only a short history and few traditions. It is a fuel of the twentieth century and offers the potter new ways of working with new effects to be discovered and used. As I hope this book shows, many potters have found ways of producing handsome and elegant work from the electric kiln which reflects both the qualities of the firing and gives ample scope for individual expression and idea.

Eric James Mellon; dish, stoneware. 'Persephone and Pluto, cat and birds.' Elm ash glaze with painted oxide decoration. 34.3 cm (13½ in) diameter

14 Glaze and slip recipes

Glazes and slips firing in the range 1200–1280°C (2192–2336°F)

(All amounts are given in parts by weight, and references are to potash feldspar, unless stated otherwise)

Clear and white glazes

Smooth semi-clear glaze   1260°C (2300°F)

Feldspar	65
Calcium borate frit	3
Whiting	25
Talc	4
Titanium dioxide	3

Works well over iron slips to give rich colours and varied effects.

Clear/green glaze   1260°C (2300°F)

Nepheline syenite	50
China clay	6
Flint	25
Whiting	5
Dolomite	14

A clear glaze with a pronounced crackle on porcelain, a semi-frosty matt glaze on stoneware. With an addition of 1.5% copper oxide, a dark green glaze with small black and gold crystals results.

Smooth White   1250–1260°C (2282–2300°F)

Potash feldspar	64
Talc	13
Dolomite	13
China clay	12
+Tin oxide	5

A smooth opaque white on stoneware and porcelain; on iron bodies it gives iron speckles.

White/cream with iron speckle   1260°C (2300°F)

Nepheline syenite	35
Dolomite	14
Whiting	7
Zinc oxide	5
China clay	22
Flint	17

A smooth semi-matt glaze with small iron speckles on stoneware. A creamy-white smooth glaze on porcelain. Good with small additions of coloured oxides.

Greens and Blues for stoneware and porcelain

Pale green crackle, porcelain   1260°C (2300°F)

Soda feldspar	85
Dolomite	5
Whiting	10
+Copper carbonate	0.5%

For a more subtle green substitute black pigment (0.5) for the copper. Other colouring oxides can be substituted for the copper carbonate. Colour faint on stoneware.

Porcelain celadon   1260°C (2300°F)

Cornish stone	50
China clay	5
Flint	25
Dolomite	3
Zinc oxide	2
Whiting	15
+Copper carbonate	1%

A smooth, even, shiny glaze, pale green on porcelain and stoneware. Addition of small quantities of other oxides instead of the copper will vary the colour.

Broken dark blue   1260°C (2300°F)

Calcium borate frit (gerstley borate)	45
China clay	20
Flint	35
+Cobalt oxide	1

A broken blue green black on stoneware; a runny topaz colour on porcelain.

Blue/white/cream   1260°C (2300°F)

Talc	12
Whiting	20
Feldspar	32
China clay	16
Flint	20
+Rutile	8

Rich, shiny smooth glaze, runny especially on porcelain; mottled blue, white cream. An addition of 5% flint makes a more stable glaze.

Celadon porcelain glaze   1260°C (2300°F)

Soda feldspar	45
Wollastonite	18
China clay	18
Flint	9
Calcium borate frit	9
+Copper carbonate	0.5
Red iron oxide	0.5

A matt cream cream glaze with iron speckles on porcelain.

Smooth blue/green/grey   1250°C (2282°F)

Barium carbonate	4
Calcium borate frit (gerstley borate)	12
Whiting	2
Feldspar	47
China clay	7
Flint	25
Zinc oxide	3
+Manganese carbonate	2%
Red iron oxide	2%
Rutile	2%

A smooth, mottled glaze coloured blue/green-/grey; runny on porcelain, more even on stoneware.

Turquoise   1200–1250°C (2192–2282°F)

Feldspar	52
Whiting	8
Zinc oxide	8
Barium carbonate	21
Ball clay	8
Bentonite	4
+Rutile	1.5%
Copper carbonate	0.75%

A smooth, semi-matt glaze with subdued highlights; an attractive mottled green turquoise.

Special Glazes

Runny crystal glaze   1260°C (2300°F)

Alkaline frit	45
China clay	5
Flint	18
Zinc oxide	24
Titanium dioxide	8

Very runny. Cream white background with pale silver-green crystals with pink edges. Can be coloured with oxides.

Ash type   1220–1240°C (2228–2264°F)

Calcium borate frit (gerstley borate)	16
Barium carbonate	25
Lithium carbonate	4
Whiting	14
Red clay	27
Flint	9
Feldspar	5

A broken, runny ash-type surface but which does overfire very easily and become too runny. Effects may vary according to the body on which it is put.

Cloudy red   1260°C (2300°F)

Soda feldspar	56
Whiting	13
Talc	5
Calcium borate frit (gerstley borate)	2
China clay	6
Flint	18
+Tin oxide	0.5%
Copper carbonate	0.5%
Silicon carbide (fine)	0.5%

A frosty, stiff, red/grey glaze on porcelain and stoneware.

Crystalline glaze   1260°C (2300°F)

Alkaline frit	46
China clay	4
Flint	18
Zinc oxide	24
Titanium dioxide	8

A runny glaze which, on porcelain, gives a pale cream coloured background with darker crystal formation, without any soak period. A more yellow glaze on stoneware.

White textured glaze   1260°C (2300°F)

Alkaline frit	12
Lithium carbonate	6
Flint	60
China clay	22

A textured, volcanic-type white glaze on stoneware and porcelain. Apply thickly for best results. With an addition of 4% tin oxide a whiter glaze results with orange flashings.

Dry textured glaze   1260°C (2300°F)

Barium carbonate	20
Dolomite	20
Soda feldspar	35
China clay	15
Flint	10

A dry, opaque white glaze with a textured surface on stoneware, smooth on porcelain. With an addition of cobalt oxide 0.5% and red iron oxide 1% a speckled blue/yellow smooth glaze results on porcelain, a dry blue purple on stoneware.

Red reduction   1260°C (2300°F)

Soda feldspar	44
Calcium borate frit (gerstley borate)	10
Whiting	15
China clay	5
Flint	26
+Tin oxide	1%
Copper carbonate	0.5%
Silicon carbide	0.5%

A smooth firing glaze which gives deep red colours and blue chun effects where thick. Can run if too thickly applied; colour can disappear if too thin.

Brown/black iron glazes

Hare's fur type   1220/1240°C (2228–2264°F)

Basalt	70
Whiting	5
Flint	15
Red clay	10

A runny, streaky glaze on stoneware which should not be overfired. Very runny on porcelain.

Bone ash red glaze   1260°C (2300°F)

Feldspar	45
Whiting	6
Dolomite	10
Bone ash	10
Flint	22
China clay	7

With an addition of 4% red iron oxide a speckled yellow cream bronze glaze results; with 8% red iron oxide a richly coloured, even red-brown glaze is obtained.

Red brown   1250/1260°C (2282–2300°F)

Soda feldspar	25
Flint	28
Whiting	10
Dolomite	10
China clay	20
Bone ash	7
+Red iron oxide	12%

A smooth, semi-matt red-brown glaze. Good for functional ware.

Hare's fur type, speckled brown   1260°C (2300°F)

Feldspar	5
Whiting	4
Basalt	65
Flint	11
Red clay	15
+Red iron oxide	4

A semi-matt, red-brown speckled glaze on stoneware and porcelain.

Textured black brown   1260°C (2300°F)

Basalt	50
Feldspar	34
Fremington clay (Albany slip)	12
Borax frit	4
+Red iron oxide	6

A smooth, semi-matt, black glaze with brown/gold specks on porcelain and stoneware.

Brown/red   1260°C (2300°F)

Ball clay	10
China clay	5
Whiting	14
Wollastonite	19
Flint	20
Feldspar	32
+Red iron oxide	8

A smooth, shiny brown-yellow glaze, darker on stoneware, brighter on porcelain.

Satin matt red mottled yellow   1260°C (2300°F)

Potash feldspar	55
Zinc oxide	8
Barium carbonate	20

Whiting	12
China clay	5
+Red iron oxide	8

A smooth surfaced matt glaze which is a pleasant mottled red/brown/yellow on stoneware.

Black satin flecked glaze   1260°C (2300°F)

Basalt	80
Feldspar	5
Fremington clay (Albany slip)	10
Rutile	5
+Red iron oxide	8

A smooth, semi-matt black glaze with golden specks on stoneware and porcelain.

Smooth semi-matt black   1260°C (2300°F)

China clay	14
Feldspar	65
Wollastonite	4
Whiting	4
Calcium borate frit (gerstley borate)	9
Flint	4
+Copper carbonate	3
Manganese carbonate	4
Cobalt oxide	2
Nickel oxide	1

A semi-matt black glaze with a slight green cast which sometimes breaks with gold specks on stoneware and porcelain.

Streaky brown   1260°C (2300°F)

Basalt	96
Bentonite	4

A smooth, subdued brown glaze on stoneware. More runny on porcelain.

Rust red ash slip glaze   1260°C (2300°F)

Ball clay	50
Mixed wood ash	25
Whiting	10
Feldspar	15
+Red iron oxide	7

A smooth rust red glaze which breaks well on porcelain. The high content of plastic clay can make this glaze difficult to apply on biscuit fired pots.

Slips

S1 Black brown slip

China clay	28
Ball clay	28
Flint	28
Red iron oxide	10
Crocus martis	6

S2 Black slip

Red clay	60
Yellow ochre	30
Red iron oxide	10

S3 Blue black slip

Stoneware body	80
Red iron oxide	12
Manganese oxide	5
Cobalt oxide	3

S4 White slip

Ball clay	40
China clay	60

Glaze supplied by Lucie Rie   1250°C (2282°F) cone 8

Feldspar	58
Whiting	8
China clay	14
Flint	8
Zinc oxide	10

This is a reliable semi-transparent base glaze useful for added oxides. Lucie Rie fires very slowly. She suggests that experiments with different sorts of feldspar are worth trying. Additions of 5–10% tin oxide give opaque whites, 2% copper oxide gives a rich green and 2% tin oxide and 2% zinc oxide gives a pale creamy white.

Glazes supplied by Sarah Bodine   Orton cone 6

Floating blue

Nepheline syenite	47
Calcium borate frit (gerstley borate)	27
China clay	6
+Red iron oxide	2%
Cobalt oxide	1%
Dark rutile	4%

A variable, shiny, rich blue glaze; a thin application gives a darker blue, when thicker, a lighter blue. Holds to throwing marks if well defined.

Randy's red

Flint	30
China clay	5
Soda feldspar	20
Talc	14
Calcium borate frit (gerstley borate)	31
+Red iron oxide	15%

A rich, almost ox blood colour if applied relatively thickly and fired to exactly the right temperature.

Hatch base matt
Potash feldspar	40
Zinc oxide	15
China clay	20
Whiting	25

A very even matt when well applied. Below cone 6 can be dry and scaly. The success of this glaze depends very much on the clay body.

Colour additions
Granular manganese 1–2% ⎫ speckled off-white
Cobalt oxide 0.8% ⎬ light blue
Rutile 3.5% ⎭ with flecks
Copper carbonate 3% ⎫ green
Nickel oxide 1% ⎭
Red iron oxide 2% yellow with small, lighter flecks

Glazes supplied by Alex Leff (U.K. materials in brackets)

Y Blue Orton cone 9
Barium carbonate	27
Nepheline syenite	57
Flint	7
Lithium carbonate	2
E.P.K. (China clay)	7
+Copper carbonate	4%

Stone matt glaze with beautiful surface. Brilliant turquoise colour.

Plum red Orton cone 8–9
Flint	30
E.P.K. (China clay)	5
Cornwall stone (Cornish stone)	20
Talc	14
Calcium borate frit (gerstley borate)	31
+Red iron oxide	15%

Dark red satin. Silver and light-red crystal surface.

Black Oil Spot Orton cone 8–9
Albany slip (Fremington red clay)	75
Nepheline syenite	15
Spodumene	10
+Red iron oxide	2%
Cobalt oxide	2%

Lustrous, deep black and silver oil spots. Very

good on porcelain and light bodies. Also works at cone 7.

Ash No. 6 Orton cone 8–9
Cornwall stone (Cornish stone)	42
Mixed Wood ash	42
Volcanic ash	16

Waxy cream colour with speckled surface.

White Orton cone 8–9
Potash feldspar	37
Calcium borate frit (gerstley borate)	7
Dolomite	6
Talc	13
China clay	8
Flint	21
Zinc oxide	8

At cone 8 this is a veil-like translucent white. At cone 9 it becomes opalescent, streaky and transparent at the edges. Smooth, very good on porcelain.

Colour additions
Red iron oxide	5% tobacco brown
Nickel oxide	3% soft green
Cobalt carbonate	0.25% lavender blue

Orange Orton cone 8–9
Potash feldspar	43
Whiting	19
Cornwall stone (Cornish stone)	24
China clay	11
Zinc oxide	3
+Red iron oxide	4%
Titanium oxide	8%

Mottled cream brown breaking to blue satin matt.

Glazes supplied by John Loree   Orton cone 6–7

These glazes were originally designed for Orton cone 6, but the glazes proved richer, more varied and consistently more interesting at cone 7. They were tried on many clay bodies, from pseudo-porcelains to dark bodies containing a great deal of earthenware clays. John Loree found that the best browns and rusts and oranges from bodies which contained healthy amounts of earthenware clay gave the more interesting results; also the white bodies. What he found least interesting were stoneware bodies pale yellowish in colour.

Slip

China clay	25
Ball clay	25
Flint	20
Nepheline syenite	15
Borax frit	15

Colour additions

'Ultrox' (or zirconium silicate)	10% white
Black stain	8% black
Yellow stain	10% yellow
Red Iron	5% brown
Cobalt oxide	2% blue
Copper oxide	5% green
Deep crimson stain	6% pink

6/7 C

Ball clay	22.2
Nepheline syenite	22.2
Bone ash	16.6
Magnesium carbonate	11.1
Talc	11.1
Wollastonite	5.6
Flint	5.6
Lepidolite	5.6

Opaque, soft-shine (lost with some colour combinations). Yellowish cast; subtle colour combinations, taking oxide decorations very nicely.

Colour additions

C-1: 1% copper oxide, $\frac{1}{2}$% nickel oxide

C-2: $\frac{2}{3}$% cobalt oxide, 2% granular ilmenite

C-3: 4% red iron oxide, 2% yellow ochre

C-4: 1% nickel oxide, $\frac{1}{8}$% cobalt oxide

C-5: 4% manganese dioxide, 2% rutile

C-6: 6% praeseodymium zirconium yellow stain, 1% rutile

C-7: 1% chrome oxide, 2% yellow iron oxide

C-8: 7% red iron oxide, 4% rutile

6/7 F

Ball clay	21.0
Nepheline syenite	21.1
Bone ash	15.8
Talc	26.3
Wollastonite	5.3
Flint	5.3
Lepidolite	5.3

Similar but different from the C. A much easier glaze – physically – because there is no light, fluffy and awkward magnesium carbonate to handle. Opaque, shinier than C, yellowish cast to the base.

Colour additions

1% copper oxide, $\frac{1}{2}$% granular iron oxide

2% yellow iron, 2% rutile

$\frac{1}{4}$% cobalt oxide, $\frac{1}{2}$% nickel oxide

3% manganese dioxide, 1% granular manganese

5% rutile, 1% copper oxide

Superglaze (from Wayne State University)

Georgia kaolin (China clay)	9.9
Flint	18.2
'Ultrox' (Zirconium silicate)	17.3
Zinc oxide	15.8
Lithium carbonate	8.5
Nepheline syenite	15.0
Whiting	15.3

A very fine, strong white glaze, with a soft sheen. (In some colour combinations one gets the effect of a lustre.) Has a slight crystalline cast. Quite opaque.

Colour additions

$\frac{1}{2}$% chrome oxide, $1\frac{1}{2}$% copper oxide
$1\frac{1}{2}$% granular ilmenite

$\frac{3}{4}$% copper oxide, $\frac{1}{6}$% cobalt oxide
$\frac{1}{2}$% granular manganese

2% rutile, 1% titanium dioxide, $\frac{1}{2}$% granular manganese, 2% granular ilmenite (one of the best.)

$\frac{1}{3}$% chrome oxide, $\frac{1}{3}$% cobalt oxide, 1% granular ilmenite (greener: more chrome; bluer: more cobalt.)

4% yellow iron oxide, $1\frac{1}{2}$% rutile, 1% granular iron, $\frac{1}{2}$% granular manganese

Super-dry matt: Li

Nepheline syenite	59.6
Barium carbonate	21.1
Calcined kaolin (molochite)	7.7
Flint	5.8
Lithium carbonate	5.8

Best sprayed; thickness results in flaws, notably bubbling, some crawling. Needs improvement, but is worth it, for the colour response is *very* intense, and it takes surface decoration handsomely, with patterns created by iron, copper, rutile, etc. standing out with great clarity. Interesting edges typical of alkaline glazes. Intense colour reactions from small percentages of copper, cobalt, chrome, etc. At its present stage, best for non-functional pieces.

Loree clear (This glaze is measured by volume)
4 parts potash feldspar
4 parts whiting
3 parts flint
3 parts georgia kaolin (China clay)
2 parts gerstley borate (calcium borate frit)

Consistently successful; I've used it at many different temperatures, both oxidation and reduction. Clearer and glassier the higher the temperature. This glaze will fire to cone 8.

Colour additions
Capable of *many* colour combinations. A few of the best:
5% red iron, 5% yellow iron

12% 'Ultrox' (Zirconium silicate). Strong opaque, slight shine, white.

2% cobalt oxide, 2% chrome oxide, 3% black iron oxide, 3% copper oxide. Handsome silvery black.

Decorating oxide mixtures: For brush decorating (or spraying) on top of glazes:
1. Blue-black: Roughly, equal parts of Loree Clear, Albany clay, and 4 parts black iron oxide, 1 part cobalt oxide. At this point it should be a barely liquid sluggish mass; add enough water to get brushable consistency. He found that it was necessary to start in with a clear glaze in order to fuse slightly the oxides to the previously applied glaze, and not have them sit harshly on the surface of the fired piece.
2. Dark brown: Clear, Albany clay, red iron oxide. Add water.
3. Tan-gold: extra Clear, a small amount of yellow ochre, rutile. The refractory nature of the rutile requires greater amounts of Clear – to fuse it. One of the best. Changes the most heavily dependent for its effect on the colour of glaze underneath; can be almost white to yellow to orange – to tomato-red (on chromium glazes). Crystallized haloes often form. Never moves, stays in place.

There are no guarantees for the following formulae but they proved interesting with small amounts of cobalt, iron, copper and rutile in them.

Feldspar	50	Superb matt, great
Whiting	22	break-up,
Georgia kaolin (China clay)	13	excellent colours.
Zinc oxide	9	
Flint	6	
Bentonite	2	

Feldspar	49	Very, very dry;
Whiting	26	flat colour.
Georgia kaolin (China clay)	18	
Spodumene	7	

Feldspar	39	For insides only;
Zinc oxide	25	running, but
Whiting	16	lovely crystals.
Flint	14	
Georgia kaolin (China clay)	7	

Nepheline syenite	43	Dry but varied and
Georgia kaolin (China clay)	16	interesting; over-laps attractive;
Flint	14	good colour
Barium carbonate	11	responses.
Whiting	10	
Zinc oxide	4	
Talc	2	

Soda feldspar	63.1	Silky matt; great
Whiting	12.7	colour, especially
Barium carbonate	10.0	gorgeous cobalt
Flint	7.4	blue.
Georgia kaolin (China clay)	6.8	

John Loree   Orton cone 8

Talc matt

D.F. Stone (Cornish stone)	12.7
Colemanite (Calcium borate frit)	1.8
Nepheline syenite	1.8
Zinc oxide	4.5
Calcined kaolin (molochite)	6.8
Georgia kaolin (China clay)	6.8
Whiting	17.3
Custer feldspar	39.2
Talc	9.1

Matt, with sometimes a hint of soft shine on a second application. The colours are very subtle, greyed, but not dull. It takes decoration superbly. Rutile mixtures produce haloed crystalline blooms on the surface; copper, iron, cobalt-rutile mixtures are all good.

Colour additions
2% nickel oxide, 2% red iron oxide, $\frac{1}{2}$% granular manganese

2% nickel oxide, $2\frac{1}{2}$% red iron oxide, $\frac{1}{4}$% cobalt oxide, $\frac{1}{2}$% granular manganese

2% nickel oxide, 4% black iron, $\frac{1}{5}$% cobalt oxide, $\frac{1}{2}$% granular manganese

2% nickel oxide, $\frac{1}{5}$% cobalt oxide, 1% granular manganese. (This, and the first colour, are his favourites in this glaze)

2% nickel oxide, 2% manganese dioxide, 2% granular ilmenite, $\frac{1}{2}$% granular manganese

Dolomite matt

D.F. Stone (Cornish stone)	12.7
Colemanite (calcium borate frit)	1.8
Nepheline syenite	1.8
Zinc oxide	4.5
Calcined kaolin (China clay)	6.8
Georgia kaolin (China clay)	6.8
Whiting	17.3
Custer feldspar	39.2
Dolomite	9.1

A close relative of the Talc Matt, but quite different. Much more matt, more textural, dryer to the touch.

Colour additions

$2\frac{1}{2}$% red iron, $\frac{1}{2}$% cobalt oxide, $\frac{1}{4}$% granular manganese

5% red iron, $\frac{1}{2}$% cobalt oxide, $\frac{1}{4}$% granular manganese

6% red iron, 4% rutile, 1% granular ilmenite

$\frac{3}{4}$% copper oxide, $\frac{1}{5}$% cobalt oxide, 2% granular ilmenite

$1\frac{1}{2}$% nickel oxide, $1-\frac{3}{4}$% copper oxide, $\frac{1}{2}$% granular manganese

$\frac{1}{2}$% copper oxide, $\frac{1}{2}$% granular manganese

Barium matt

D.F. Stone (Cornish stone)	12.7
Colemanite (calcium borate frit)	1.8
Nepheline syenite	1.8
Zinc oxide	4.5
Calcined kaolin (molochite)	6.8
Georgia kaolin (China clay)	6.8
Whiting	17.3
Custer feldspar	39.2
Barium carbonate	9.1

A close relative of the Talc and Dolomite matts, it was developed later, and yields a much brighter, lighter more vivid palette of colours, including peach, yellow, orange, bright blues and greens. It is best applied very thinly. All three of these closely related glazes have a tendency to form cracks on second applications, so speed in applying is important. However, since they are all at their best thin, it is another reason for not getting the glaze on too thickly. Calcining the zinc helps.

Some colour additions

$1\frac{1}{2}$% red iron oxide, $\frac{1}{5}$% cobalt oxide, 1% granular ilmenite

2% nickel oxide, $\frac{1}{5}$% cobalt oxide, $\frac{1}{2}$% granular manganese

$1\frac{1}{2}$% nickel oxide, $\frac{1}{8}$% cobalt oxide, 2% granular ilmenite

$1\frac{1}{2}$% yellow ochre, $\frac{1}{4}$% chrome oxide, 1% granular ilmenite, $\frac{1}{4}$% granular manganese

$\frac{1}{4}$% copper oxide, $\frac{1}{5}$% chrome oxide, $1\frac{1}{4}$% granular ilmenite

$\frac{1}{4}$% copper oxide, $\frac{1}{6}$% cobalt oxide, $\frac{1}{4}$% granular manganese

2% iron chromate, $\frac{1}{4}$% granular manganese, 1% granular ilmenite

$1\frac{1}{2}$% nickel oxide, $\frac{1}{5}$% cobalt, $2\frac{1}{2}$% black iron oxide

$1\frac{1}{5}$% copper, $\frac{1}{6}$% cobalt, $\frac{1}{4}$% chrome, 1% granular ilmenite

$1\frac{3}{4}$% nickel, $\frac{1}{6}$% cobalt, $\frac{1}{2}$% granular manganese, $\frac{3}{4}$% granular ilmenite

26–9 dry white matt

4 parts nepheline syenite
2 parts dolomite
$1\frac{1}{2}$ parts China clay
1 part flint
$\frac{1}{4}$ part spodumene

A stark white, very dry looking matt. It does unusual things with decorating oxides, changing normal hues you would expect from cobalt, rutile. It is ultra-sensitive to copper mixtures, sometimes producing strange orange-pinks on very thin applications.

Satin white

6 parts feldspar
4 parts flint
3 parts whiting
2 parts China clay
2 parts talc
1 part spodumene

A favourite white glaze; its nicest advantage is that it looks identical on stonewares and porcelains. Colour trials proved disappointing. Oxide decorations on top of glaze work very well.

Barium 29

5 parts barium carbonate
4 parts whiting
4 parts custer feldspar
3 parts calcined kaolin (China clay)
2 parts flint
1 part Georgia kaolin (China clay)

Very intense jewel-like colours, probably best on porcelains. Any texture (such as a throwing ridge) will actively show in the glaze texture and patterning.

Colour additions

5% jet black stain

5% pink stain

8% red iron oxide

$\frac{1}{2}$% chrome oxide, 2% yellow ochre

2% nickel oxide, 2% red iron oxide

2% copper oxide

$\frac{2}{3}$% copper oxide, $\frac{1}{3}$% cobalt (brilliant blue)

3% red iron, $\frac{1}{4}$% cobalt oxide, 2% granular ilmenite

White decorator

3 parts feldspar
2 parts flint
1 part whiting
1 part dolomite
1 part Georgia kaolin (China clay)

Immature by itself, but great for on-glaze decoration, especially on the shiny glazes, where it will do some fusing (depending on the under glaze, but will still register strong white effects).

John Loree: Orton cone 9
(U.K. materials in brackets)

18–6 White Matt

China clay	25
Feldspar	25
Dolomite	25
Nepheline syenite	10
Flint	7
Whiting	4
Colemanite (calcium borate frit)	4

Slip glaze
(This glaze is particularly effective under glazes, particularly the many coloured ones developed in the C-10 Matt glaze.)

Barnard clay (Fremington red clay)	86
Whiting	14

Colour additions

SG-2	red iron oxide	5%
SG-4	cobalt oxide	2%
SG-5	cobalt oxide	1%
	black iron oxide	4%
SG-6	chrome oxide	1%
	cobalt oxide	0.5%
SG-7	yellow ochre	10%

LY-H Matt

Feldspar	47
Barium carbonate	24
Flint	5
Dolomite	10.5
Ball clay	5
Lithium carbonate	0.5
Bentonite	2
Zircon Opacifier (such as 'Zircopox')	4
Super pax Ultrox	6

Colour additions

Copper carbonate	1.5%
Granular manganese	0.25%
Red iron oxide	8%
Rutile	4%
Copper carbonate	2%
Rutile	3%
Red iron oxide	6%
Copper carbonate	2.5%
Cobalt oxide	0.2%
Granular manganese	0.2%
Cobalt oxide	0.5%
Granular ilmenite	2%

C-10 Matt

Feldspar	43
Cornwall stone (Cornish stone)	14
Whiting	19
China clay	15
Zinc oxide	5
Nepheline syenite	2
Colemanite (calcium borate frit)	2

Colour additions

Cobalt oxide	0.5%
Yellow ochre	2%
Granular ilmenite	1%
Red iron oxide	2.5%
Granular ilmenite	1%
Granular manganese	0.25%
Copper carbonate	0.75%
Granular manganese	0.25%

Cobalt oxide	0.50%
Red iron oxide	2%
Rutile	8%
Red iron oxide	3%
Granular manganese	0.25%
Chrome oxide	0.50%
Copper carbonate	0.50%
Granular ilmenite	1%
Cobalt oxide	0.25%
Copper oxide	0.25%
Cobalt oxide	0.20%
Nickel oxide	2%
Granular ilmenite	3%
Rutile	1%
Granular manganese	0.25%

Stephenson blue-green matt

Nepheline syenite	45
Barium carbonate	20
Flint	12
China clay	10
Dolomite	8
Whiting	5
+ Copper carbonate	2

Sedoestrom Matt

Nepheline syenite	56.6
Whiting	18.8
Zinc oxide	5.1
China clay	9.5
Flint	9.5

Glazes supplied by Debbie Shapiro

Blue reduction effect 1260°C (2300°F)

Soda feldspar	80
Whiting	10
Zinc oxide	5
Bone ash	5
+ Red iron oxide	1
Silicon carbide	2

Pale blue/grey, smooth china-type glaze on porcelain; a darker blue/grey on stoneware.

Sung Yellow   Orton cone 6–8

Cornwall stone (Cornish stone)	73
Whiting	16
Nepheline syenite	4
Gerstley borate (calcium borate frit)	7
+ Vanadium yellow stain	4
or Uranium oxide	4

This is an excellent base glaze; at cone 6 it crazes slightly, but is smooth at cone 8 and slightly flinty.

KM 46   Orton cone 7–8

Nepheline syenite	43
Whiting	16.5
Bone ash	7
Talc	5
China clay	12.5
Flint	10.5
Gerstley borate (calcium borate frit)	5.5
+ Yellow iron oxide	1.10
Copper carbonate	0.4

A cream matt glaze with a slight turquoise tone.

D.S. III   Orton cone 7–9

Feldspar	21
Wollastonite	31
Whiting	13
Cornwall stone (Cornish stone)	22
Tennessee ball clay (or O.M.E. Kentucky clay)	10
Bentonite	3

A satin matt with a large craze on porcelain.

Tenmoku DS II   Orton cone 6–8

Feldspar	27
Flint	24
Wollastonite	22
Whiting	15
Ball clay	12
+ Red iron oxide	9
Calcined Albany clay (calcined Fremington clay)	0.5

Celadon   Orton cone 7–9 (Porcelain)

Soda feldspar	50
Wollastonite	20
China clay	10
Flint	10
Gerstley borate (calcium borate frit)	10
+ Copper carbonate	0.5%
Black pigment	0.2%

Black pigment

Cobalt carbonate	31
Chrome oxide	7
Red iron oxide	37
Manganese dioxide	12
Nickel oxide	13

Black gloss glaze   Orton cone 6–8

Feldspar	77
China clay	5
Wollastonite	5
Whiting	4
Gerstley borate (calcium borate frit)	9
+ Copper carbonate	3%

Manganese carbonate	4%
Cobalt oxide	2%
Nickel oxide	1%

A slightly fluid glaze at cone 8 on porcelain; excellent on both stoneware and porcelain.

Useful information

Ceramic Materials

Name	Chemical formula	Molecular weight (MW)	Oxides entering fusion
Albite (soda feldspar)	$Na_2O.Al_2O_3.6SiO_2$	524·6	Na_2O Al_2O_3 SiO_2
Alumina	Al_2O_3	102·0	Al_2O_3
Alumina hydrate	$Al(OH)_3$	Eq.wt. 78	Al_2O_3
Amblygonite	$Li.AlF.PO_4$	147·9	Li_2O Al_2O_3 P_2O_5
Anorthite (lime feldspar)	$CaO.Al_2O_3.2SiO_2$	278·3	CaO Al_2O_3 SiO_2
Anorthoclase (mixed feldspar)	$NaKO.Al_2O_3.6SiO_2$	540·7	$NaKO$ Al_2O_3 SiO_2
Antimonate of lead	$Pb_3(SbO_4)_2$	993·2	PbO Sb_2O_3
Antimony oxide	Sb_2O_3	291·6	Sb_2O_3
Baria (baryta)	BaO	153·3	BaO
Barium carbonate (Witherite)	$BaCO_3$	197·4	BaO
Bauxite	$Al_2O_3.2H_2O$	138·0	Al_2O_3
Bentonite	$Al_2O_3.4SiO_2.H_2O$	360·4	Al_2O_3 SiO_2
Bone ash	$Ca_3(PO_4)_2$ or $3CaO.P_2O_5$	310·3 Eq.wt. 103	CaO P_2O_5
Borax	$Na_2O.2B_2O_3.10H_2O$	381·2	Na_2O B_2O_3
Boric acid	$B_2O_3.3H_2O$	61·8	B_2O_3
Boric oxide	B_2O_3	69.6	B_2O_3
Boro-calcite	$CaO.2B_2O_3.6H_2O$	304	CaO B_2O_3
Calcia	CaO	56·1	CaO
Calcite	$CaCO_3$	100·1	CaO
Calcium borate	$Ca(BO_2)_2$	125·7	CaO B_2O_3
Calcium carbonate (Whiting)	$CaCO_3$	100·1	CaO
Calcium chloride	$CaCl_2$	111·1	CaO
Calcium phosphate	$Ca_3(PO_4)_2$	310·3	CaO P_2O_5
Calcium sulphate	$CaSO_4$	136·2	CaO
Chalk	$CaCO_3$	100·1	CaO
China clay	$Al_2O_3.2SiO_2.2H_2O$	258·2	Al_2O_3 SiO_2

Name	Chemical formula	Molecular weight (MW)	Oxides entering fusion
Chromite	$FeO.Cr_2O_3$	223·8	Fe_2O_3 Cr_2O_3
Chromium oxide	Cr_2O_3	152·0	Cr_2O_3
Cobalt carbonate	$CoCO_3$	118·9	CoO
Cobalt oxide	CoO	74·9	CoO
Colemanite	$2CaO.3B_2O_3.5H_2O$	411·0 Eq.wt. 206	CaO B_2O_3
Copper carbonate	$CuCO_3$	123·5	CuO
Copper oxide black (cupric oxide)	CuO	79·5	CuO
Copper oxide red (cuprous oxide)	Cu_2O	143·0	CuO
Copper sulphate	$CuSO_4.5H_2O$	249·6	CuO
Cristobalite	SiO_2	60·1	SiO_2
Crocus martis	$FeSO_4$	151·9	Fe_2O_3
Cryolite	Na_3AlF_6 or $3NaF.AlF_3$	210·0 Eq.wt. 420	Na_2O Al_2O_3 F_2
Dolomite	$CaMg(CO_3)_2$ or $CaCO_3.MgCO_3$	184·4	CaO MgO
Epsom salts	$MgSO_4.7H_2O$	246·4	MgO
Feldspar lime (anorthite)	$CaO.Al_2O_3.2SiO_2$	278·3	CaO Al_2O_3 SiO_2
Feldspar mixed (anorthoclase)	$NaKO.Al_2O_3.6SiO_2$	540·7	$NaKO$ Al_2O_3 SiO_2
Feldspar potash (orthoclase)	$K_2O.Al_2O_3.6SiO_2$	556·8	K_2O Al_2O_3 SiO_2
Feldspar soda (albite)	$Na_2O.Al_2O_3.6SiO_2$	524·6	Na_2O Al_2O_3 SiO_2
Ferric oxide	Fe_2O_3	159·6	Fe_2O_3
Ferrous oxide	FeO	71·8	Fe_2O_3
Ferrous sulphate	$FeSO_4.7H_2O$	277·9	Fe_2O_3
Flint	SiO_2	60·1	SiO_2 CaO
Fluorspar	CaF_2	78·1	CaO
Galena (lead sulphide)	PbS	239·3	PbO
Gerstley borate (Ulexite)	$Na_2O.2CaO.5B_2O_3.6H_2O$	405·1	Na_2O CaO B_2O_3

Name	Chemical formula	Molecular weight (MW)	Oxides entering fusion
Haematite	Fe_2O_3	159·6	Fe_2O_3
Ilmenite	$FeO.TiO_3$	151·7	Fe_2O_3 TiO_2
Iron chromate	$FeCrO_3$	155·8	Fe_2O_3 Cr_2O_3
Iron oxide black	FeO	71·8	Fe_2O_3
Iron oxide red	Fe_2O_3	159·6	Fe_2O_3
Iron pyrites	FeS_2	120·0	Fe_2O_3
Iron spangles	Fe_3O_4	231·4	Fe_2O_3
Kaolinite	$Al_2SiO_5(OH)_4$	258·2	Al_2O_3 SiO_2
Lead bisilicate	$PbO.2SiO_2$	343·4	PbO SiO_2
Lead monosilicate	$PbO.SiO_2$	283·3	PbO SiO_2
Lead oxide red	Pb_3O_4	685·6	PbO
Lead oxide yellow (litharge)	PbO	223·2	PbO
Lead sesquisilicate	$2PbO.3SiO_2$	626·7	PbO SiO_2
Lepidolite	$Li_2F_2.Al_2O_3.3SiO_2$	334·1	Li_2O Al_2O_3 SiO_2
Limestone (Whiting)	$CaCO_3$	100·1	CaO
Lithia	Li_2O	29·8	Li_2O
Lithium carbonate	Li_2CO_3	73·8	Li_2O
Magnesia (periclase)	MgO	40·3	MgO
Magnesium carbonate (magnesite)	$MgCO_3$	84·3	MgO
Magnesium carbonate light	$3MgCO_3.Mg(OH)_2.3H_2O$	365·2	MgO
Malachite	$CuCO_3.Cu(OH)_2$	221·0	CuO
Manganese carbonate	$MnCO_3$	114·9	MnO
Manganese dioxide (pyrolusite)	MnO_2	86·9	MnO
Microcline (potash feldspar)	$K_2O.Al_2O_3.6SiO_2$	556·8	K_2O Al_2O_3 SiO_2
Mineralised stone	$K_2O.Al_2O_3.8SiO_2$	782·48	K_2O Al_2O_3 SiO_2
Mullite	$3Al_2O_3.2SiO_2$	426·2	Al_2O_3 SiO_2
Natron	$Na_2CO_3.10H_2O$	286·0	Na_2O

Name	Chemical formula	Molecular weight (MW)	Oxides entering fusion
Nepheline syenite	$K_2O.3Na_2O.4Al_2O_3.8SiO_2$	1169·0 Eq.wt. 389	K_2O Na_2O Al_2O_3 SiO_2
Nickel oxide	NiO	74·7	NiO
Petalite (lithium feldspathoid)	$Li_2O.Al_2O_3.8SiO_2$	612·6	Li_2O Al_2O_3 SiO_2
Plaster of Paris	$2CaSO_4.H_2O$	290·4	CaO
Potash	K_2O	94·2	K_2O
Potassium carbonate	K_2CO_3	138·2	K_2O
Potassium dichromate	$K_2Cr_2O_7$	294·2	K_2O Cr_2O
Potassium permanganate	$KMnO_4$	158·0	K_2O MnO
Praseodymium oxide	PrO_2	172·9	PrO_2
Quartz	SiO_2	60·1	SiO_2
Red ochre	Fe_2O_3	159·6	Fe_2O_3
Rutile	TiO_2	79·9	TiO_2
Silica	SiO_2	60·1	SiO_2
Silicon carbide	SiC	40·1	SiO_2
Sillimanite	$Al_2O_3.SiO_2$	162·1	Al_2O_3 SiO_2
Sodium carbonate (soda ash)	Na_2CO_3	106·0	Na_2O
Sodium silicate (waterglass)	Na_2SiO_3	122·2	Na_2O SiO_2
Spodumene (lithium feldspathoid)	$Li_2O.Al_2O_3.4SiO_2$	372·2	Li_2O Al_2O_3 SiO_2
Stannous oxide	SnO	134·7	SnO_2
Strontia	SrO	103·6	SrO
Strontianite (strontium carbonate)	$SrCO_3$	147·6	SrO
Talc	$3MgO.4SiO_2.H_2O$	379·3 Eq.wt. 126·7	MgO SiO_2
Tin oxide (stannic oxide)	SnO_2	150·7	SnO_2
Titanium dioxide (titania)	TiO_2	79·9	TiO_2
Ulexite	$NaCaB_5O_9.8H_2O$ $(Na_2O.2CaO.5B_2O_3 6H_2O)$	405·1	Na_2O CaO B_2O_3
Uranium oxide	U_3O_8	842·0	U_3O_8
Vanadium oxide	V_2O_5	181·8	V_2O_5
Washing soda	$Na_2CO_3.10H_2O$	286·0	Na_2O

Name	Chemical formula	Molecular weight (MW)	Oxides entering fusion
Whiting	$CaCO_3$	100·1	CaO
Witherite	$BaCO_3$	197·3	BaO
Wollastonite	$CaSiO_3$	116·2	CaO SiO_2
Yellow ochre	$2Fe_2O_3.3H_2O$	373·2	Fe_2O_3
Zinc oxide (zincite)	ZnO	81·4	ZnO
Zirconia	ZrO_2	123·2	ZrO_2
Zirconium silicate (zircon)	$ZrSiO_4$	183·3	ZrO_2 SiO_2

Analysis of tree ashes

	Apple	Cherry	Chestnut	Damson	Privet	Lime	Maple	Mistletoe	Hazel	Walnut
Fe_2O_3	0.70	2.62	3.89	3.26	4.26	2.56	2.39	1.06	0.12	1.26
MnO	34.69	—	0.80	0.51	0.42	0.10	0.43	traces	0.08	0.41
Al_2O_3	1.98	—	—	—	0.56	0.26	0.68	traces	0.10	0.06
CaO	54.20	30.24	32.00	20.62	23.63	26.11	28.36	20.04	26.62	40.00
MgO	3.25	8.72	16.46	8.21	12.55	11.24	12.55	10.16	15.20	6.59
K_2O	0.89	21.63	27.82	34.17	15.62	12.52	6.32	42.03	36.19	14.68
Na_2O	4.90	1.84	10.61	6.10	8.36	8.33	6.44	5.06	10.22	4.86
P_2O_5	1.57	7.56	2.31	10.36	6.31	7.52	7.07	18.13	4.20	6.44
SO_3	—	2.62	3.10	1.91	3.22	1.24	1.24	1.51	1.00	8.17
Cl	—	0.81	1.11	0.86	1.54	0.65	0.73	0.40	0.61	0.82
SiO_2	2.65	24.96	12.82	14.00	23.53	29.44	13.79	1.61	9.66	16.71

	Pear	Plum	Ash	Beech	Birch	Box	Elder	Elm	Gorse	Hawthorn
Fe_2O_3	1.20	5.21	3.92	0.62	1.26	1.06	0.36	1.17	2.61	1.52
MnO	—	—	0.41	4.52	0.34	0.34	0.09	—	0.52	0.33
Al_2O_3	—	—	0.63	—	—	—	—	—	0.63	0.50
CaO	7.99	6.39	25.52	42.00	29.62	30.12	35.96	47.80	30.14	31.10
MgO	5.42	9.25	12.00	8.20	14.28	14.00	15.62	7.71	10.62	9.24
K_2O	55.00	56.99	16.02	24.29	22.62	19.80	15.55	21.90	26.42	20.55
Na_2O	8.69	5.24	7.65	8.34	9.00	8.26	1.22	13.72	11.86	3.61
P_2O_5	13.93	12.09	7.00	6.20	7.90	7.11	12.11	3.33	3.66	8.52
SO_3	5.73	3.33	2.52	2.10	2.00	2.46	5.78	1.28	1.48	2.60
Cl	0.52	0.20	1.03	0.72	1.00	1.23	0.26	—	1.32	0.53
SiO_2	1.52	1.30	23.30	3.90	11.52	12.62	12.80	3.07	10.74	21.50

	Heath	Hornbeam	Horse Chestnut	Holly	Ivy	Laburnum	Larch	Bay Laurel	Cedar	Mountain Ash
Fe_2O_3	4.00	2.16	1.53	2.59	2.46	2.96	4.21	3.65	1.00	1.92
MnO	—	0.12	0.21	0.36	0.54	0.54	10.32	0.24	0.26	traces
Al_2O_3	—	0.14	0.56	0.41	0.12	0.42	0.59	0.36	0.52	0.65
CaO	16.23	32.04	20.00	15.61	24.61	29.42	25.63	14.96	44.21	49.34
MgO	8.93	10.21	16.01	15.42	8.00	2.21	8.23	6.53	6.00	10.55
K_2O	7.61	15.02	23.00	16.39	25.53	15.96	20.16	5.77	4.24	18.96
Na_2O	9.40	8.63	14.61	12.13	20.08	4.56	9.05	8.99	3.61	1.21
P_2O_5	4.19	12.96	8.65	11.41	5.61	12.73	7.76	8.02	10.62	5.72
SO_3	11.10	3.00	1.20	2.00	1.03	3.86	3.24	4.61	4.00	1.00
Cl	2.12	1.21	0.81	1.99	0.64	1.04	0.26	0.35	1.20	0.31
SiO_2	35.22	14.51	13.42	21.69	11.38	26.09	10.55	26.72	24.28	10.34

	Noble Silver Fir	Norway Spruce	Pine	Poplar	Willow	Upright Cypress	Oak Wood	Oak Leaves
Fe_2O_3	2.02	2.46	4.00	1.20	1.25	2.46	2.40	1.03
MnO	9.09	8.65	5.06	0.23	0.18	3.88	0.10	0.20
CuO	—	—	—	—	—	—	0.05	—
Al_2O_3	3.56	2.19	0.43	0.16	0.05	1.69	0.13	—
CaO	30.09	30.83	25.00	16.53	20.21	24.97	30.02	18.02
MgO	12.56	8.56	6.32	10.21	8.26	7.00	12.01	2.00
K_2O	12.47	10.99	26.50	54.23	49.81	12.51	14.00	54.63
Na_2O	6.31	6.53	8.60	2.34	2.50	6.04	9.12	12.00
P_2O_5	5.88	8.99	8.88	10.21	10.00	9.24	13.08	4.07
SO_3	0.99	1.23	4.63	1.31	1.22	2.10	2.61	3.20
Cl	0.53	0.56	0.52	0.12	0.08	0.46	1.18	0.81
SiO_2	15.49	19.01	10.00	3.46	4.44	19.65	15.30	4.00

Mixed wood ash (average)	
Fe_2O_3	1.60
MnO	6.57
Al_2O_3	0.11
CaO	30.66
MgO	10.17
K_2O	28.44
Na_2O	7.53
P_2O_5	7.60
SO_3	3.06
Cl	0.60
SiO_2	9.35

From *Manures for Fruit and other Trees*, A. B. Griffiths, London, Robert Sutton, 1908.

Bituminous coal ashes

Constituent	U.S.A.	England	Germany
SiO_2	20–60	25–50	25–45
Al_2O_3	10–35	20–40	15–21
Fe_2O_3	5–35	0–30	20–45
CaO	1–20	1–10	2–4
MgO	0.3–4	0.5–5	0.5–1
TiO_2	0.5–2.5	0–3	—
$Na_2O + K_2O$	1–4	1–6	—
SO_3	0.1–12	1–12	4–10

An average composition for West Virginia coal ash is Li_2O 0.075, Na_2O 1.78, K_2O 1.60, Rb_2O 0.030, CaO 2.76, SrO 0.38, BaO 0.22, MgO 0.98, Al_2O_3 29.9, SiO_2 43.9, Fe_2O_3 15.9. TiO_2 1.52, Ag_2O 0.0010, As_2O_3 0.07, B_2O_3 0.12, BeO 0.008, Bi_2O_3 0.004, Cb_2O_5 0.010, CoO 0.010, Cr_2O_3 0.023, CuO 0.061, GaO 0.022, GeO_2 0.011, HgO 0.011, La_2O_3 0.030, MnO 0.046, MoO_3 0.016, NiO 0.047, P_2O_5 0.35, PbO 0.048, Sb_2O_3 0.005, SnO_2 0.020, V_2O_5 0.050, WO_3 0.01, ZnO 0.053, ZrO_2 0.029.

This is an average over all coals, whatever type, in West Virginia. (With thanks to Peter Brown for analysis.)

Colour in chamber of electric kilns

°F	°C	Usual firing temperatures	
32–752	0–400	no colour in kiln	
842	450	black	
932	500	first visible heat	
1022	550	darkest glow	
1112	600	dull red	
1292	700	dark red	
1472	800	deep red	
1652	900	cherry red	raku glazes
1832	1000	bright red	studio biscuit
1922	1050	orange	earthenware glazes
2012	1100	bright orange	earthenware glazes
2102	1150	pale orange	earthenware glazes
2120	1160	pale orange yellow	industrial biscuit
2192	1200	light yellow	medium stoneware/bone china
2252	1250	yellow white	stoneware /porcelain
2372	1300	white	porcelain
2462	1350	bluish white	

Temperature equivalents: Centigrade and Fahrenheit

°C	°F	°C	°F	°C	°F	°C	°F	°C	°F	°C	°F
0	32	600	1112	950	1742	1120	2048	1210	2210	1316	2400
100	212	650	1202	982	1800	1130	2066	1220	2228	1350	2462
120	248	700	1292	1000	1832	1140	2084	1230	2246	1400	2552
200	392	704	1300	1038	1900	1149	2100	1232	2250	1500	2732
250	482	750	1382	1050	1922	1150	2102	1240	2264	1600	2912
300	572	760	1400	1060	1940	1160	2120	1250	2282	1700	3092
350	662	800	1472	1070	1958	1170	2138	1260	2300	1710	3110
400	752	816	1500	1080	1976	1177	2150	1270	2318	1800	3272
450	842	850	1562	1090	1994	1180	2156	1280	2336	1900	3452
500	932	871	1600	1093	2000	1190	2174	1288	2350	2000	3632
550	1022	900	1652	1100	2012	1200	2192	1290	2354		
573	1063	927	1700	1110	2030	1204	2200	1300	2372		

Health and safety

Any equipment if mishandled, badly installed or carelessly maintained presents potential dangers, but with correct operation such dangers can be avoided. Electric kilns carry four hazards: electrocution, either by being badly installed with inadequate wiring, poor earthing or by being carelessly maintained; fire, from overheated supply wires or bad siting (too close to walls or ceilings); burns from an outside surface which gets too hot (the spit test is a common measure – if spit or water sizzles on the surface it it too hot); toxic fumes, given off by the clay in an inadequately ventilated room.

All educational establishments lay down strict guidelines for the installation, maintenance and use of kilns. Ideally these are sited away from working and teaching areas, even in a separate room; the kiln should be fitted with a door lock, a temperature indicating pyrometer, a heat safety fuse and an isolation switch. An operating light is often sited outside the room to serve as a reminder that the kiln is in operation. Where kilns are installed in a working area, especially one used by young children, they should be surrounded by a protective wire cage to prevent access.

Few potters, however, feel they need such protective equipment, but all electrically operated kilns in the U.K. are subject to the Electricity (Factories' Acts) Special Regulations. Potters have to be aware of the potential hazard and should consider all the danger points, so that their kilns can be operated safely. Kilns need to be situated with good space on all sides. This not only allows access for maintenance work but helps to prevent fire. Combustible materials should not be stored in this space, and shelving near the kiln should be metal rather than wood. On kilns fitted with a roof damper the gap between it and the ceiling should be at least a yard and preferably more. The ceiling should be fitted with a heat resisting board (a double layer of plasterboarding is a good fire prevention). Also useful is a heat baffle made out of a material like asbestos, fitted some 13 cm (5 in) from the ceiling. Metal canopies fitted over the kiln with a flue to the outside of the building or up a chimney will help to remove heat and fumes given off during firing. This is especially useful if a reduction firing is planned. In any case, adequate ventilation to remove fumes during firing is essential. Open windows and/or a powerful extraction fan should be installed to keep the atmosphere clear.

Maintenance of the kiln is essential. During firing the high temperatures involved and the fumes and steam given off have a powerful effect on both the fabric and the wiring of the kiln. Regular maintenance includes care of the brickwork and furniture, the metal structure and the wiring elements, connections and electronic equipment. Frequent cleaning of the inside of the firing chamber with a vacuum cleaner will remove particles of grit and dust. A coat of aluminium paint over the brushed-down metal cladding and frame of the kiln will protect it from rust and lengthen its working life. Regular inspection of the wiring to check for any loose connections and so on will help to ensure efficient working. Ideally this work should be carried out by a qualified electrician who can carry out necessary repair work. Local education authorities usually insist that these surveys are carried out regularly by suitably qualified fitters.

Operation of electric kilns, if correctly carried out, will prevent accidents. When any work whatsoever is done on the kiln when it is being cleaned or packed, it must be turned off at the mains using the isolation switch. It is not sufficient to switch off the kiln at the electronic control. When major repair work is carried out the fuses should be removed. Pots should be packed at least 2.5 cm (1 in) from the elements. The kiln door or doors should be firmly closed and, if necessary, locked in position before the kiln is switched on. All metal parts must be effectively earthed with devices which cannot be interfered with or broken. Control panels should be positioned so they can be clearly seen and should be protected from enquiring hands.

Fires, with electric kilns are rare, but remain a danger. Badly installed or incorrect wiring which can overheat by being overloaded are the main dangers, as the kiln itself has neither flames nor any combustible material (unless introduced for a reduction atmosphere). Electrical fires *must* be put out with special fire extinguishers. Ordinary water-based fire extinguishers can cause severe electric shocks to the operator and must never be used. Turn off the electricity immediately if there is any sign of danger and do not turn it on until all danger is past and the installation has been checked by a qualified electrician.

The design, installation and operation of any electric kiln should be in strict accordance with manufacturers' instructions. Electrical loading on most kilns is heavy and can only be safely carried out on electric wiring specially designed and installed for this purpose, fitted with correct isolation switches and proper fuse systems.

Electricity

While only a minimum amount of information is needed about why electricity works, some understanding of how it works and how it is measured is useful. Electricity is a form of energy brought about by the movement of electrons. The current from the terminals of a battery (the live, L, and neutral, N) is known as direct current (DC) while that supplied from the grid system usually moves in cycles and is known as alternating current (AC).

Electric current can be conducted through different sorts of materials. An efficient conductor is a substance which allows the current to pass with ease. The opposite is an insulating material (such as potted clay or rubber) which does not allow the electric current to pass through at all. Metals are by far the most efficient conductors;

they are only affected by a rise in temperature and depending on the particular sort, thickness and length of wire, they put up different levels of resistance. It is in trying to overcome this resistance to the flow of electricity that light and heat is generated, and it is this heat which is obtained from the electric elements in the kiln, where wire must be chosen which will put up resistance to give the amount of heat required. Too much resistance, or too much current, will cause the wire to get too hot and burn out.

The unit of resistance is known as the ohm. The electric potential (sometimes thought of as pressure) of a conductor, measured in *volts*, always relates in the same proportion to the current, or flow of electricity, measured in amperes (*amps*), according to the resistance. Volts = amps (current) × ohms (resistance).

The thicker the wire the less resistance it will put up and therefore the greater the current that can move along it. (Inversely, the larger the length of wire, the more resistance it will offer, and this will restrict the current that will flow.) So a long length of thin wire will pass less current and produce less heat than a short thick one of the same type of metal. The total amount of electrical power transformed into heat, or other energy forms, is measured in *watts*, a unit which combines volts and amps. Watts = volts × amps.

Bibliography

Health & Safety in Ceramics: A Guide for Educational Workshops and Studios. The Institute of Ceramics, 1981.
   A clear, concise outline of potential dangers, with sensible recommendations.

Cooper, Emmanuel, *The Potters' Book of Glaze Recipes*, Batsford, 1980.
   Over 500 recipes with full descriptions of how they work in both oxidation and reduction.

Cooper, Emmanuel, *A History of World Pottery*, Batsford, 1981.
   An outline history which describes techniques, styles and working methods from the potters' point of view. Many illustrations (some in colour) and maps.

Cooper, Emmanuel and Royle, Derek, *Glazes for the Studio Potter*, Batsford, 1978.
   A theoretical and practical guide to making and understanding glazes with an emphasis on medium- and high-temperature effects in the electric kiln.

Fournier, Robert, *Electric Kiln Construction for Potters*, Van Nostrand Reinhold, 1977.

A step by step guide to building different sizes and types of electric kiln, with many clear and explanatory drawings.

Fournier, Robert, *Illustrated Dictionary of Practical Pottery*, Van Nostrand Reinhold, 1977.

Much useful information on many aspects of pottery, most of which is presented from the electric kiln potter's point of view.

Hamer, Frank, *The Potter's Dictionary of Materials and Techniques*, Pitman, 1975.

Excellent and reliable reference book for techniques and technical information.

Lane, Peter, *Studio Porcelain*, Pitman, 1980.

A survey of techniques and styles of potters, many of whom fire in electric kilns, who work in countries throughout the world. Many colour illustrations, also black and white, plus technical information.

Fraser, Harry, *Electric Kilns and Firing*, Pitman, 1980.

A practical guide to the different sorts of kilns available on the market, as well as to the various electronic controls now in production.

Rhodes, Daniel, *Kilns: Design, Construction and Operation*, Pitman, 1972.

One chapter on electric kilns which is presented very much as the poor relation of reduction flame burning kilns.

Suppliers

U.K.

Joseph Arnold & Son Ltd Billington Road Leighton Buzzard Bedfordshire	Fine silica sand
C. H. Brannan Barnstaple Devon	Fremington red earthenware plastic clay
English China Clay John Keay House St Austell Cornwall	Ball clays and china clays
Podmore Ceramics 105 Minet Road London SW9 7UH	Clays, raw materials, kilns
Fulham Pottery 184 New Kings' Road London SW6 4PB	Clays, raw materials, kilns
Wengers Ltd Garner Street Etruria Stoke on Trent Staffs. ST4 7BQ	Clays, raw materials, kilns
Harrison Mayer C & E Division Campbell Road Stoke on Trent ST4 4ET	Clays, raw materials, kilns
Watts Blake Bearne & Co. Courtenay Park Newton Abbott Devon	Ball clays and plastic bodies
Kilns and Furnaces Tunstall Stoke on Trent Staffs ST6 5AS	Electric kilns
Potclays Ltd Brick Kiln Lane Etruria Stoke on Trent	Clays and raw materials
Cromartie Kilns Park Hall Road Stoke on Trent ST3 5X	Kilns and electronic firing equipment, shelves, props
Moira Pottery Co. Ltd Moira Burton on Trent	Stoneware and terracotta clays with glazes to fit

U.S.A.

American Art Clay Co. (AMACO) 4717 W. 16th Street Indianapolis IND 46222	Materials and kilns
Capital Ceramics Inc. 2174 S. Main Street Salt Lake City UT 84115	General suppliers
Carborundum Co (Fiberfrax) Box 337 Niagara Falls NY 14302	Ceramic fibre insulating materials

Cedar Heights Clay Co. 50 Portsmouth Road Oak Hill OH 45656	Ball clays; clay bodies
Edgar Plastic Kaolin Co. Edgar Putman Co, FLA 32049	China clays
Ferro Corporation Frit Division 4150 East 56th Street Cleveland Ohio 44150	Raw materials, ferro frits
Georgia Kaolin Co. 433 N. Broad Street Elizabeth NJ 07207	China clay
Harrison Bell (associate company of Harrison Mayer Ltd) 3605A Kennedy Road South Plainfield New Jersey	Potters basic materials; colours, etc
O Hommel Co. PO Box 475 Pittsburgh PA 15230	Hommel frits
House of Ceramics 1011 North Hollywood Memphis TN 38108	Potters' supplies; raw materials
Leslie Ceramics Supply Co. 1212 San Pablo Ave Berkley CA 94706	Raw materials; colours etc.
Ohio Ceramic Supply Inc. Box 630 Kent OH 44249	Various raw materials
Pemco Division Glidden Company 5601 Eastern Avenue Baltimore MD 21224	Pemco frits
Rovin Ceramics 6912 Shaefer Dearborn MICH 48126	Potters' materials

Standard Ceramic Supply Co. Box 4435 Pittsburgh PA 15205	Raw materials, etc.
Van Howe Ceramic Supply Co. 11975 E. 40 Ave. Denver Co 80239 *or* 4860 Pan American Freeway N.E. Albuquerque NM 87107	Potters' raw materials and equipment
Western Ceramic Supply 1601 Howard Street San Francisco CA 94103	Potters' equipment, raw materials, clays

CANADA

Barrett Co. Ltd 1155 Dorchester Blvd W. Montreal 2 Quebec	Potters' raw materials
Clay Crafts Supply 1004 Taylor Street Saskatoon Sas.	Potters' raw materials
HIRO Distributors 518 Beatty Street Vancouver BC	Potters' materials
Pottery Supply House PO Box 192 Oakville Ontario	Potters' equipment, clays, raw materials

Index